The Global Vampire

CRITICAL EXPLORATIONS IN SCIENCE FICTION AND FANTASY
(a series edited by Donald E. Palumbo and C.W. Sullivan III)
Earlier Works: www.mcfarlandpub.com

Recent Works: 42 *The Heritage of Heinlein* (Thomas D. Clareson and Joe Sanders, 2014)
43 *The Past That Might Have Been, the Future That May Come* (Lauren J. Lacey, 2014)
44 *Environments in Science Fiction: Essays* (ed. Susan M. Bernardo, 2014)
45 *Discworld and the Disciplines: Critical Approaches to the Terry Pratchett Works* (ed. Anne Hiebert Alton, William C. Spruiell, 2014)
46 *Nature and the Numinous in Mythopoeic Fantasy Literature* (Christopher Straw Brawley, 2014)
47 *J.R.R. Tolkien, Robert E. Howard and the Birth of Modern Fantasy* (Deke Parsons, 2014)
48 *The Monomyth in American Science Fiction Films* (Donald E. Palumbo, 2014)
49 *The Fantastic in Holocaust Literature and Film* (ed. Judith B. Kerman, John Edgar Browning, 2014)
50 *Star Wars in the Public Square* (Derek R. Sweet, 2016)
51 *An Asimov Companion* (Donald E. Palumbo, 2016)
52 *Michael Moorcock* (Mark Scroggins, 2016)
53 *The Last Midnight: Essays* (ed. Leisa A. Clark, Amanda Firestone, Mary F. Pharr, 2016)
54 *The Science Fiction Mythmakers: Religion, Science and Philosophy in Wells, Clarke, Dick and Herbert* (Jennifer Simkins, 2016)
55 *Gender and the Quest in British Science Fiction Television* (Tom Powers, 2016)
56 *Saving the World Through Science Fiction: James Gunn* (Michael R. Page, 2017)
57 *Wells Meets Deleuze* (Michael Starr, 2017)
58 *Science Fiction and Futurism: Their Terms and Ideas* (Ace G. Pilkington, 2017)
59 *Science Fiction in Classic Rock: Musical Explorations of Space, Technology and the Imagination, 1967–1982* (Robert McParland, 2017)
60 *Patricia A. McKillip and the Art of Fantasy World-Building* (Audrey Isabel Taylor, 2017)
61 *The Fabulous Journeys of* Alice *and* Pinocchio: *Exploring Their Parallel Worlds* (Laura Tosi with Peter Hunt, 2018)
62 *A* Dune *Companion: Characters, Places and Terms in Frank Herbert's Original Six Novels* (Donald E. Palumbo, 2018)
63 *Fantasy Literature and Christianity: A Study of the Mistborn, Coldfire, Fionavar Tapestry and Chronicles of Thomas Covenant Series* (Weronika Łaszkiewicz, 2018)
64 *The British Comic Invasion: Alan Moore, Warren Ellis, Grant Morrison and the Evolution of the American Style* (Jochen Ecke, 2019)
65 *The Archive Incarnate: The Embodiment and Transmission of Knowledge in Science Fiction* (Joseph Hurtgen, 2018)
66 *Women's Space: Essays on Female Characters in the 21st Century Science Fiction Western* (ed. Melanie A. Marotta, 2019)
67 *"Hailing frequencies open": Communication in* Star Trek: The Next Generation (Thomas D. Parham, III, 2019)
68 *The Global Vampire: Essays on the Undead in Popular Culture Around the World* (ed. Cait Coker, 2019)

The Global Vampire
Essays on the Undead in Popular Culture Around the World

Edited by CAIT COKER
Afterword by Amanda Jo Hobson *and* U. Melissa Anyiwo

CRITICAL EXPLORATIONS IN SCIENCE FICTION AND FANTASY, 68
Series Editors Donald E. Palumbo *and* C.W. Sullivan III

McFarland & Company, Inc., Publishers
Jefferson, North Carolina

ISBN (print) 978-1-4766-7594-7
ISBN (ebook) 978-1-4766-3733-4

LIBRARY OF CONGRESS AND BRITISH LIBRARY
CATALOGUING DATA ARE AVAILABLE

Library of Congress Control Number 2019051450

© 2020 Cait Coker. All rights reserved

No part of this book may be reproduced or transmitted in any form or by any means, electronic or mechanical, including photocopying or recording, or by any information storage and retrieval system, without permission in writing from the publisher.

Front cover images © 2020 Ruta Production /Shutterstock

Printed in the United States of America

McFarland & Company, Inc., Publishers
  Box 611, Jefferson, North Carolina 28640
    www.mcfarlandpub.com

For Candace

Acknowledgments

It takes a village to raise a child; apparently it takes a conference to raise a scholar.

My thanks go out to my "Aca-Superheroines" U. Melissa Anyiwo, Amanda Jo Hobson, Anna Gal, Lisa Nevárez, and Lauren Rocha. I met them at PCA ten years ago and we never stopped talking. They have provided me with support beyond measure, have been willing to answer questions and pleas at all hours, supply feedback, recommendations and the occasional (okay, more than occasional) cup of coffee at odd moments. This book would not be here if not for them.

Heartfelt thanks as well to Sheila Coyazo and Rhea Uhl, friends of Candace Benefiel and fellow fangirls, and to Renee Kelley, Candace's niece, for her encouragement to make this book happen.

To my constant companions and colleagues, Todd Samuelson and Kate Ozment, who always know, somehow, the right thing to say when I need to hear it.

Finally, to Scott Zrebiec, my better half and husband, for his endless support.

Table of Contents

Acknowledgments — vi

Preface (and In Memoriam) — 1

Introduction—Texts and Contexts: The Global Vampire in Popular Culture
   CAIT COKER — 3

The Americas and Canada

Biting, Sex and Blood: The New American Vampire Narrative
   CANDACE R. BENEFIEL — 11

"I'll give you blood to drink": The New Vampire in Novels About the Salem Witch Trials
   MARTA MARÍA GUTIÉRREZ-RODRÍGUEZ — 23

Wes Craven's *Vampire in Brooklyn*: A Passing Narrative
   KENDRA R. PARKER — 35

The Transmediated Lesbian Vampire: LGBTQ Representation in a Contemporary Adaptation of J. Sheridan Le Fanu's *Carmilla*
   NATALIE KRIKOWA — 48

Éternelle Colonization: The Figure of the Vampire as Colonizing Factor in 21st-Century Québec
   MAUREEN-C. LAPERRIÈRE *and* JULIEN DRAINVILLE — 60

viii Table of Contents

Europe and the Mediterranean

"The creatures of the night, what bad jokes they make!": Racism, "True" Humor and the Nationalistic Vampire on Film
   SIMON BACON   77

Amid and Beyond Gender(s): The Vampire as a Locus of Gender Neutrality in John Ajvide Lindqvist's *Let the Right One In*
   MARIE LEVESQUE   90

The Economic Miracle and the Italian Undead in *Tempi duri per i vampiri*
   FERNANDO GABRIEL PAGNONI BERNS   104

"Time is an abyss": The Role of History in Werner Herzog's *Nosferatu* (1979)
   THOMAS PRASCH   116

There's Water Here: Cities, Safety and the Global Environment in Jim Jarmusch's *Only Lovers Left Alive*
   KAREN E. VIARS   128

Asia and Australia

From Sunnydale to Seoul: The Vampire "Fan" in Korean Dramas
   CAIT COKER   143

"Don't adjust your life to mine": *Moon Child*, Homoeroticism and the Vampire as Multifaceted Other
   MIRANDA RUTH LARSEN   153

Aboriginal Australian Vampires and the Politics of Transmediality
   NAOMI SIMONE BORWEIN   165

"In need of vitamin sea": The Emergence of Australian Identity Through the Eyes and Thirst of Kirsty Eager's Vampires
   PHIL FITZSIMMONS   177

Globalism: Real and Virtual Worlds?

The Ecohorror of *The Strain*: Plant Vampires and Climate Change
  as a Holocaust
    TATIANA PROROKOVA-KONRAD   189

"Set to drain": Vampirism as Mechanic and Metaphor
  in *The Elder Scrolls IV: Oblivion*
    TREVOR DODGE   200

Afterword
    AMANDA JO HOBSON *and* U. MELISSA ANYIWO   211

About the Contributors   215

Works Cited   219

Index   235

Preface
(and In Memoriam)

This book has two origin stories.

The first, more straightforward one, is that it began as a roundtable session for the Vampire in Literature, Culture, and Film Area of the Popular Culture Association 2017 meeting. I had been attending the area for the better part of a decade, along with a number of colleagues who had become friends over the years: Candace R. Benefiel, U. Melissa Anyiwo, Amanda Jo Hobson, Lisa Nevárez, Anna Gal, Lauren Rocha, and Rho Nichol. We call ourselves "Aca Superheroines" half jokingly and half seriously; we have come to recognize one another's strengths (superpowers) in research that can be depended upon for fixing this or that problem, whether looking for a forgotten book title or the need to pinch-hit a book chapter for a collection. In the summer of 2016, I put together a proposal for "Familiar and Strange: International Vampires Onscreen" and submitted it to the conference with our names, excited about the possibilities for discussion when we all met once again.

The second origin story is much sadder, and follows closely on the heels of the first. In early 2017, Candace was diagnosed with cancer. While the early prognosis was optimistic, she was unable to come to PCA, despite the prep work she had begun to do for her paper there. By summer, however, her condition had worsened: the cancer had metastasized and was now terminal. She passed a few weeks later, mourned by family, friends, and colleagues. She left behind a legacy of friendship, academic rigor, and scholarly work, some of which was unfinished. With the help of Candace's niece, Renee Kelley, I was given her flash drives with her research files, and permission to edit her work for publication.

This collection is intended as a memoriam to our dear friend and colleague. Many of the scholars included here knew Candace personally as well as through her work. She was always a voice for the importance of popular culture scholarship in academia, and advocated for using popular texts to foster critical thinking and academic engagement with students. She was also a prolific scholar, with numerous articles in print and online on topics ranging from the figure of the vampire to matters of academic librarianship. At the time of her passing she was concluding work on her doctoral dissertation, "Stakeholders in a New Tradition: Vampires and the American Woman at the Beginning of the Twenty-First Century." Though Candace focused particularly on American popular culture, we had begun discussing the possibilities inherent in investigating the "global vampire" more broadly in popular culture. To that end, consider this collection a first step toward finishing work she had only just begun.

Introduction

Texts and Contexts: The Global Vampire in Popular Culture

CAIT COKER

The vampire is an expansive figure in folklore, and perhaps even more so in popular culture. Whether as a figure of horror or romance, as friend or foe, the vampire appears in one form or another across the world. Indeed, the global popularity of the media vampire goes well beyond the usual Anglo-American suspects, from its origins in *Nosferatu* (1922) and *Vampyre* (1932) to the more recent *A Girl Walks Alone at Night* (Iran, 2014). Television dramas go even farther afield: Korean shows like *The Scholar Who Walks the Night* (2015) and *Orange Marmalade* (2015) play with the common interpretations of the sexy and heroic vampire that varies greatly from the folkloric *giangshi*, while American shows like *The Strain* (2014–2017) present terrifying creatures that have more in common with science fiction than fantasy or folklore. In Australia, the aboriginal monster namorroddo has been presented in popular culture through both film (*Outback Vampires* [1987], *Bloodlust* [1992]) and through novels like Kristy Eager's *Saltwater Vampires* (2010). Other films like *Only Lovers Left Alive* (2014) and the web series *Carmilla* (2014–2016) emphasize the vampiric figure as a globetrotting citizen *du monde* rather than as an isolated monster. These and many other texts demonstrate that the popularity of the vampire remains strong even without a multimillion-dollar Hollywood franchise at the helm.

This collection defines "text" broadly, encompassing novels both print and electronic, films and television, comics and video games. In a world in which the consumption of texts is exceeded only by the desire for more, new, and *different* media which might just manage to fill in the gaps and the erasures of representation in everyday life, the "vampire" is a convenient trope both familiar and strange, utilized in all places and all times. It is curious, then, how much of the scholarship has been constrained by largely considering only the specifically American vampire, and so creating an ahistorical narrative that more or less reads as "from *Dracula* to *Twilight*." This volume was created to resist the American-centric narrative both in studies of the vampire generally and in media specifically. This book is meant as a remedial text, if you will, in which global cultures and global travel include but are not subsumed by the American culture complex.

Instead, this book has reconceived of the American vampire as a launching point for a world tour, traveling north to Canada, then east to Europe, East Asia, and the Pacific Rim, before concluding with a duo of essays that rethink the vampire in "our" world as a figure of eco-horror in the natural world and as a creature of terror and danger in the virtual world of popular video games. Echoes of the American interpretation of the vampire haunt other cultures, showcasing colonial afterlives that continue on in the export of popular culture—even as Bram Stoker's classic anxieties regarding the immigrant other in the United Kingdom have for so long informed American conceptions of the vampire's purpose and pedigree.

Despite my best efforts and intentions, however, telling gaps remain both in critical and popular exploration. In this book, there are no examinations of the vampire in Africa, effectively erasing an *entire continent* from our global jaunt. There are no Mexican, Latin or South American, or Caribbean vampires, nor any from India, Pakistan, or other parts of South Asia. Indigenous vampires from Australia are examined, but not those from the myriad cultures of the Americas. This is not for lack of examples in folklore and myth: the Indian vetalas, Soucouyant of Trinidad, the Tunda and Patasola of Colombia, the Tagalog Mandurugo and the Visayan manananggal, the Ashanti asanbosam and the Ewe adze, to say nothing of the Greek vrykolakas, Icelandic draugar, or the Spanish guaxa. Perhaps speaking to a primal, even Jungian fear, the "living undead" or the "bloodsucker" is omnipresent in every culture. It behooves us, then, to think about why such figures are not reflected in mass culture or on the scholarship of popular culture. With any luck, this is something we can revisit in a future volume.

What this collection does contain, however, are over a dozen essays that explore the vampire as a reflection of issues ranging from the lingering class problems of the Old World in the new economies of 20th-century Europe to anxieties regarding queer love in Japan. Contributors discuss fan fiction, comic books, young adult novels, music, film, and television, all of which seem to feed on one another rather like the vampire and his willing, or unwilling, prey.

While this collection has geographical and national boundaries, it has nonetheless gathered interdisciplinary work that stretches from traditional literary and cinematic studies to video game scholarship and ecocriticism, and in doing so demonstrates the wide body of "texts" in which the popular vampire appears. The lack of disciplinary constraints reflects that the global vampire is freed from typical readings of monstrosity and otherness into variegated possibilities that include the cute and the beautiful as well as the horrific and sickening.

The first section, "The Americas and Canada," explores the vampire in its new home territory in North America. It encompasses five essays that examine novels, film, and television. Pointedly, it includes no mega-franchises like *Buffy the Vampire Slayer* or *Twilight*, and focuses instead on works that span the Americas, including the L.A. of the TV series *Moonlight*, the Salem, Massachusetts, of Meredith Allard and Frank R. Godbey's novels; and the Montreal of *Éternelle* (2004). Candace R. Benefiel's "Biting, Sex and Blood: The New American Vampire Narrative" examines how popular American fiction reconfigures the vampire from monster to romantic hero. Marta María Gutiérrez Rodríguez's "'I'll give you blood to drink': The New Vampire in Novels About the Salem Witch Trials" looks at contemporary novels that complicate the history of the Salem Witch Trials with vampires who are responsible for its horrific events. Kendra R. Parker's "Wes Craven's *Vampire in Brooklyn*: A Passing Narrative" revisits the horror classic of the mid–1990s as an examination of problematic racial politics and HIV/AIDS anxiety. Natalie Krikowa's "The Transmediated Lesbian Vampire: LGBTQ Representation in a Contemporary Adaptation of J. Sheridan Le Fanu's *Carmilla*" brings us up-to-date on a web series that plays with queerness and adaptation in contemporary Canada. Finally, Maureen-C. LaPerrière and Julien Drainville's "*Éternelle* Colonization: The Figure of the Vampire as Colonizing Factor in 21st-Century Québec" provides a postcolonial reading of a Québecois horror film which features the historical figure Erszebet Báthory as a vampire.

The second section, "Europe and the Mediterranean," ventures across the European Union past and present, exploring films made in Sweden, Poland, Belgium, Germany, Italy, and Morocco, the last of which has long been the traditional gateway between Europe and Africa. The works explored explicitly link problems of nationalism and transnationalism to the vampiric figure. Simon Bacon's "'The creatures of the night, what bad jokes they make!': Racism, 'True' Humor and the Nationalistic Vampire on Film" looks at a trio of comedies whose jokes articulate and complicate the anxieties of a postwar Europe in transition. Marie Levesque's "Amid and Beyond Gender(s): The Vampire as a Locus of Gender Neutrality in John Ajvide Lindqvist's *Let the Right One In*" explores the complications of biological sex and gender identities of the vampire in the 2004 Swedish novel. Fernando Gabriel Pagnoni Berns's "The Economic Miracle and the Italian Undead in *Tempi duri per i vampiri*" is a case study of a popular vampire comedy from the 1970s. Thomas Prasch's "'Time is an abyss': The Role of History in Werner Herzog's *Nosferatu* (1979)" reconsiders that movie as not just a remake of Murnau's famous 1922 film, but as an explicit response from the context of 1979 Germany. Finally, Karen E. Viars's "There's Water Here: Cities, Safety and the Global Environment in Jim Jarmusch's *Only Lovers Left Alive*" reads Jim Jarmusch's 2013 film as an exploration of anxieties around urban decay and increasingly depleted and polluted national resources.

The third section, "Asia and Australia," encompasses popular film, television, and novels from across Korea, Japan, Australia, and New Zealand. Four essays explore the widespread use of the vampire in these varying contexts, both as a specifically Western figure transformed in an Eastern context and as a folkloric figure explored in the popular culture of specific nations. My essay, "From Sunnydale to Seoul: The Vampire 'Fan' in Korean Dramas," explores South Korean revisions of the romantic vampire hero in conjunction with the role of the vampire fan in popular culture. Miranda Ruth Larsen's "'Don't adjust your life to mine': *Moon Child*, Homoeroticism and the Vampire as Multifaceted Other" provides a queer reading of a contemporary Japanese film and how it utilizes J-pop to orchestrate a secondary text through popular music. Naomi Simone Borwein's "Aboriginal Australian Vampires and the Politics of Transmediality" examines the depiction and usage of a folkloric figure in movies and novels. Finally, Phil Fitzsimmons's "'In need of vitamin sea': The Emergence of Australian Identity Through the Eyes and Thirst of Kirsty Eager's Vampires" looks at how a popular series of Young Adult novels revises real events in Australian history to complicate the popular "myth" of that country's founding as a colonial state.

The fourth and final section, "Globalism: Real and Virtual Worlds?" consists of two essays that think globally in the sense of real-world ecology and in the expansive possibilities of virtual worlds. These two pieces stand apart from the rest of the collection but in many ways bring it full circle as they both ask: How is the vampire utilized as a global symbol? Tatiana Prorokova's "The Ecohorror of *The Strain*: Plant Vampires and Climate Change as a Holocaust" uses eco-critical theory to examine the television show where "vampires" are rendered as parasites whose impact on the natural environment, and thus humanity, is explicitly paralleled to the genocidal and nuclear horror of World War II. Trevor Dodge's "'Set to drain': Vampirism as Mechanic and Metaphor in *The Elder Scrolls IV: Oblivion*" examines the impact of vampirism on players' characters, and thus their actions and game-play strategies, in the game.

As is amply demonstrated here, the popular vampire is so much more than what is casually seen in American television and film. The vampire in global popular culture is a truly transnational entity whose boundaries are not limited by geography, language, or medium. Its cultural dominance therefore reflects global anxieties and preoccupations that are as familiar to readers in the U.S. as they are to Japan. The vampire is not only here to stay in popular culture, but has become truly omnipresent.

The Americas and Canada

Biting, Sex and Blood

The New American Vampire Narrative

CANDACE R. BENEFIEL

> We are told to be wary of vampires. Some critics remind us that vampires can infect us with their otherness, beguile us with their depraved intimacy, and exhaust us with their embraces. Others warn us against accepting the images of fear that the vampire is held to represent. The vampires of the West exist to frighten us into acquiescence, to reassert patriarchy, racial superiority, family values, and chaste heterosexual sexuality. We have long been urged to exorcise the vampire from our imaginations—or, at least, not to get too carried away with it.
> —Williamson 2005, 1

In the continuing debate on the significance and use of the figure of the vampire in literature, the gap between the vampire as fearsome enemy and the vampire as romantic hero has become increasingly gendered by and for American audiences. Both critics and authors tend to take a stance on the vampire based on their own gendered identities, in several directions. If, as Auerbach observed, the vampire is a product of the times and society that produce his peculiar narrative, the present state of the vampire in literature and television would appear to indicate that the dawn of the 21st century is seeing a more open dialogue on the uses of the vampire to fulfill the needs of a fragmented audience.

While the traditional producers of cultural artifacts fight a rear-guard action to maintain the vampire narrative established by Bram Stoker with the publication of *Dracula* over a century ago as a representation of heterosexual patriarchy fighting against the Otherness of this dweller in the shadowlands between life, death, gender, and race, women writers and consumers of vampire literature, and authors outside those narrow boundaries, are shaping the vampire into their own construct. He is still an Other, still a figure who presents as the embodiment of an ideal beyond humanity, but his danger is in his very attractiveness, not in his agency of destruction. The vampire has always held a certain allure, from his roots in Romantic literature until the present day. And yet, with traditional 19th century literary vampires such as Lord Ruthven, Varney, and Dracula, the allure was a danger, not a refuge from the vicissitudes of life. In *Dracula*, when the going got tough, Lucy Westenra got staked, and Mina Harker got sent off to bed while the men hunted the big, bad vampire. Female characters in contemporary vampire narratives, on the other hand, are more likely to be either out staking the vampires themselves, or in bed with them exploring sexual territory Bram Stoker could not even begin to depict in 1897. Once subjects to be protected, these women have become agents in their own stories.

Women in the Traditional Vampire Narrative

Lord Ruthven, the original Byronic vampire in John Polidori's 1819 novella, *The Vampyre*, has limited use for women. While upon his first appearance in London society he pays little heed to the more wanton women of the nobility, he does spend time with virtuous maidens. However, his acquaintance and sometime traveling companion, Aubrey, quickly discovers that Ruthven delights in the ruination of innocence. It is said of him that "he had required, to enhance his gratification, that his victim, the partner of his guilt, should be hurled from the pinnacle of unsullied virtue, down to the lowest abyss of infamy and degradation" (37–38). But it is not against women alone that he employs his talent for corruption; he is said also to have destroyed the fortunes of many affluent young men at the card table. The vampire is never depicted, as later members of his species so often are, in the act of feeding upon a human—male or female. In some way, it is as though the destruction of innocence is his sustenance, more than any physical ingestion of blood. As Aubrey and Ruthven travel through Europe together, Aubrey foils Ruthven's plan to debauch a young woman in Rome, but he fails to prevent the vampire's murder of the beautiful Greek girl Ianthe. And his promise to Ruthven, at the time of the nobleman's assumed death, keeps him from alerting his own sister to the dangers of the vampire's wiles. Aubrey's sister serves as a bond between the vampire and the mortal man who is his true prey. She is never more than a sketch in the story, without voice or personality; a young woman who should be, but is not, protected from the monster Ruthven, until it is too late.

Another important vampire text from the 19th century, the "penny dreadful" *Varney the Vampire: or, The Feast of Blood* (1845–1847), features a vampire who is more direct in his assaults upon women. The very first chapters of the narrative show him attacking Flora Bannerworth in her bedroom on a dark and stormy night. Varney is an exceptionally long and repetitive text, and while it eventually comes out that the vampire's motives for attacking young Miss Bannerworth go beyond a simple desire for her blood (he is scheming to re-acquire his ancestral home from the Bannerworth family), nonetheless, Flora is the victim here, and there is no question of her being able to protect herself. As Lucy Westenra and Mina Harker are in *Dracula*, Flora is a fragile creature who must be protected. Her blood is necessary to Varney, but she is even more useful as a pawn in his quest to regain what he considers rightfully his. The other female characters in the sprawling serial novel come and go, but they are all very similar.

Sweet, young, mid–Victorian damsels in distress, they are worried above all about the protection of their purity, and their worthiness to be loved by the mortal young men in their lives—a purity threatened by the lurking presence of the vampire. There is much discussion that anyone bitten by such a foul fiend is doomed to live a debauched life, regardless of prior character or inclination, and to become a vampire at death.

Published in 1872, Sheridan Le Fanu's novella *Carmilla* is something of an exception to the rule, but nevertheless important for its depiction of a female vampire who works her way into the confidences of a family through her supposed frailty. As it transpires, the vampire, Carmilla, is apparently in the habit of preying on young women. The main part of the story details the growing closeness between Carmilla and Laura, an innocent young woman of eighteen. Laura and her father take in the victim of a carriage accident which has occurred near their house, and Laura quickly grows very fond of the girl, who appears to be about her own age. Daringly enough for the time of this publication, Carmilla sometimes makes what can only be construed as romantic advances toward Laura. Eventually, it is discovered that she is, in fact, an ancient vampire, Countess Karnstein; and Laura's father, with the aid of friends, is instrumental in discovering the tomb of Carmilla so that the vampire can be destroyed. One of the more disturbing aspects of *Carmilla*, naturally, is not only that the vampiric villain of the piece is a female, but that she seeks out other women as lovers/victims. Women in *Carmilla* are not only the objects of desire, but the agents of corruption and destruction.

The final landmark text, of course, is Bram Stoker's *Dracula* (1897). The question of women in this complex narrative has been widely discussed, particularly in the past thirty years. In one of the most influential articles on the topic, "'Kiss Me with Those Red Lips': Gender and Inversion in Bram Stoker's *Dracula*," Christopher Craft situates women as a locus of displaced sexuality, using them as societally acceptable intermediaries that nevertheless serve to enable the performance of sexual desire between men. For example, in the earlier part of the novel, Lucy serves as a chalice to be drained by Dracula. Her veins are refilled with the blood of the mortal men surrounding her, only to be drunk once more; and in this way, Dracula is able to drink the blood of young men he desires without the impropriety of penetrating them with his fangs.

After Lucy's death and subsequent rising as a vampire, she forfeits the mantle of male protection, and the same group of suitors who once banded together to protect her with their blood now pursue and ultimately destroy her, in what almost every critic has perceived to be a highly sexualized act of violence. While they claim that this is done to restore her innocence and provide her with peace, nonetheless the gory staking has the more primary benefit of removing a sexualized and dangerous woman from the community.

At first glance, Mina appears to be a different case. She is active at first, and included in the plans of the Crew of Light, even if her activity is restricted to providing secretarial support. Fleissner has argued that Dracula is, in many ways, a secretarial novel, and that much of the successful resolution of the plot is dependent upon Mina's able organization of the mass of documents relating to the vampire's activities in England. Nevertheless, it is precisely Mina's exclusion from a meeting of the male constituents of the Crew of Light that provides Dracula with an opportunity to attack her in her bed, while her husband lies in a stupor next to her. Once she has been made, in her own term, "unclean," she is relegated to the status of an object to be protected. She is no longer even an ancillary member of the Crew of Light.

Women in vampire narratives for the next three-quarters of a century following the publication of *Dracula* remain primarily damsels in distress, or disposable victims. They are the reward for the vampire hunter who has successfully dispatched his prey and saved the community from further depredation. There are, of course, exceptions to this rule—for instance, in Murnau's 1922 film, *Nosferatu*. When other attempts to destroy the vampire have failed, the courageous Ellen sacrifices her chastity to entice Count Orlock to stay with her until sunrise, when he will meet his doom. She achieves, with her female body, what the men have been unable to do.

The New American Vampire

The 1970s see the beginning of a transitional period for women as both readers and writers of vampire narratives. The unprecedented success of Anne Rice's *Interview with the Vampire* (1976) presents not only a new paradigm for the vampire narrative—one which focuses on the subjective experience of the vampire, rather than casting him primarily as the antagonist—but also introduces the chilling figure of a vampire who is not only female, but trapped in the body of a child. In this novel, a young Louisiana planter, Louis de Pointe du Lac, is turned into a vampire by the demonic Lestat, a recent immigrant from France. Claudia, a child vampire created by Lestat as a means of binding Louis to him, gradually matures mentally, yet, as is traditional with literary vampires, she is unable to attain a physical form to match her psychological age. In some ways, Claudia's plight mirrors the status of women in Western civilization: possessed of adult mental faculties, yet condemned by physiology to remain children in the eyes of the dominant forces in society. Claudia's fury at her state leads to her attempt to kill Lestat, and eventually to her death at the hands of a coven of vampires in Paris, who cannot abide the presence in their midst of this grotesquely ancient child.

Beginning publication not long after Rice's reinvention of the vampire narrative, Chelsea Quinn Yarbro's series of historical vampire novels detailing the long life of the Comte St. Germain brings a decidedly feminist outlook to the genre. Beginning with *Hotel Transylvania* (1978), women in the novels are presented as strong intelligent personalities, although often they find themselves at the mercy of restrictive, if not downright repressive, patriarchal societies. The vampire in these novels functions as an outside observer of society, one who is capable of appreciating women on their own terms, and he works diligently to free them from the bonds their society has placed upon them. If he rescues a damsel in distress, it is only with her cooperation and assistance, and she is not his reward for his good deed. In fact, her freedom, and whatever autonomy she can achieve, are his goals.

Women as Vampire Hunters and Lovers

Beginning in 1993 with *Guilty Pleasures*, Laurell K. Hamilton's series *Anita Blake, Vampire Hunter* showed a supernaturally empowered woman "kicking butt and taking names" among creatures who should be far more powerful than she. Over the twenty years and two dozen novels of the series, Anita has evolved to the point where she questions her own humanity as she accretes more and more preternatural resources. In the beginning, she is presented as a largely normal young woman, possessed of dual attributes which enable her success as a vampire executioner: she has inherited an innate ability to raise zombies (her primary job in the first few novels is as a reanimator), and she carries within her a deep anger, which she channels outward to enable her survival against unlikely odds. With her knowledge of preternatural creatures, this no-holds-barred attitude often gives her the element of surprise in fights: no one (prior to the Age of Buffy) expects a small woman, young and pretty, to be so overwhelmingly ruthless. Later, her metaphysical bonds to a powerful vampire and a number of were-creatures transform her further. She becomes, if not physically impervious, at least inhumanly strong, and her gifts in reanimation strengthen into full-fledged necromancy.

Particularly in the early novels of the series, Anita represents an idealized everywoman. While she is possessed of extraordinary gifts, she is also forced to work hard in order to be able to utilize those gifts. Operating in the largely male milieu of law enforcement, time and again she needs to prove herself worthy to be in the game with the big boys. She works out to enhance her physical strength, and frequently comments that her ability to shoot straight or run fast is what saves her life. Later, she comes to be accepted for her expertise and her deadly competence by local law enforcement, although in the course of her work as a federal marshal she still faces prejudice and skepticism from male colleagues. It may be indicative of the societal change in viewpoint toward women that, as the series has progressed, Anita's position in her profession has also changed. Where once she drove to crime scenes on her own, and was often turned away by officious local deputies who assumed her presence was an intrusion, in later novels she often arrives like a celebrity, complete with an entourage. The law enforcement officials with whom she works are not necessarily any happier to see her than they ever were, but as her status has evolved from consultant to the Regional Preternatural Investigative Team (RPIT) and marginally tolerated vampire executioner to licensed federal marshal and nationally celebrated expert, she has transformed from a figure of contempt into a figure of intimidation. In the 2012 novel *Kiss the Dead*, the police do not like her, but they acknowledge that she is the best person to have on hand in dangerous situations involving vampires and other preternatural creatures.

In many ways, readers are invited to see Anita as a sort of amped-up version of the modern American woman. When the series opens, she is a young, college-educated, single career woman, trying to navigate the demands of a job, relationships, and life in general. She has a small apartment, an overbearing boss, and a beat-up car. Through the progression of the novels she gains a number of live-in lovers, a house, more autonomy in her reanimating job, and much more authority in her side career as a police consultant and later marshal. She suffers through a pregnancy scare and at least one badly failed relationship. Throughout this, she matures and develops, gaining strength and self-knowledge. Over the course of twenty-six (and counting) novels, Anita comes into her own and functions as a power in the sphere of her activities.

Similar to Anita Blake, the narrator and main character of Charlaine Harris's *Southern Vampire* series, Sookie Stackhouse, at first appears to be a fairly typical young woman. Although possessed of a natural intelligence and attractiveness, she has never had many opportunities in life. Orphaned at an early age and raised by her grandmother, she has been forced by economic necessity to work as a waitress in her tiny hometown of Bon Temps, Louisiana. She has one other difficulty: she is telepathic. In the world of these novels, beginning in 2001 with *Dead Until Dark*, vampires not only exist, but have "come out of the coffin," revealing their existence to the world at large. They are tolerated in American society, although the government is still struggling with questions of their citizenship and status. As the series opens, Sookie meets her first vampire, Bill Compton, a Civil War veteran returning to the town where he was born. After a lifetime of hearing the unwanted thoughts of all those around her, Sookie realizes that she cannot read the mind of this vampire. She and Bill quickly become lovers, and she is drawn into the world of supernatural politics. As with many contemporary paranormal series, Harris's novels are populated not only with humans and vampires, but a number of other supernatural creatures as well. It is eventually revealed, in fact, that Sookie herself has a trace of faerie blood, which is the probable source not only of her telepathy, but also of the attraction most vampires feel for her.

Despite the supernatural shenanigans that surround her, Sookie continues to be concerned with such mundane matters as new gravel for her driveway, her continued employment at Merlotte's Bar and Grill, and returning her library books on time. While she does have a psychic talent that is out of the ordinary, she presents as an everyday, small-town woman, doing what she needs to do to get by. While the love interests in her life are definitely extraordinary—shape-changers and vampires as they are—readers can easily see themselves in her situation, perhaps with hopes that they would be able to react as sensibly as she.

Willing Freshies and Fangbangers: Vampire Relationships with Human Women in Contemporary Television

The act of feeding for the vampire in literature and film has often been eroticized, with the act of the bite either substituting for heteronormative or homoerotic sexual activity, or accompanying it. With the rise of the increasingly romanticized vampire in popular genre fiction, television, and film, this tendency has been given more graphic expression. In recent media depictions, the television series *Moonlight* and *True Blood*, the humans willing to feed vampires are generally characterized in terms paralleling prostitutes, and the main love interests of the vampires in these series risk falling into that category of perception.

The vampire, by his nature, is transgressive against the natural order of life and society; his need to drink the blood of the living puts him outside the bounds of normal human activities. Yet while the bite of the vampire may represent transgressive sexuality, the burden of participation in that transgression against societal norms is placed on the woman feeding the vampire in these contemporary television interpretations of the genre, with implications for the vampire/human love relationship. This perceived onus resting more heavily on the human part of the mixed couple serves as a both a reinforcement and an ironic subversion of patriarchal hegemony, with the vampire acting both as a replacement for the iconic heteronormative masculine, and as a representative of the Other, outside the norms and mores of contemporary culture. If women in ordinary human relationships are perceived as less than morally upright when they have any sexual relations outside wedlock, and are subsequently characterized as "sluts" or "whores," then how much more degrading it must be, in these narratives, to have sex with dead men, and bear the visible scars of that degradation. Feeding the vampire is an activity that leaves marks, and not just those neat little puncture scars on the throat. In the vampire narrative, whether on the page or onscreen, blood is never just blood.

Interestingly, every constructed world where vampires are present now seems to include some recognition of the willing human blood donor, often with a particular term attached. In *Moonlight* (2007–2008), the putative secrecy of the vampire nation means that the term "freshie" is known and used only by vampires (and presumably those relatively few humans in the know). On the other hand, the term "fangbanger," used in *True Blood* (2008–2014), seems to have more common currency among humans—presumably because vampires have renounced their secrecy. Fangbangers, or vampire groupies, are mostly habitués of vampire clubs, and seem to be there as much for the sex as for the bite. In *True Blood*'s world of legal vampirism, vampire clubs and fangbangers are known not only to the vampires and a select group of humans, but also to the general public, who regard the vampire-addicted humans with contempt. Further, the violent societal reaction against vampires, best exemplified by the radical evangelical Fellowship of the Sun, certainly seems to place the vampire as an outcast from righteous and right-thinking society, who must be shunned or destroyed since he cannot be reclaimed. The Fellowship is not terribly keen on humans who consort with vampires, either, and about the mildest epithet they have for such people is "fangbanger whore," a term that is, in fact, applied to main character Sookie Stackhouse.

Meanwhile, in *Moonlight*, reluctant vampire Mick St. John explains the concept of freshies to his human girlfriend, Beth Turner ("Sonata," 1.16). At a charity function, they have just met up with his vampire best friend, Josef Kostan, and his date Simone. Josef, without much regard for propriety or anything else, has hauled Simone off into a corner for a drink, as he says, "because the champagne just ain't cuttin' it." There's very little romance there; Josef simply takes her arm and leads her away, as she stammers a somewhat embarrassed comment to Mick and Beth. Beth begins to query her vampire lover as to what the situation is, exactly, and Mick explains that people who feed vampires are called freshies. Beth presses, asking, "Is it a paid arrangement, or like 'friends with benefits'?" Mick's answer is equivocal at best; Beth is not terribly amused, and presses him further, asking Mick if he's ever had freshies. Mick evasively replies, "I've been a vampire for over fifty years." The conversation has an obvious overtone of "have you ever been to a prostitute," but it's unclear whether freshies can be more than just blood donors and casual flings. Later in the same episode, when Beth asks if Josef would become seriously involved with Simone, Mick's response is, "Not with a freshie. Josef has rules."

In both *True Blood* and *Moonlight*, the existence of the willing blood donor, and society's general attitude toward them, is established in the first episode of each series. In *Moonlight*, vampire private investigator Mick pays a visit to Josef, who is presented as a ruthless businessman, surrounded by the trappings of wealth and power. At his futuristic, palatial house, one can see naked women lounging by the pool outside the glass-walled living area. During the course of Mick's conversation with Josef, the older vampire asks if Mick would "care for any liquid refreshment?" and shouts a command, "Hungry!" whereupon an attractive young woman appears ("No Such Thing as Vampires," 1.01). Josef handles the woman carelessly, never speaking directly to her, and comments to his friend that she's "delicious." Mick declines the offer, and Josef admonishes him for denying his "inner vampire." After Mick leaves, Josef lifts the young woman's gracefully offered wrist, allows his vampire side to emerge, and sinks his fangs into her forearm, to her evident and erotically charged delight.

Later in the same episode, the term freshie is used for the first time to denote human blood donors. In another episode ("Arrested Development," 1.05), the connection between freshies and prostitutes is underlined by a comment from Mick. While investigating the murder of a woman euphemistically characterized as an "escort," he states, "Between willing freshies and basic vamp appeal, vampires don't normally need to patronize 'women of the trade.'" He seems to have some disdain for freshies; in "Fever" (1.04), when circumstances dictate that he must drink Beth's blood to save his life, he responds to her offer with "Not yours! Not like this!"—a comment that has inspired endless discussion by fans of what he really meant by that.

Similarly, the first episode of *True Blood* features a discussion of fangbangers in Sookie's kitchen, with her brother Jason and her grandmother ("Strange Love," 1.01). This is one of those fascinating "good women are interested in prostitution" conversations, reminiscent of the respectable little old Southern ladies so interested in the interior of the scandalous Belle Watling's house in *Gone with the Wind*. When they learn of the death of a woman named Maudette Pickens, Jason comments that a murder in their tiny town is not unexpected, now that they have a vampire in residence. Sookie, already rather taken with "Vampire Bill" Compton, protests that it's not necessarily the vampire's fault, and Jason counters with a story about how fangbangers go missing all the time in the city, and everyone knows the vampires kill them and dispose of the bodies. Gran, not quite as up-to-date with modern slang, asks, "What's a fangbanger?" and Sookie explains that they are vampire groupies, "men and women who like to get bitten." Jason goes on to expound on hookers who specialize in vampires, and follows up with salacious details while the women listen in fascinated disgust, surprised to learn that Maudette would do such a thing.

Before long, though, Sookie has been bitten herself. In "Mine" (1.03), Bill lays formal claim to her as his own, not to be touched by his vampire friends. The other humans present act very much as slavish whores, ordered by the vampires to provide oral sex and blood at will. It seems to be almost a given in the contemporary vampire narrative that, when vampires have sex, biting and blood are involved. There is an allusion to this in *Moonlight* as well, when Mick tells Josef one of the obstacles to his romance with Beth is that "I tend to bite down when I—" and before he can finish his comment, Josef interrupts him with a smirk, saying, "Some women like that" ("Fated to Pretend," 1.13). One suspects the four-hundred-year-old hedonist Josef would know.

In *True Blood*, when Bill and Sookie make love, there is biting and there is blood: it's just part of the deal. (And, since the series ran on Cable TV, it's directly and graphically portrayed, whereas *Moonlight*, a broadcast series, could only allude to the more intimate aspects of vampire sex and feeding.) In both series, there is the question of whether being bitten by the vampire means that the woman is "damaged goods," whether freshie or fangbanger. In episode "B.C." (1.06) of *Moonlight*, Mick is getting beaten by an older, wilier vampire in a fight. Things are not going well for Mick, at least until his opponent, who is maybe not quite as wily as we thought, makes a comment about Mick's "little freshie friend." There is an immediate transformation: Mick is clearly upset, rallies, and the tables turn rapidly. You don't insult his girl by calling her a filthy name.

The depiction of freshies in *Moonlight* definitely parallels prostitutes, or at least party girls. In "Sleeping Beauty" (1.10), Josef, in need of blood and stuck in Mick's apartment, does not deign to drink his friend's bottled supply, but rather gets out his little black book (or rather, his little Blackberry) and calls in three young ladies. When Mick returns to his apartment, he finds the party in full swing. As he approaches the door, he hears glasses clinking, music, and Josef saying, "All right, we're going to play a little game. The rules are, you kiss her..." Mick righteously comes in and throws out the three freshies before Josef has a chance to feed. One must in fairness point out, however, that these women are not treated badly; upon leaving, each of them kisses Josef, and murmurs affectionately to him (the last one even says, "Love you, Josef"). Party girls, yes. Willing donors, most definitely. Blood prostitutes, perhaps not. The difference in attitudes toward freshies and fangbangers between the two series seems to parallel the difference between a somewhat repressive, small-town Southern society and a sophisticated, upscale, urban area such as Los Angeles.

In both *Moonlight* and *True Blood*, there is a price to be paid for a relationship with a vampire, which has nothing to do with losing blood. Beth was perhaps saved by the premature cancellation of *Moonlight* from experiencing much social disapprobation concerning her relationship with Mick, but Sookie definitely sees the effects almost immediately. She must, among other things, submit to Bill proclaiming her "owned" status (1.03), and to being called a fangbanger, as though a woman who would sleep with one vampire would therefore agree to be bitten by *any* vampire. In *Moonlight*, that's seen a little more clearly in the character of Josef's freshie, Simone, in "Sonata" (1.16). Beth herself comments to Mick that she suspects "blood isn't the only bodily fluid [Josef and Simone] are sharing." At another point in the episode, when Josef insists on Mick tasting Simone's blood to determine her blood type, they are interrupted by Beth, who interprets the scene of Mick, with his mouth on Simone's wrist, as "making out," despite Mick's protests to the contrary. When Beth has an opportunity to speak with Simone privately, however, the freshie insists that feeding is not as intimate for vampires as it seems for the humans, because vampires cannot afford to become emotionally attached to short-lived mortals.

These differences between humans and vampires threaten to tear apart the relationships in both series. During an emotional scene in *True Blood*, Sookie says to Bill, "I always thought as different as we are, somehow, we could still be together," but worries that she is not sure if they can overcome his ease with taking human life (2.01). His response is that he will never apologize for what she has awakened in him; that "for the first time in a hundred and forty years, I felt something I thought had been lost to me forever.... I love you." Meanwhile, in *Moonlight*, Beth has decided that she cannot go on with the relationship, because vampire culture is just too alien to her notions of justice. She tells Mick that his assertion that they live in different worlds means they cannot be together, and she has come to agree. Mick leaves her, but comes back to say that he has realized she was right all along, that it isn't about being a vampire, or a human, but "this is about us, how we feel about one another, right here, right now" (1.16). In both cases, the music swells, and kissing and lovemaking ensue.

Conclusions: Romancing the Vampire

In Judith Halberstam's *Skin Shows: Gothic Horror and the Technology of Monsters*, she comments that in contemporary horror films, "Gothic monstrosity has become Gothic masculinity and fear is coded as the female response to masculine desire" (1995, 108). In the contemporary vampire narrative on television, the fear resides not so much in the female, who loves the vampire and welcomes his desire, but in society's fear that the monstrous masculinity of the vampire will replace the need for traditional masculinity. Fearing the vampire, the brunt of disapproval of the monstrous is displaced onto the women who find little to fear within his arms. For Sookie and Beth, vampires become both the reason for their estrangement from normal human society and their protection from society's stones. If their actions are transgressive, they differ little from those of heroines of literature and film down through the ages, who have risked all for lovers standing outside the restrictions and bounds of culture or country.

The vampire, as configured in this modern romance narrative, is overwhelmingly male, and has a strong compulsion to protect his mated female. In this sort of portrayal, he becomes the quintessential bigger, badder predator who can effectively guard a weaker female from the dangers and depredations of the modern world. In the fantasy landscape of escapist literature, then, the vampire becomes one of the best protectors a woman can find, regardless of her desire to remain independent and self-determining. In addition, in these contemporary narratives, if the vampire serves as a protector for his chosen woman from the vicissitudes of the world, she fulfills an equally important function in maintaining the vampire's well-being. The vampire romance presents the heroine not as a helpless mortal female at the mercy of the vampire hero (or villain), but instead as an empowered partner whose very mortality, whose blood, is vital to her beloved.

"I'll give you blood to drink"
The New Vampire in Novels About the Salem Witch Trials

MARTA MARÍA GUTIÉRREZ-RODRÍGUEZ

> I am no more a witch than you are a wizard and if you take away my life, God will give you blood to drink.
> —Calef 2002, 358

Introduction

Sarah Good, one of the first persons accused of witchcraft during the Salem Witch Trials, pronounced the words above when she was about to be executed and the Reverend Nicholas Noyes was trying to convince her to confess her alliance with the Devil. Several years afterwards, the Puritan Minister died of an internal hemorrhage; the curse that the supposed witch put on him before dying was fulfilled (Baker 2015, 32). Although there were no vampires in Salem in 1692, novelists "disagree" with the historical reality and this essay is going to examine the relationship that writers have established between vampires and this historical event.

The town of Salem, Massachusetts, has been known worldwide as "the witch city," since the year 1692, when the most famous witch-hunt of colonial America took place. Despite the more than two hundred accusations of witchcraft, hardly any scholar has been able to prove that there were real witches in Salem. Nonetheless, in the last decades, authors of historical fiction and romance novels have included female characters with supernatural powers as protagonists of their literary works, with an important emphasis placed in showing that having unnatural abilities can benefit the community and that the use of magic is not necessarily linked with indulging harm and provoking catastrophes. Consequently, these fictional representations of the Salem witch-hunt vindicate the innocence of the people who were hanged in 1692 while they introduce the (fictional) possibility of supernatural forces being present at that time.

Due to the notoriety that vampires have enjoyed in the last decades, some of the writers who have made use of this historical event in their novels have decided to accompany the supposed witches with these other supernatural beings. There are many reasons that explain the pairing of these two mythic/folkloric creatures. First, they have been identified as servants of Satan and symbols of everything that is evil. Second, throughout history, they have been demonized and considered monsters and heretics. Finally, as symbols they stand for a wide range of social, political, and cultural aspects in moments of crisis. Consequently, when there are suspicions of their presence, they are hunted and destroyed. Finally, there is a historical relationship between New England and vampires: during the 18th and 19th centuries there were reports of vampirism, mostly associated with the disease that was called consumption at the time, and that we currently know as tuberculosis.

This essay examines the figure of the vampire in three novels about the Salem Witch Trials to see what these creatures add to the fictional construction of this historical event. The works analyzed are *Jonathan Hale: The First American Vampire* (2009) and its sequel *Salem Lost* (2010) by Frank R. Godbey, Jr., and *Her Dear and Loving Husband* (2011) by Meredith Allard, the first book of the trilogy under the same name. I pay special attention to what elements of the mythical or folkloric vampire have been used in these novels, as well as the type of vampire—i.e., romantic, charming and gentle, or villainous, hideous and grotesque—that has been introduced. The two authors have decided to use different genres in their fictional construction of the Salem Witch Trials: Godbey's work is a traditional historical novel set in 1692 while Allard's is a paranormal romance set in contemporary Salem. This difference is going to affect the type of vampire that each author is going to introduce as well as the role that it will play in relation with the historical events.

From Folklore to Literature: The Transformation of the Vampire

The vampire is conceived differently in different countries denoting different beings and coming from different origins (Beresford 2008, 7–8; Gelder 1994, 24). As Nina Auerbach says, "vampires are easy to stereotype, but it is their variety what makes them survivors" (1995, vii). Nonetheless, what all the definitions and descriptions have in common is their relation to "fear, horror, revulsion, as well as fascination and even reverence" (Kratter 1998, 32). Vampires have adapted and developed as humanity has progressed (Curran 2012, intro, Kindle LOC 53; Kratter 1998, 32). They have adjusted to changes in political circumstances and this versatility "attests to its vitality as a contemporary myth" (McClelland 2009, 17).

Originally, vampires were far from supernatural entities, shape-shifters or any sort of mythological or demonic being. The first vampires were connected, it appears, with a refusal to abandon beliefs and practices that were considered anathema by the Eastern Church. Consequently, the term was used as a pejorative label for people practicing rituals unacceptable to Christianity (Beresford 2008, 41–42, 45). These first vampires were just members of a village community who simply refused to abandon their religious practices (Beresford 2008, 48). Nevertheless, in time, these villagers were transformed into bloodsuckers, greedy and infectious men. However, these individuals were anonymous and when literature and cinema started paying attention to them, vampires acquired a face and a personality.

The literary vampire was born in the 19th century with classical works such as Polidori's *The Vampyre* (1819), which established the prototype of the vampire that most later creations seem to follow in the Ruthven formula (Beresford 2008, 118); James Malcolm Rymer's *Varney, the Vampire* (1847), which can be considered the first attempt to make the reader empathize with the vampire, and hence a precedent to Anne Rice's *Vampire Chronicles* (Beresford 2008, 124); Sheridan Le Fanu's *Carmilla* (1872), which included lesbian vampirism; and Bram Stoker's *Dracula* (1897), the novel that established the construction of literary vampires for nearly a century. The result of these works is the figure of the Victorian vampire, a male aristocrat with cape, fangs, and the ability to shape-shift (Beresford 2008, 8).

Up to the 1970s, the vampire was commonly represented as a "blood-draining monster" (Chaplin 2017, 10). The publication in 1976 of Anne Rice's *Interview with the Vampire* initiates a tradition of texts "that strive to represent the vampire as a more sympathetic, or even tragic protagonist" (Chaplin 2017, 2). Rice's novels should be considered the starting point of "the process by which the demon/monstrous vampire is transformed into a hero" (McClelland 2009, 28). This shift has been widely discussed by scholars such as Beresford (2008), Chaplin (2017), Mutch (2013) and Zanger (1997), among many others. What these authors commonly accept is the fact that vampires become more human, moving from the predators depicted in previous texts such as *Dracula, I Am Legend* or *'Salem's Lot* "to the tortured, sympathetic and often highly romanticized hero-vampires of contemporary culture" (Chaplin 2017, 3). Consequently, the vampire is no longer the feared being that it once was mainly because it has undergone a process of domestication (Gordon and Hollinger 1997, 2), "[…] of humanization and, indeed, romanticization"

(Chaplin 2017, 17). The humanization of the literary vampire may be seen in their loss of the ability to transform themselves into bats, mist or wolves; the lack of effect of mirrors and crucifixes on them (Zanger 1997, 18); and the possibility of moving around in daylight (Gelder 1994, 35). The new vampire has also been stripped of its metaphysical characteristics of magical "other," as well as of its metaphorical construction as the Anti-Christ (Zanger 1997, 17), hence deleting some of the religious connotations that originally gave this creature much of its appeal. Therefore, the new vampire's evil acts are the expression of its individual personality and condition, and not of any cosmic conflict between God and Satan. Accordingly, we can find both good and bad vampires.

Anne Rice's novels changed the course of the vampire's evolution. She created a personality for the vampire, a kind of desperate being that was continually struggling to understand its cursed existence (Beresford 2008, 145–149). Consequently, the new vampire is not only evil, but it shows more complexity as it can experience tension, rivalries, betrayals and even love (Zanger 1997, 22). In addition to this transformation, Rice is probably the first writer to give them a voice; they are the ones who narrate their own history, in a clear contrast with the epistolary style of Bram Stoker's *Dracula*. After Rice, many authors started to narrate their stories from the vampire's perspective, hence creating empathy between the "monster" and the reader— something that would have been unthinkable in previous decades (Gordon and Hollinger 1997, 2).

Susan Chaplin (2017, 38–39) adds two more elements to the characteristics of the new vampire. The first one refers to vampires becoming communal, i.e., they are no longer lone predators but creatures who struggle to assert their personality within conflicted societies. It is common to find communities of vampires who fight together against intolerance and violence. The second one is related to blood-feeding. Although it continues being the substance that guarantees immortality, in some instances it becomes a commodity, as in the case of *True Blood*, where a chemically produced substance replaces human blood and the necessity to hunt people or animals. The result of this transformation is that, as Matthew Beresford argues, "we no longer fear the vampire" (2008, 145). The multimedia proliferation of the last decades has also influenced this transformation (Zanger 1997, 17) in the sense that it has been exploited until it has become a "household product" (Beresford 2008, 145).

Fearing Evil: Witches and Vampires

From the very beginning of the incorporation of the vampire into the European literary tradition, ample equivalence has been established between the witch and the vampire. When the tragic witch-hunt of the early modern period was still fresh in memory, the role of the witch was replaced by the one of the vampire. Proof of this are the hysterical vampire epidemics that happened at the end of the 18th century in areas that had been contaminated by contemporary ideas about witches and witchcraft (McClellan 2009, xi, 4).

They were caused by rumors of strange vampire phenomena brought by travelers and returning soldiers from the fringes of the Balkans and the Transylvanian region to western countries (Beresford 2008, 4, 53–76). Consequently, when the projection of evil onto the figure of the witch had been suppressed, the vampire arose to stand in as the perfect helpless victim of communal violence (Beresford 2008, 51–52; McClelland 2009, xiv). Witches and vampires are manifestations of evil in the sense that they are somehow related with the Devil or Satan. As Western society became more secular, these two figures were increasingly used to accentuate the negative pole of Christianity. Both are represented as enemies of all that is good; the witch is portrayed as indulging in corrupt inversions of Christian ritual and behavior, and vampires are destroyed by sacred implements of Christian magic. Among the many forms of evil that can attack humanity, the one that cannot be clearly identified is considered the most dangerous, and the witch and the vampire are very difficult to distinguish from common people. Further, it is difficult to assign blame for society's misfortunes, were it not for the presence of people with superior abilities that allow them to identify these mysterious creatures. In the case of witches, the Inquisition and the cohort of witch-hunters were the ones endowed with these powers, even though in most of the cases the only defining feature of the people whom they accused were their "erroneous belief and unholy actions" (McClelland 2009, 24). Regarding the undead, vampire hunters and/or slayers were summoned in order to identify them, as they are the only ones who possess "the necessary insight to recognize a vampire and the knowledge of the necessary rituals to destroy one" (McClelland 2009, 6).

Both witches and vampires have thus been transformed, even "mythologized," by such collective persecutions because they can be considered clear incarnations of both physical deformity and moral monstrosity (McClelland 2009, xiv). However, we can also find differences between these two creatures. To begin with, the witch is alive and has a social status, whereas the vampire is dead or, rather, undead, and has "no valid identity, no evident social position" (McClelland 2009, 24). While witches are mainly identified as women, vampires are seen as men (McClelland 2009, 30), though we can find both genders represented in both groups of creatures. Moreover, witches are related with conspiracies, through their relationship with Satan and their assembly on what is known as the Witches' Sabbath[1] to plot against Christianity or even the whole humanity. On the contrary, vampires do not tend to assemble.

This difference can be easily linked with the position of the witch within the community and the one of the vampire "from without" (Kratter 1998, 37). As John Demos notes: "The witch ... is discovered ... inside the host community. [...] Thus, too, witch-hunting has an intensely countersubversive, anti-conspiratorial tone. Always and everywhere, its goal is to root out the hidden enemy within" (2008: 3). In any case, both vampires and witches are invisible enemies in the sense that normally there are no external marks that help to identify them.[2] Nonetheless, when it comes to formal accusations, the witch's invisibility disappears in the form of confessions obtained through torture or by evidence of the possession of supernatural powers or knowledge in the sense of healing or herbology (Beresford 2008, 51).

At the symbolic level, witches and vampires incarnate our darkest fears and perceptions and work as night visitors that torment people. Curran (2012) and Demos (2008) agree on how these two creatures embody "xenophobia within some areas of the world" (Curran 2012, intro, Kindle LOC 159). In the case of the vampire, "anyone who was foreign, anti-social, or had strange ways about them was almost certain to become a vampire upon death" (Curran 2012, intro, Kindle LOC 162). Similarly, "witch-hunting ... belongs to a still more capacious terrain that also includes racism, sexism, and anti–Semitism, as well as pogroms, lynching, genocide, and ethnic cleansing" (Demos 2008, 3). Examples of this can be clearly seen in the connections established between witch-hunting and the McCarthy Era (Demos 2008, 266–274), the child sex-abuse crisis of the 1980s and 199s (Demos 2008, 274–281), and the "demonization" of the Muslim community after the September 11, 2001, terrorist attacks in New York (Hill, 2004). In the case of vampirism, since the mid–20th century, it has been associated with the transmission of virus and infections (Chaplin 2017, 88), diseases and plagues (Beresford 2008, 100–101) and, consequently, with AIDs/HIV (Kratter 1998, 35).

Vampires in Fictional Salem

Jonathan Hale, The First American Vampire opens in the late 1630s with the protagonist arriving in the colony of Massachusetts and discovering that he has been buried alive. He felt ill while on board his ship, the *Arabella*, and he seemed dead when they arrived; consequently, he was put into a tomb (Godbey 2009, chap. 1, Kindle LOC 41). Soon we discover the reasons for his travel: he was excommunicated in the Old World and he decided to search for freedom in the New one. When he awakes in his grave, he feels that something has changed in him: he is able to see in the dark, he has an overwhelming desire for blood, and he learns that he cannot cross a stream and that there is no reflection of him on the water. When he meets other human beings, he can hear people's thoughts, and realizes that bullets do not hurt him. He is fascinated with his supernatural powers:

> The whole experience was new and to a degree frightening to Jonathan. He did not know what it all meant, but it was fascinating. He felt for the first time in his life that he was completely in control. He feared nothing and no one. He could go wherever he wanted and do whatever he desired. This was true power in his eyes [Godbey 2009, chap. 5, Kindle LOC 426].

However, the downsides of his new condition are soon revealed: "Yet with all his power, he was alone. The loneliness of his solitude was a terrible feeling" (Godbey 2009, chap. 10, kindle LOC 965). This conflict between the fascination with his powers and the doom of his new condition will accompany him for the rest of his days.

Jonathan finds an ally in Richard Bennet, a carpenter, to conceal his condition. Although their alliance starts under a threat of killing the man if he reveals his true identity, they finally become friends. Bennet helps him to recover his coffin from the ship and agrees to take him into his house, keeping him safe while he sleeps during the day. Jonathan starts feeling a sudden fascination for Sally, his first victim. He talks to her through his mind so that she starts feeling the same. There is no violence when he attacks her: "Jonathan stood up and went over to her. He pushed her long red hair from her neck and ran his fingers down her cheek. It was as though she was under her spell" (Godbey 2009, chap. 1, Kindle LOC 159). She is turned into a vampire so that Jonathan will have a companion with whom to spend the rest of eternity.

However, it is his thirst for blood that transforms him into a violent creature when he realizes that he needs it to survive. This necessity makes him start questioning his own humanity: "What kind of creature am I that I need another human's blood to sustain my own life [...] Surely a monster such as I will burn in Hell forever" (Godbey 2009, chap. 1, Kindle LOC 170). The people he bites do not react to his attacks; they obey him and go back to their lives: "It seems that all my victims are under my complete control. As if, [sic] I had utterly hypnotized them" (Godbey 2009, chap. 6, Kindle LOC 561). Nonetheless, when he feels his integrity is at risk or when someone discovers his true identity, the monster inside takes over, and he does not deal so gently with people. This is the case of the sailors who recognize him as the man they buried before they reached land or the Indian camp he burns to ashes.

Due to all the strange deaths and disappearances happening in the town, authorities start to suspect that "there is an evil among us and I do not know what to do about it. I cannot fight something I cannot see" (Godbey 2009, chap. 15, Kindle LOC 1557). In Salem, this sentence takes an important significance, because several decades before the witch-hunt, the inhabitants of this place experienced a feeling like the one provoked by the suspicion of the practicing of witchcraft. However, this anxiety disappears when Sally and Jonathan decide to enjoy a quiet life without raising any suspicion about their condition. After 48 years living in the same place with unchanged appearances, they decide to move to Salem Village in the year 1690. Soon afterwards they are involved in the witch-hunt and play an important role in the fictional development of these events.

Their first acquaintances are Sarah and Edward Bishop, tavern owners who suffer the verbal attacks of the strict Puritans who consider their business evil. Since Jonathan was excommunicated because of his rejection of the established faith in the Old World, he does not feel any sympathy for Puritans, and all his rage is directed toward one of them: the minister Samuel Parris: "The hypocrisy of Parris's preaching considering what he had done to his woman left Jonathan with a disgusted feeling in the pit of his stomach" (Godbey 2009, chap. 26, Kindle LOC 2227). The woman Jonathan refers to is Tituba, whose tragic story he sees in her mind as he bites her, reminding Jonathan of memories of the suffering that his sister had to endure after being raped by their minister. However, Jonathan's rage toward Puritans is diverted toward Indians when one of them kills Sally, condemning him again to the loneliness of his condition. He slaughters all but one member of the tribe, making him feel the pain of losing his dear ones. At this point in the story, he is so desperate that he jumps into the river to kill himself.

The sequel, *Salem Lost* (2010), focuses on the role Jonathan played in the Salem Witch Trials. It begins with him realizing that his suicide attempt has failed. His new helpers are Sarah and Edward Bishop; their tavern is going to provide him with the blood he needs—mainly through the maids who work there—without drawing attention from the villagers or the authorities. In return, he frees them from those who attack their tavern as a place of evil dealings. His rage against Samuel Parris continues unabated, and he plans to use Tituba to destroy Parris. This involves controlling the mind of the slave to divide the family of the minister: first, by uncovering the attraction that Parris feels for Tituba to make his wife jealous, and, second, by telling the girls stories about her native land, Barbados, some of them involving magical practices that were forbidden by the Puritan doctrine. Because of Jonathan's orders, Tituba teaches the girls a "fortune telling game" (Godbey 2010, chap. 2, Kindle LOC 341) to discover the profession of their future husbands. Historians use this incident to explain the strange behavior of the girls that led to the witch-hunts. In this novel, Jonathan is consequently responsible for their behavior, as Tituba taught the girls this "magic" trick following his instructions.

Jonathan's plan against Parris seems to work. However, the girls from the village discover his cellar and coffin, and he must use his ability to control their minds to prevent them from revealing his secret. He loses control of the situation and the girls are terrified by what they see in their minds: a man dressed in black who entered a coffin. Once again, Jonathan is responsible for the fits that the girls suffered and that, in this novel, are real. The girls are telling the truth of what they see in their visions; their behavior is the result of something real. When Jonathan wants to stop the first accusations, people whose minds he had never controlled join the group of girls. Consequently, "the whole witch-hunt hysteria was his making because of the hate that he had for Parris. Nothing went, [sic] as it should have" (Godbey 2010, chap. 21, Kindle LOC 3960).

In these two novels we see a mixture of the old and the new vampire. On the one hand, he is still an independent being, with no need to belong to a community, keeping his true condition undercover. On the other hand, these two novels follow Anne Rice's tradition and tell the story from the vampire's point of view. One of the most frequent feelings he experiences is remorse for his beasty behavior; we can see some degree of domestication in him, as he does not kill if he is not attacked, but just takes the blood he needs to survive. He is nevertheless presented as the one responsible for the accusations of witchcraft because he wanted to take revenge on a man who represented everything he hated: hypocrisy and bigotry. However, he was acting just like the Puritans he was criticizing, and it is this behavior that provoked guiltless people to be accused of witchcraft and the shedding of innocent blood.

Accordingly, he is presented as the evil that destroyed Salem in 1692 because, were it not for him, the witch-hunt would not have happened. By placing him as the origin of the strange behavior of the girls, this novel is filling in one of the unknown areas of this historical event; to this day, there is no definitive explanation of what led a group of girls to accuse so many people of being witches.

Meredith Allard's *Her Dear and Loving Husband* (2011) introduces us to a supernatural modern-day Salem where witches, vampires, and werewolves walk the streets of the city without being noticed by humans. The protagonist of this novel is Sarah Alexander, who discovers that she is the reincarnation of one of the women accused of being witches: Elizabeth Wentworth. Not only this, she also discovers that her husband in her past life, James Wentworth, is still alive because he is a vampire.

The vampires in this novel could be, as Jules Zanger argues, "our next-door neighbor" (1997, 19). James Wentworth is a college teacher at Salem State who only teaches evening classes. He was turned in 1692 while his pregnant wife was in jail, accused of being a witch; she was not hanged but died while waiting for her execution. Among his unnatural abilities he can hear people's minds, and his senses, mostly his hearing, are more developed than in average humans. He wears fake glasses—like Superman—to hide his paleness and the dullness in his eyes.

With the passing of time, his behavior as an undead has suffered a dramatic transformation. In his early years as a vampire he can be described as the blood-sucker monster of folklore; as the years passed, he became more humanized and domesticated, reducing his attacks for mere survival; even this stops when he is provided with human blood in bags taken from the hospital by a nurse who knows about his condition. However, his violent side comes to light when he or his beloved are in danger. When he reveals his true condition to Sarah, she is rejected, mainly because she felt that he had been lying by concealing such a big secret from her for months. Discovering her identity as the reincarnation of Elizabeth helps her to better understand the supernatural world, and the love she feels for him is stronger that her reluctance toward being in love with a vampire.

Nonetheless, James is not the only vampire living in Salem. One of his students, Timothy, is "tired of having to hide" his true nature (Allard 2011, 58) and thinks that people in general will react in a positive way if the world learns of their existence. James, because he lived through the Salem Witch Trials, thinks that "people aren't ready to know. Bad things happen when people are confronted with things they don't understand" (Allard 2011, 58).

James teaches him everything he needs to get used to his new condition, something that James did not have, as he does not know who turned him into a vampire. Eventually he meets his creator: Geoffrey, who only reveals himself because there is a threat to their kind that must be stopped, and he needs James' help. There is also a dentist, Jocelyn, who is also a vampire and has been married with a human for several decades; this gives hope to our protagonists that the love they feel for each other can overcome all the difficulties derived from belonging to two different races.

This book includes an element that did not appear in the other novels but that is typical of the vampire genre: a vampire hunter or slayer. In fact, there is an interesting debate in the novel about the difference between hunting vampires and slaying them, focusing on what role Van Helsing played in the novel *Dracula*: "I don't want to slay vampires. I want to hunt them, flush them into the open" (Allard 2011, 71). Kenneth Hemple is a staff writer working for *The Salem News* who is doing field research about the presence of vampires in Salem: "I'm not interested in literary vampires, Professor. I'm interested in real vampires that walk the streets right here in Salem and probably all over the world" (Allard 2011, 62). He knows James is a vampire but cannot prove it. Hemple pursues James relentlessly to find physical evidence of his true identity. When he publishes an article explaining his suspicions, he is severely criticized. The vampire-hunter in this novel has a personal motive in his desire to reveal the existence of vampires: his father was murdered by one. Hemple witnessed the dramatic attack when he was a teenager, and ever since has suffered the accusation of being mentally disturbed because of his insistence in blaming a vampire for his father's death. By proving the truth, he will demonstrate that there is nothing wrong with his mind and that vampires are real.

James, in his present condition, is not evil. On the contrary, he risks his life to prevent a new hunt from happening in Salem. He agrees to meet Hemple in daylight to prove that he is a normal human being. James has already experienced the consequences of such exposure years before, and what he remembers is an unendurable pain. With the help of the other supernatural beings living in Salem, he manages to go to his appointment at noon, keeping Salem's underworld safe and preventing the city from suffering another dramatic hunt.

The revenants in this novel clearly conform to the new vampires typical of the twenty-first century, as communality has been established as one of the most common tropes of postmillennial vampires (Chaplin 2017, 11; Gelder 1994, 106). Although they continue being lone individuals, they stay in contact with other members of their kind. However, the conflicts they must fight do not only come from outside, as Jonathan must come to terms with Timothy to keep their condition secret. Accordingly, this novel foregrounds "a community of vampires beset by conflict from within (…) and without" (Chaplin 2017, 11). Though they have some unnatural skills far beyond the capacity of any human being, such as being able to hear people talk at a distance, they do not display any supernatural power such as shape-shifting. There are a few hints of violent behavior but this only happens when they feel threatened or someone they care about is in danger. Though we do not know much about Jocelyn's feelings, both Timothy and Jonathan feel that immortality is a punishment rather than a gift at the beginning of the novel. However, James changes his mind when he recovers the love of his life and sees the possibility of spending eternity with her. He encourages Timothy to be patient and wait for his opportunity to find his place in the world.

Finally, in this novel, the Salem Witch Trials are just the backdrop against which the danger of a new hunt is presented. The unjust death of James's wife and unborn child is what encourages him to put all his efforts into preventing something similar from happening again in the present. Accordingly, James has nothing to do with the evil of Salem in 1692. Quite the contrary; James tried to save the lives of his wife and his friends, arguing against what was happening and trying to expose the irrationality of what was occurring. He failed in the past, but he refuses to fail again in the present.

Conclusions

The novels examined in this essay demonstrate the coexistence of traditional and new attributes of the vampire. Although in general they seem to have been domesticated and humanized, they still retain some hints of violence and blood-sucking instincts, though these are mainly relegated to moments when they feel threatened or for their survival. The narrative techniques used by both novelists derive from the tradition initiated by Anne Rice of showing the vampires' perspectives. The reader cannot but sympathize with these creatures who were forced to abandon their human condition without warning, and who must cope with new situations they have not been prepared to face. When reading from within, these literary vampires hide their inner beasts, and justify their violent behavior through the difficult situations they must survive.

Each novel assigns them a different role in the Salem Witch Trials. In the case of Godbey's novels, the vampire is used to incorporate fictional reasons to explain the Salem witch-hunt. As has already been pointed out, Jonathan's desire to get rid of Samuel Parris as the incarnation of the Puritan doctrine he hates leads him to use his supernatural powers on the minds of the girls who eventually would start the accusations. In a clear contrast, the vampire in Allard's novel incarnates the distress derived from the possibility of a new hunt happening in contemporary Salem. He clearly seems to have learned the lessons of the past and he does not want to go through a new persecution again—to the point that he prefers to die and sacrifice himself rather than allow the city to suffer the madness of a community drawn by prejudices. This may relate to the current tendency in which "more and more victims of collective persecution are being rehabilitated and brought to light" (Kratter 1998, 35). Witches and vampires are used in this novel as stand-ins for the people who have been persecuted just for being or thinking differently. By presenting them as innocent victims of their own time and circumstances, what the novel is claiming is that when reason triumphs over superstition and when the most genuine human feelings prevail, no more scapegoats would be necessary to explain the unexplainable or to assign blame for the miseries of the world.

Notes

1. The rituals practiced in these sabbaths involved the inversion of many of the Christian rituals (Gibson 2018, 8) and in them "witches not only paid homage to the Devil but also engaged in a variety of gluttonous, lewd, infanticidal and cannibalistic practices, all of which represented an inversion of the moral standards of society" (Levack 1995, 8).

2. In the case of witches, once a person was arrested he/she was examined in search for what is known as a "witch's mark" or "devil's mark" that is a distinctive mark that the Devil imprinted on the witch's body as a sign of their allegiance (Levack 1995, 27). However, these marks are in hidden parts of the body and confirm the identity of a witch after the accusation.

Wes Craven's *Vampire in Brooklyn*

A Passing Narrative

Kendra R. Parker

Wes Craven's *Vampire in Brooklyn* (1995) focuses on finding one's self and re-claiming a lost, fractured, or hidden heritage. In the film, Maximilian or "Max" (Eddie Murphy) is the lone survivor of the Caribbean vampire race exterminated by humans, and he searches for the last vampire female to reproduce his ancestral line. Maximilian knows that the female child born from a vampire-human union lives in New York, and he arrives in Brooklyn to find her. Rita Veder (Angela Bassett), a New York–based police detective in danger of losing her job and unknowingly a half-vampire, learns about her vampire heritage from Max, and by the film's end, she chooses between human and vampire, a choice that becomes increasingly complicated when placed in the larger context of passing. *Vampire in Brooklyn* functions as Rita's passing narrative by comparing it with early 20th-century passing narratives that take passing as their central trope or motif. In considering Rita as a "passing subject," she occupies several intermediate positions, characterized by Homi Bhabha as "not quite/not white" (Bhabha 1984, 132), including human/vampire, white/black, cop/criminal, sane/insane, and Madonna/whore. By considering *Vampire in Brooklyn* as Rita's passing narrative, I grapple with troubling messages the film supports (whether deliberately or not) concerning race, gender, nationality, and disability which are linked to Rita's vampire heritage.

Passing: Lost, Fractured Heritages

Vampire in Brooklyn concerns itself with the dilemmas of being a "half-breed," and the vampire half is demonized and coded not only as Black, but also as immigrant, criminal, disabled, and sexually lascivious. The dilemma of being a "half breed" when coupled with the context of Rita's life allows me to consider her as an embodiment of the tragic mulatto, a popular trope in early African American literature. To uncritically suggest racial passing is akin to human/vampire hybridity is dangerous; blackness inevitably becomes linked to being non-human. Equally dangerous is an uncritical approach to all forms of passing as akin to vampire/human hybridity because the "non-normative" entity will always be considered the non-human. However, *Vampire in Brooklyn* is a speculative world, and the genre of the film cannot be ignored. Speculative fiction, as a genre, employs the non-human to offer social critiques.

Having addressed the dangers of uncritically approaching passing, I interrogate the film's subscription to historically persistent stereotypes of Black people as non-human, Black people as feeble-minded, and Black people as sexually lecherous. Further, if we imagine vampirism in *Vampire in Brooklyn* as an imagined discussion centering on real-world issues, then the notion of social invisibility, best highlighted in Ralph Ellison's *Invisible Man* (1952), is pertinent with this discussion of racial passing, particularly since vampires in this film do not have reflections. Rita's life mirrors the lives of passing characters from the late 19th and 20th-century passing narratives, notably *Autobiography of an Ex–Colored Man* (1912), *Passing* (1929), and *Quicksand* (1928). Like these novels, *Vampire in Brooklyn* is deeply rooted in issues of miscegenation, identity, and psychological angst, all of which occur from the conflicting loyalties that come from being mixed race.

As a passing subject, Rita's choices are not easy, and I do not discount the issues that arise concerning passing narratives. Do passing narratives, for instance, subvert or reinforce the systems of power that disenfranchise Black people, or do they do both? Should passers be condemned or condoned? For Frances E.W Harper and Janice Kingslow, passing is to be condemned because it causes the passer to suffer. In *Iola Leroy* (1892), Harper argues for racial solidarity, and she privileges the characters that consciously choose to live as Black. In 1950, a Hollywood studio offered Kingslow an enticing contract contingent upon her changing her racial identity and her name, but she refused, explaining: "What good was fame or money if I had lost myself? … This [passing] meant stripping my life clear of everything I was. Everything that had ever happened to me" (Wald 2000, 117). For others like Langston Hughes and Walter White, passing is the ultimate ploy and ultimate mode of subversion. In "Jokes on Our White Folks," Hughes discusses how Black people who pass (whether of their own volition or because other whites did not recognize them as Black) serve alongside whites in the army and donate blood to the Red Cross. Hughes speculates how "white plasma and black plasma must be hopelessly scrambled together, and it amuses [him] how the

Red Cross will ever get it straightened out" (Hughes 1995, 98). White, fair-skinned with blue eyes, considered himself Black, and he often infiltrated white communities to investigate lynchings and to collect evidence to deliver to newspapers as a way to make the American public aware of the brutality African American people endured ("Walter Francis White," 2004). Passing reveals the instabilities of the color line, but passing and those who pass also benefit from these instabilities. These instabilities either assume there is a certain combination of physical characteristics and behaviors that represent the system that the passing subject can "pass" into or they exploit society's assumptions about these characteristics. I do not reduce Rita's choice to moral terms. Instead, I raise one question about Rita's passing: What are we to make of the film's connections between disability, criminal, vampire, Afro-Diasporan subject, and sexual activity? The film relies on a narrative of "good" over "evil," one that becomes complex given the nexus of race, sexuality, disability, and nation.

What becomes harrowing is the film's association of the Afro-Diasporan vampire with what the film portrays as evil—bloodlust, sexual licentiousness, disability, and evil.

Passing: Converging Definitions

To discuss the passing narrative in *Vampire in Brooklyn*, I draw on five working definitions of "passing." First, Elaine Ginsberg frames passing in terms of theft and trespassing, or an act of illegal or illicit commandeering for personal gain. The racial Other, when passing, moves "from a category of subordination and oppression to one of freedom and privilege, a movement that interrogate[s] and thus threaten[s] the system of racial categories and hierarchies established by social custom and legitimated by the law" (Ginsberg 1996, 1–2). Second, Gayle Wald considers passing a conscious act of subversion in which the racial other (the passer) appropriates the racial majority's power. Passing does not undermine the power of the dominant race, but it gives others access to that power. Wald proffers: "The interest of narratives of racial passing lies precisely in their [the passing narrative's] ability to demonstrate the failure of race to impose stable definitions of identity, or to manifest itself in a reliable, permanent, and/or visible manner" (Wald 2000, ix). Next, Brooke Kroger defines those who pass as "effectively presenting themselves as other than who they understand themselves to be" (Kroeger 2003, 7) and she specifically focuses on those who pass "in order to bypass being excluded unjustly in their attempts to achieve ordinary, honorable aims and ambitions" (Kroeger 2003, 2). Additionally, Marcia Dawkins examines passing used in rhetoric and the relationship between rhetoric and passing: "Rhetoric is all about identity, symbolic expression, and how our identities and expressions can change when we encounter situations and social networks. Passing ... is about using rhetoric to grapple with crises of meaning produced when images, identities, and categories diverge" (Dawkins 2012, 8–9). Finally, according to Amy Robinson's triangulated dramatic theatrical model, passing requires three participants or perspectives: "the passer, the dupe, and the clairvoyant" (Robinson 1993, 17–18). The passers choose to define themselves as one thing, and the dupe perceives the passer as such; however, the in-group clairvoyant sees the passers for who they are but lets the passers pass. Thus, the success of a pass depends on the reaction of the clairvoyant. In *Vampire in Brooklyn*, the passer is Rita; she understands herself to be human. The dupe is Justice; he understands and categorizes Rita the way that she sees herself—as human. Max is the in-group clairvoyant; he knows Rita's "true" identity, so he recognizes and understands her in a way different from herself and Justice. With these definitions in mind, passing is, for Rita, an attempt to assimilate or to ingratiate herself into a society, embodied by the NYPD force whose social expectations of sanity, rationality, and literal thinking position her as disabled—as an outsider—because of her "insane" mother, her "irrational" visions, and her belief in the paranormal.

Vampire in Brooklyn *and 20th-Century African American Passing Narratives*

Traditional passing narratives generally portray a mixed-race protagonist who willingly identifies as white and knowingly conceals his or her Black heritage to access social and economic privileges attributed to whiteness. Increasingly popular during the Harlem Renaissance, passing novels explored the psychological and emotional quandaries involved in passing for white. Early 20th-century passing narratives share several features: the protagonist denies his or her families, conceals his or her ancestry, relocates to different cities or states, and inserts himself or herself into a white community while pursuing relationships with white partners. The passing protagonist remains haunted by fears of discovery, guilt, and betrayal, and he or she struggles to establish an identity. Nella Larsen's *Quicksand* (1928) follows Helga Crane— the daughter of a Danish white woman and deceased West Indian man. From the Southern United States to Denmark, to Chicago, to New York, and back South, Helga searches for a community of people with whom she feels comfortable and fulfilled—where white people do not sexually objectify her and where the African American bourgeoisie does not surround her. The novel ends in Helga's marriage to an African American Southern preacher and her disillusionment with marriage and motherhood. Larsen's *Passing* (1929) is written from the perspective of Irene Redfield, a woman who passes for white out of convenience but is married to an African American man. Irene receives a letter from a childhood friend, Clare Kendry. Clare, married to John Bellew, a white man who does not know of her African American ancestry, wants to reconnect with Irene and the African American community. The novella ends with the Bellew discovering Clare's "Blackness" and Clare's subsequent death. In James Weldon Johnson's *The Autobiography of an Ex-Colored Man* (1912), the un-named protagonist discovers he is a "nigger" after being corrected in school for standing when the white schoolchildren stand (Johnson 2014, 798). Afterward, the protagonist first finds community among various African Americans in different socioeconomic classes, but he decides to pass after witnessing a lynching, recalling: "All the while I understood that it was not discouragement or fear or search for a larger field of action and opportunity that was driving me out of the Negro race. I knew that it was shame, unbearable shame. Shame at being identified with people that could with impunity be treated worse than animals" (Johnson 2014, 863). These passing narratives convey the inner angst that plagues many mixed-race writers of Afro-Diasporan and European descent, revealing the social and psychological uncertainties that occur with conflicting loyalties birthed from a racial twoness. In many cases, the protagonists question their ability to turn from their Africanness and survive.

Rita's life compares to the lives of several passing characters African American novels. Just as the ex-colored man unknowingly passes for white as a child because his parents, a Southern white man and an African American woman, conceal it from him and raise him as white until the ex-colored man is corrected in school, Rita also unknowingly passes. Her mother, impregnated by a vampire, returns to the United States and places Rita in foster care; Rita remains unaware of her vampire heritage until Max's arrival in Brooklyn. Rita is plagued by premonitions and visions, both of which are "gifts" from her dormant vampire gene, gifts that mark her as "different" from her police comrades and therefore "unstable." Rita's difference becomes coded as disability, and not only do her coworkers stigmatize and tease her, but her different abilities result in her supervisor placing her on administrative leave. Several features of Rita's familial history—her mother's confinement in an insane asylum, her mother's work with the paranormal, and Rita's preference for the night—lead Rita to believe that she is different from her peers. Such evidence, circumstantial though it may be, leads viewers to realize that Rita knows something is amiss with her identity. The suspicions of her difference are confirmed when Max arrives in Brooklyn. While she does not know the truth of how or why she is "othered," Rita is aware of her difference, and her intentional attempts to conceal that difference and pass herself off as "normal," with assistance from her detective partner Justice (Allen Payne), likens her to both Irene and Clare.

Further, like the ex-colored man, who learns of his mixed-race heritage after being told to "sit down for the present, and rise with the others [the Black students]" during class (Johnson 2014, 808), Rita learns about her vampire past after Max reveals it to her. Resembling Helga, who is an "illegitimate" daughter and who is disowned by her uncle, Rita, too, is "illegitimate" and disowned when her mother places her in foster care. Like Helga, Rita feels alienated from both of her "selves," and she experiences social and psychological discomfort because of the alienation. Just as Helga neither fits in at school nor in the South as a housewife to the Reverend Pleasant, Rita's coworkers ridicule her "behind her back," and her partner, Justice, warns her: "If [Captain] Dewey heard you talking that crazy mess [about evil spirits in Brooklyn], she'd have you wrapped in a straitjacket." Justice's comment, while intended to warn Rita about keeping her job, contributes to the denial of part of herself. Like Larsen's protagonists, Rita "assume[s] [a] false identit[y] that [should] ensure social survival but [will] result in psychological suicide" (Wall 1995, 89). Justice's comment speaks to stereotypes attached to passing subjects, specifically the increased experiences of psychological trauma and tendencies toward madness.

When threatened with exposure, the passing subject has opportunities to reconcile with his or her past, but he or she does not always do so. For example, the ex-colored man's internal dilemma—deciding whether or not to reveal his African American heritage—arises when he falls in love with a white woman. He reveals he is passing, and though she initially leaves him, she eventually returns, and they marry and have two children. Conversely, Clare flits between the separate spheres of Black and white, and when her husband discovers she is a "nigger, a damned dirty nigger" (Larsen 1997, 111) she does not attempt to reconcile or to respond—she is unable to; she dies. The ex-colored man laments his passing: "I am an ordinarily successful white man who has made little money. They are men who are making history and a race. I, too, might have taken part in a work so glorious" (Johnson 2014, 883). Just as Iola, Clare, and the ex-colored man are presented with an opportunity to reconcile with their Blackness, their "darker" selves, Max's arrival in New York becomes Rita's opportunity to accept the severance from her vampire heritage, but she refuses: "I gotta go back, go back to my life, you can't stop me. You can't" (Craven 1995).

Passing Subject: Revealed

Vampire in Brooklyn uses the Madonna-whore dichotomy, a trope common in the mulatto woman's passing narrative, as a mode of representing Rita's passing. In passing narratives with female protagonists, the mulatto's mixed race is often considered a catalyst for her licentious sexual appetite or at least a confusion of multiple sexual desires. Larsen certainly illustrates this in both *Quicksand* and *Passing* with Helga, Clare, and Irene. Before Max bites Rita, the Madonna-whore dichotomy is represented by Rita and her roommate, Nikki (Simbi Khali), and after Max bites Rita, Rita herself embodies the Madonna-whore dialectic. Rita, the virtuous woman, protects virtue; her profession as a detective who polices others (and ostensibly herself) is no accident. When Justice comes to Rita's apartment, the two argue about the existence of vampires, and Nikki comments: "You finally get a man in the apartment, and you're gonna kick his ass. Interesting approach. Well, from the way y'all was arguing, I'd swear you was in love" (Craven 1995). Nikki's comment not only suggests Rita's demureness and sexual inexperience, but it also mocks proper roles for womanhood and rejects sexual inhibitions for herself. Nikki's "interesting approach" comment reveals that instead of verbally arguing with Justice, she would offer herself sexually to him, an offer she makes to him once Rita steps out of the room. Rita, unlike Nikki, refuses to acknowledge her sexuality. Rita learns by her social assimilation and training to suppress sexual desire, and she immerses herself in social respectability.

Conversely, Nikki emerges as the sexually active woman, and her licentious behavior displayed as improper. Upon introducing herself to Justice, Nikki attempts to brush her breasts against his chest. Justice rebuffs her advances, and hastily exits the apartment, forgetting his car keys. "You know what Freud would say," Nikki remarks as she follows Justice outside, "if you leave something this important behind," as she dangles his keys, "it uh means you really don't want to go" (Craven 1995). The last of her words are muffled slightly as she begins to kiss his neck. Justice pushes her away, chiding: "Whoa! Two words: cold shower" (Craven 1995). Max quickly reassures a visibly disappointed Nikki. "Now he's obviously a man of poor taste," Max offers, and Nikki responds, "My sentiments exactly ... do you want to warm up with some coffee or some *other* refreshment?" (Craven 1995, emphasis mine). The implied promise of sex is not lost on Max, and he acquiesces, allowing Nikki to lead him inside where they begin having sex, which culminates in Nikki's death.

After Max bites Rita, her dormant vampire side awakens, and she struggles between two facets of her sexual identity she cannot reconcile: a virtuous, sexually repressed cop and a sensual, lustful vampire. Following Max's off-screen seduction and biting of Rita, Rita sleeps on her bed until Justice enters her apartment, wakes her, and reveals that other police officers found Nikki's dead body. Grief-stricken, Rita cries and nuzzles her face to Justice's neck; the scent of his blood triggers her (blood)lust, and she kisses him, pushes him back on the bed, and mounts him; she rips his shirt open and leans forward, fangs protracted, ready to penetrate his flesh. As her fangs extend, Rita glimpses her reflection in a mirror; she sees her fangs and yellow eyes, and then her reflection disappears. As a fledgling vampire, Rita loses the ability to project a reflection. Thus, the lack of a reflection for Rita suggests that she does not see herself (the vampire/monster) reflected in the faces of others (humans). Rita always felt "different" from others, and as a fledgling vampire, her difference is rendered visible by the absence of her reflection in a mirror. Screaming, Rita pushes Justice away, breaks the mirror, and runs out into the night in search of Max. Max explains the new lusts (blood and sex) she feels, and he tells her that she must join him by feeding on flesh to complete her vampire transition before the full moon or die. Refusing, Rita asks for her old life back, and Max appeals to her sense of difference and alienation: "Then go. Go back to your little shoe-box apartment filled with those empty dreams. Go back to church and don't forget the collection plate, the preacher's whiskey is running low. Go back to your job! Where they laugh and call you crazy! Or you face the truth: that you have no place left to go but to me." Rita then asks, "What if I don't want it?," and Max counters, "But what if you do?" (Craven 1995). Max appeals to Rita's latent desires for belonging and acceptance, and she goes with him so that he can show her "the world" as a vampire. He isolates a woman in the park, bites her, and encourages Rita to join him, but again she refuses, screaming "No!" These back-to-back scenes of Rita wavering between her simultaneous attraction to and revulsion at the lust for blood, sex, and power are indicative of her shared attraction to both Max and Justice. Leslie Tannenbaum offers, "After her seduction by Max, [Rita] must police her own unruly body by refusing to feed on the blood of others and by [later] driving a stake through Maximilian's heart" (Tannenbaum 2002, 72). Indeed, Rita does "police" her own body, but her self-policing is more than just about becoming a full vampire; it is about policing all forms of "difference," chief among these being expressions of promiscuity. Rita, in a DuBoisian state of double consciousness, cannot help but see her identity as fractured between human/vampire, good/bad, and Madonna/whore.

Rita's vacillation and horror at her sexual self (and perhaps as an explanation for Nikki's violent death) came at an opportune time in African American communities. HIV/AIDS impacted African Americans since the 1980s, but Magic Johnson's public revelation of his HIV-positive status in 1991, rapper Easy E's death from HIV/AIDS related complications in 1995, and the Center for Disease Control's (CDC) surveillance of people with HIV/AIDS "pushed [black Americans] into the forefront of the epidemic as a population 'in crisis'" (Weekley 2010, 26). 1995, the year of *Vampire in Brooklyn*'s release, was also the year that "for the first time, the proportion of persons reported with AIDS who are black was equal to the proportion who are white (40 percent)" (Center for Disease Control, 1995). Further, Ayana Weekley reminds us that the "[c]ontrolling images of the jezebel, sapphire, hot momma, and welfare queen have long histories in the U.S., and in the context of HIV/AIDS they serve as implicit explanations for the high rates of HIV/AIDS in black women" (Weekley 2010, 101).

Given these contexts, Rita's horror at her "almost but not quite" sexual self and Nikki's lack of sexual restraint may be considered as part of a larger social commentary on the containment of women's sexuality in an acceptable space. The dichotomy between Rita and Nikki's "sexual selves" is reminiscent of Harriet Jacobs's battle to control her sexual space in *Incidents in the Life of a Slave Girl* (1861) and Helga Crane's attempts to reconcile her sexuality with the cult of true womanhood in *Quicksand*. Further, the Madonna/whore dynamic embodied by Rita and Nikki reflects the conflict surrounding the navigation of women's sexuality considering the value placed on "virtue" and "womanhood"—terms representative of women's value within a patriarchal framework. Linda and Rita navigate this space and make efforts to control their sexuality, but Helga Crane and Nikki do not.

Nikki's apparent salaciousness gets her killed, and Rita would "rather die" before succumbing to such desires. Rita's disgust with her fledgling vampire-self suggests that she longs for purity, cleanliness, or redemption if you will. Black women in the United States, particularly throughout the nineties, were portrayed in public policies as wanton and lascivious. Given this portrayal, it is not surprising that Rita possesses an ambivalence (if not the complete shunning of) non-normative expressions of sexuality, nor is it surprising that the sexually active woman is killed during one of her sexual exploits. Therefore, Rita's passing for "human" includes a shunning of "illicit" sexual conduct. The film's portrayal of the Madonna/whore dynamic, embodied by both Rita and Nikki, limits their sexual expression and implies that to be protected, Rita must remain a Madonna—she must choose to be human instead of a vampire—or she will be punished (by death) like Nikki. By the end of *Quicksand*, Helga shuns illicit sexual desires in her marriage to the Reverend Pleasant Green, but at the end, Helga is overcome with repressed sexuality and is symbolically killed by the bearing of children, just as Rita's vampire side dies with Max's death.

Rita's attitude toward passing—a passing that will become permanent in the event of Max's death—is complex. She engages several intermediate positions, what Homi Bhabha characterizes as "not quite/not white," (Bhabha 1984, 132) including human/vampire, white/Black, cop/criminal, sane/insane, and Madonna/whore. Rita's ambivalence—her attraction to and repulsion from her vampire heritage as well as her attraction to and rejection of her humanity—disturbs the authority of what her society expects her to be and what Max argues she is. While she wants the freedom not to be ridiculed and the freedom to express herself, she also fears the monster that appears when the lust rises to the surface. Interestingly, the monster, a complex being, does not confine itself to cultural limits of the normative; the monster tests, rejects, and traverses between the permeable boundaries of what is normal and what is not. The female monster (or the monstrous feminine, as Barbara Creed clarifies) embodies such refusal to be confined through her rejection of the confining laws of patriarchy, as Bonnie Zimmerman and Creed note (Creed 1993, Zimmerman 1996).

Rita, however, does not embrace the rejection of these laws that lesbian female vampires or monstrous females reject; instead, Rita seeks to adhere to them, an adherence that makes her all the more human (socially constrained and restrained) and not monstrous (free, able to traverse). On the brink of death unless she drinks human blood, Rita is confronted with a choice. Max offers Justice's throat to Rita, but she turns to Max: "Part of me loves you so much," Rita tells him, kissing his lips, "but that part of me must die," she whispers as she daggers him through the heart (Craven 1995). Max falls into his open coffin and then slowly evaporates. In killing Max, Rita chooses to permanently allow her humanity to trump the vampire within (pass as human). On the surface, Rita chooses to pass out of her desire to escape the scrutiny of her comrades in the police department, but she also passes to save the lives of others. Her passing, however, comes at Max's expense. To pass and to live, Rita must kill Max, and in killing Max, Rita kills a part of herself. In many ways, Max functions as the would-be reflection of Rita that she rejects despite the truth it renders about her identity. The name Max implies "maximum," "zenith," and "complete," all of which suggest that Max not only complements Rita but also completes her—a completion she rejects in her destruction of Max.

In destroying Max, not only does Rita reject the rising power and lust that accompany her transition from hybrid to vampire, but her murderous rejection of Max also exposes a narrative of colorism in the film. The casting of the darker-skinned men as villains (Eddie Murphy and Kadeem Hardison) and of the lighter-skinned man as the one man "Crew of Light" (Allen Payne) has striking implications. Max and Justice are binary opposites, the very embodiments of evil and good, villain and hero. Rita, in shunning her sexual desires and rejecting Max, also shuns the "darker," more dangerous part of herself. The association of darkness with evil and lightness with good are not lost in the film, and herein lies the issue: Rita destroys the visibly darker male, who, in the context of racist American history is inextricably linked to evil, to danger, and to illicit sexual desires. Such an association is nothing more than a popular vehicle for the production and reproduction of an exploitative system of racial representations that denigrates Black people. As an outsider who struggles to pass, Rita must be an active dispenser of justice; therefore, she must accept the light, the law (enforcement), and the visibly lighter Black man (her partner) who is appropriately named Justice. While casting is likely a factor, Allen Payne is the only Black actor in *Vampire in Brooklyn* with a visibly lighter skin tone than any of his counterparts who have a major role. Given the historically consistent cultural assumption that equates whiteness or near whiteness as good, and darkness and Blackness as bad, the casting of a fair-skinned man as a savior figure may very well be unintentional, but it still relies on an endorsed cultural logic.

Of course, it is plausible that Rita chooses between two facets of the African diaspora—a Black American and a Caribbean immigrant; however, if we consider *Blacula* (1972) as the context for *Vampire in Brooklyn*, we can begin to see Max as Prince Mamuwalde (William Marshall). *Blacula* begins as a movie about race and vampires; Count Dracula (Charles Macaulay) invites Prince Mamuwalde and Princess Luva (Vonetta McGee) to his Transylvanian castle, and when Dracula propositions Luva, he angers the Prince. Dracula turns Mamuwalde into a vampire and quips, "I curse you with my name. Blacula!" Awakened by a bi-racial gay couple looking to buy a house in Los Angeles, Mamuwalde uses vampirism to "create a community of the oppressed, composed almost exclusively of African Americans" (Hefner 2012, 67). As Mamuwalde creates a new race of the undead, he fights white cops and generally kills them by smashing their heads against walls. This action seems out of place in a vampire genre but functions importantly here as we recognize the limits established by Mamuwalde concerning who can "join" him as a "vampire." These limits not only exclude white men, but also white women (Hefner 2012, 67).

According to Tannenbaum, Max fights against racist hegemony, too. Tannenbaum first points out that "almost all" of Max's victims are white, and before Max attacks them, each of them uses racial epithets or euphemisms to denigrate Black people, calling Black characters "eggplant" and "Sambo," and remarking about the "black servant problem" (Tannenbaum 2002, 74). Such examples, Tannenbaum claims, suggest that Max is "really being provoked" and that "he is invoked as a hero figure, one who lashes out at modern racism, whether blatant or more subtly liberal" (Tannenbaum 2002, 74). Max enlists Julius as his ghoul, who services Max, and after Max dies, Julius becomes "the new vampire in town" (Craven 1995). Hefner and Tannenbaum's analyses both suggest that the idea of *Blacula* and *Vampire in Brooklyn* is to create someone who was a hero where he had always been a victim or villain. Both of their readings allow us to liken Max to Blacula, and by extension, to liken Justice to Dr. Thomas (Thalmus Rasulala), a Black doctor who colludes with the white law enforcement in *Blacula*—the very system that seeks to police and control Mamuwalde. Thus, if we consider *Vampire in Brooklyn* within the narrative framework of *Blacula*, and if we consider Max as an avenger much like Mamuwalde, then one possible interpretation of Justice is as an agent of or mouthpiece for whiteness, especially since the policing agent or the law protects whiteness.

I consider Rita's choice between Max and Justice as a product of her two-ness and of her confusion about whether she can turn from her heritage and survive. At the same time, I also read her choice—between human and vampire, "sanity" and "insanity," Max and Justice, Madonna and whore—as problematic given her choice's cultural implications when placed in the broad spectrum of African American history in the United States. Tannenbaum understands Rita's choice as "tied up with her sense of profession, as she is struggling to police herself as well as others" (Tannenbaum 2002, 71). Tannenbaum couches Rita's decision as coming to terms with "the cop and the criminal within herself" (Tannenbaum 2002, 72), with her choice of choosing Justice over Max as representative of choosing the cop over the criminal. However, we must read Rita as a passing subject and then look at her choice beyond cop/criminal as well as beyond human/vampire. Next, we must read her as also choosing between Madonna and whore, American and African, Justice and Max, sane and insane. After acknowledging these two steps, a problematic pattern emerges with the association of cop, human, Madonna, American, Justice, and sanity as well as of criminal, vampire, whore, Afro-Diasporan subject, Max, and insanity, especially given that Rita chooses the former of the associations. The problem with equating "humanity," "goodness," "lightness," "American," "virgin," and "sanity" with passing is that it recreates the conditions of not only racist discourse, but also sexist, ableist, and xenophobic discourses. Thus, Rita's wrestling between the dialectics of human/vampire, Madonna/whore, cop/criminal, American/African, sane/insane and insider/outsider sends troubling messages not only concerning Black women's sexual expression, but also about nation, race, and ability. The very stereotypes *Vampire in Brooklyn* perpetuates are not only troubling on account of the stereotypical images themselves but also because these images are dangerous. This movie sanctions the hierarchical placement of individuals deemed "different"—the sexually active, the criminal, the outsider, the Afro-Diasporan subject, the differently abled. *Vampire in Brooklyn* presents these binaries to an audience that is already primed and conditioned to ingest them, so much so that these images become culturally sanctioned "truths" rather than constructed images created for the sole purpose re-establishing racial, gendered, abled, and sexual social hierarchies.

Conclusion

The representation of Rita as a passing subject justifies the humiliation, assimilation, or (temporary) rehabilitation of the Black female vampire character to construct and to validate white patriarchy. Rita succumbs to normative ideologies without ever fully operating outside or against normative conditions. Rita is almost, but not quite the same as her white counterparts. Rita chooses a life of assimilation instead of setting her standards. What I hope becomes clear is *Vampire in Brooklyn* relies on palpable stereotypes that institutions and history attach to Black women, so much so that the representation of Rita is misogynistic and inextricably linked to preoccupations concerning racial, gender, and abled difference.

The Transmediated Lesbian Vampire

LGBTQ Representation in a Contemporary Adaptation of J. Sheridan Le Fanu's Carmilla

NATALIE KRIKOWA

Adaptations of classic vampire tales are not uncommon and remain popular in contemporary media production and consumption. The story of young girls succumbing to unholy and wicked temptations has found its way into many book, radio, film, stage, television, comic, video game, and music adaptations over the last one hundred and forty years. Joseph Sheridan Le Fanu's gothic novella *Carmilla* (1871–72), which predates Bram Stoker's *Dracula* as one of the first vampire narratives and which was British fiction's first female vampire, is one story that has seen many retellings. The novella is a first-person account from a young English woman, Laura, who falls prey to a beautiful and mysterious vampire. Laura recounts the curious incident that brings Carmilla, a stranger, into her home, and of how she was both frightened of and enchanted by her. What makes *Carmilla* notable, and distinct from other vampire stories of the time, is the fact that the story is centered around two female characters, whose complicated relationship is a thinly veiled lesbian romance, that ends with Carmilla's death. More recently, the classic was reimagined as a Canadian web series *Carmilla* (KindaTV 2014–2016). The series differentiates itself from its original text as it is set in our current time, takes a queer, feminist approach, utilizes camp and comedic storylines and presents nuanced and authentic representations of LGBTQ characters.

It also sets itself apart from its predecessors by giving the lesbian vampire and her human lover a happy ending. In Le Fanu's original novella, and the many adaptations since, the lesbian vampire Carmilla is killed, and her human victim Laura never recovers from the trauma she experienced at Carmilla's hands. In this most recent adaptation, however, not only do the lesbians live, but their love is celebrated.

Carmilla (co-created by Jordan Hall, Steph Ouaknine and Jay Bennett) is a romantic-comedy that puts a modern spin on the cult classic gothic vampire novella. The series takes place at the fictional Silas University in Austria and is told through single-camera video blogs recorded by Laura (Elise Bauman), a first-year journalism major. When Laura's roommate mysteriously disappears, she is assigned a new roommate, Carmilla (Natasha Negovanlis), who she later discovers to be a vampire. The exploration of the romantic relationship between Carmilla and Laura is nothing like the cautionary tale depicted in Le Fanu's novella. Carmilla and Laura fall in love, and although their relationship is strained and tested at times, it is treated as "normal." It is as much a story of the two women navigating their fantastical milieu as it is about their relationship and search for self-identity. The web series, hosted on YouTube, comprised three seasons and quickly gained a cult following online, particularly with millennials (accumulating over 73 million views at the time of writing). The series and actors have won a multitude of awards including Canadian Screen Awards, a Webby Award, a Streamy Award and a Shorty Award. The series quickly became popular with the LGBTQ community for its nuanced and respectful representation of lesbian and queer characters—something that remains lacking in mainstream media.

Using the *Carmilla* series as a case study in transmedial adaptation practice, this essay explores how contemporary representations of lesbian vampires can challenge historically negative depictions of lesbianism and reflect the current social ideologies of LGBTQ people in Western culture. It demonstrates how the story and characters have been constructed across the *Carmilla* transmedia storyworld (including the web series, film, and social media) with imbued complexity, currency and authenticity. To do this, I analyze Carmilla as a lesbian vampire within a historical literary and cinematic context, outline the adaptation processes and resulting changes, and reveal how the storyworld is expanded through transmedia practices with a highly engaged queer following. *Carmilla* demonstrates how new modes of storytelling open the story up for new interpretations and cultural relevance.

Carmilla as a Literary and Cinematic Lesbian Vampire

The lesbian vampire as a character in horror and fantasy has a rich, yet problematic past. As far back as Le Fanu's *Carmilla*, "the eponymous female had been represented as both destructive and seductive" (Leitch 2011, 8). Along with other fantastical beings such as werewolves and witches, vampires "resonate with a tradition of societal fear extending back into the nineteenth century, and beyond ... the fear of a cultural sway with the youth population that cannot be controlled" (Howe 2018, 24). In most vampire stories, women are preyed upon and ultimately meet their deaths, unless a man comes to save them. This vampire trope concurrently provided a channel for inhibiting sexual desires and a lesson in morality and the dangers of surrendering to such desires. In the original novella, Laura is the archetypal victim of vampire literature—at once drawn to and repulsed by the female vampire. She desires to both withdraw and succumb to her feelings for the mysterious and alluring creature, and is further confused by her feelings as they are for a woman. Written mostly by heterosexual men, the lesbian vampire was a cautionary tale for young women about same-sex desire. In the late 18th century in Victorian England, vampires became synonymous with sensuous and illicit sexuality. Vampires represented a willingness and even desire to be seduced; to transgress sexual morals, at least on the part of the female reader who lived vicariously through the female narrator. There is a certain mystery to the vampire and a certain allurement to the female vampire, especially when her lustful sights are set upon the innocent, young girl.

When vampires eventually found their way into cinematic stories, the embedded warnings about the dangers of lesbianism were conveyed through the sexy lesbian vampire. In the advertising for *Dracula's Daughter* (Hillyer 1936), for example, Universal Studios used the tag line "Save the women of London from Dracula's Daughter!" (Lawrence 2010, 111), which carried an obvious intentional double meaning. In the early 1970s, when the objectification of women was both desirable and profitable, the sexy lesbian vampire became a popular trope for European and Hollywood horror and sexploitation films (most of which were inspired by *Carmilla*). The lesbian vampire appeared in sensational titles such as *The Velvet Vampire* (Rothman 1971), *Lust for a Vampire* (Sangster 1971), *Twins of Evil* (Hough 1971), *Vampyros Lesbos* (Franco 1971), *The Blood Spattered Bride* (Aranda 1972), and *Countess Dracula* (Sasdy, 1971). These films implied that lesbians were literal and metaphorical vampires, predatory and intent on seducing helpless heterosexual women. Their behaviors were over-sexualized and their naked bodies used gratuitously for the heterosexual male gaze. These women were portrayed as deprived and deviant surrogates for male sexuality, and were used as targets for the heterosexual male characters to mutilate and murder. *The Vampire Lovers* (Baker 1970), while not sexploitation, was a period piece that explored the relationship between the vampire Carmilla and her romantic interest, Emma (based on Le Fanu's *Carmilla*). While Carmilla is shown to have deep feelings for Emma, she is also a predator who seduces Emma and slowly kills her. The film ends with Emma being rescued by the straight men and Carmilla being impaled and decapitated. Lesbianism is depicted as being a dangerous and destructive perversion, and curable if the woman finds the "right man."

The 1980s saw an attempt to return the vampire to a more acceptably mainstream genre character. *The Hunger* (Scott, 1983) starred Catherine Deneuve as a pansexual female vampire who seduces and eventually converts Susan Sarandon. For the next two decades, female vampires appeared on screen in a variety of new stories, including *Nadja* (Almereyda 1994) in the Noir genre, *The Addiction* (Ferrara 1995) as a metaphor for substance abuse and being closeted, and *Vampire Killers* (Claydon 2009) as satire. In *The Moth Diaries* (Harron 2011), based on the 2002 novel by Rachel Klein (an adaptation and amalgamation of both *Dracula* and *Carmilla*), the title character, Rebecca, attends an exclusive boarding school for girls, and spends most of the film warning everyone to stay away from Ernessa, a character equivalent to Carmilla. Ernessa is a captivating lead, and the film creatively balances the Gothic themes with the modern world, however it still includes the damaging trope of the predatory female vampire who destroys the female victim, depicts female homosexuality as destructive and obsessive, and shows a male love interest saving the day. In recent years, the sexy lesbian vampire returned with *We Are the Night* (Gansel 2010), bringing the trope full circle.

The character of Carmilla embodies much of the vampire lore that horror and fantasy readers will be familiar with: the gliding figure who can appear amongst the fog and disappear through thin cracks in the walls; the sharp and pointy canine teeth; and the obvious thirst for blood. The destruction of the vampire, Carmilla, with a wooden stake to the heart and decapitation is also consistent with similar portrayals from the period. Le Fanu's female vampire is the classic tale of repression, expressing the theme of the "respectable Victorian gentleman's anxieties about aggressive, unbridled female sexuality" (Miller 2006, 8). In Le Fanu's novella, Laura is depicted as the unwitting victim—the innocent who must be protected. Conversely, in the *Carmilla* series, Laura is not depicted as a victim in any way, but rather as an active protagonist. This is just one way that *Carmilla* has changed through the adaptation process—a process that by definition, requires the "new" to do something divergent from the "original."

Adapting Carmilla—*From Novella to Web Series*

Adaptation can be understood as signifying a range of structural changes that the adapter feels necessary in order to make a pre-existing story fit another medium or context. Linda Hutcheon and Siobhan O'Flynn's description of adaptation "as adaptation" is a distinctive mode of viewing that predicates a "conceptual flipping back and forth between the work we know and the work we are experiencing" (2013, 139) which Thomas Leitch asserts "invites audience members to test their assumptions, not only about familiar texts but about the ideas of themselves, others, and the world those texts project against the new ideas fostered by the adaptation and the new reading strategies it encourages" (2008, 116). It is arguable, however, that most viewers of the *Carmilla* series would not have been aware that it was an adaptation of Le Fanu's novella (unless they delved deeper into the video description on YouTube).

Even then, it would be a rare audience member who would have read this text, given its obscure form as a novella and lack of contemporary visibility within literary studies curricula. Leitch, drawing on Hutcheon's (2013) work, considers four textual markers that encourage filmgoers to see visual adaptations as "adaptations": (1) a period setting, (2) period music, (3) an obsession with authors, books, and words, and (4) the distinctive intertitles found in adaptations that establish time and place (2008a, 111–114).

Julie Sanders notes that the Victorian era is particularly desirable for appropriation (beyond these textual markers) because it highlights many of the overriding concerns of the postmodern era: "questions of identity; of environmental and genetic conditioning; of repressed and oppressed modes of sexuality; of criminality and violence; of an interest in urbanism and the potentials and possibilities of new technology; of law and authority; of science and religion; and of the postcolonial legacies of the empire" (Sanders 2016, 161). The *Carmilla* series certainly explores historically repressed and oppressed modes of sexuality, but as the series has removed itself from the Victorian setting, the moral and social concerns of female sexuality are not questioned or discussed but are an accepted, natural and positive aspect of the character's identity.

Drawing on Julie Sanders' work, Jennifer Camden and Kate Faber Oestreich suggest that canonical 19th-century novels provide another compelling opportunity for adaptation and transmedia storytelling because of the pleasures of remaining in and expanding the storyworld of a familiar novel (2018, 8). In their account of Jane Austen's *Pride and Prejudice* web series adaptation, *The Lizzie Bennet Diaries*, they suggest that the success of the series came in no small part from the built-in audience of the Jane Austen fans affectionately known as Janeites. *Carmilla*, however, is a modern adaptation, lacking Leitch's textual markers, making it challenging for audiences to view the series as "an adaptation." It had no built-in fan base from which to build on, and so the audience grew organically over time, mostly from word of mouth via social networks on Twitter and Tumblr.

Adaptation as "retelling" is a complex process. In his review of contemporary adaptation studies and publications, Thomas Leitch also highlights that two of the questions often raised are: "Does the movie in question betray its literary source?" and "Does the film depart from its literary source because of new cultural or historical contexts its addresses?" (Leitch 2003, 161). Regardless, these questions may provide the clues as to why the *Carmilla* series became so successful. When adapting a 19th-century novella into a modern-day queer and feminist story, assumptions of fidelity to the original text is negated. According to Brian McFarlane, certain narrative elements of the original literary text are transferable into audio-visuals, while some narrative elements of the text must find different equivalencies in the audio-visual medium—therefore, must be adapted to meet the obligations of the new medium or context (1996, 12). Retaining aspects of the original, such as the Victorian setting and the moral and social concerns of female sexuality, would make it unappealing (and offensive) to modern audiences. As Mario Vrbančić and Senka Božić-Vrbančić write, "an adaptation is deeply rooted in the context of its happening" (2011, 4). This is especially true when the adaptations occur centuries after the original work was first produced. The *Carmilla* web series, while lacking an emphasis on fidelity to the original story, demonstrates the challenges storytellers face when adapting texts to new audiences in new socio-cultural and political contexts. The modern retelling acts more as a critical adaptation, showing the ideological shift between Victorian England and modern North America. By positioning it within a new media space of the Internet, the new medium also predicates a new mode of storytelling for a very particular audience, one interested in deep and prolonged engagement with the storyworld. The characters and the setting of *Carmilla*, in Styria (Austria), remains the same, as does the attraction between the two lead characters. The modernization of the text, however, means that it embodies the social, cultural and political aspects of today.

Transmediating Carmilla

In their basic definitions, adaptation is the "retelling" of existing stories, whereas transmedia storytelling is the telling of "new" stories extending from the existing story. Transmedia storytelling "expands the storyworld, precipitating a very different kind of dialogical relationship with the originating text" (Harvey 2015, 78). The term "transmedia" "has been put to different purposes with different end goals depending on who is using it and in what context" (Stein 2013, 405). Using Elizabeth Evans' definition of the "popular industrial practice of using multiple media technologies to present information concerning a single fictional world through a range of textual forms" (2001, 1), *Carmilla* demonstrates both a process in adaptation and transmedia storytelling—taking an existing story and retelling it in a new medium and context, but also expanding on that text to present new stories and characters. Extensions can work by "inserting new material into the existing experience, creating a richer and more defined text, or extending the universe and deepening the user's understanding and experience of the storyworld" (Krikowa 2017, 96). It might provide character back-story or help us better understand secondary or minor characters. Expansion similarly broadens the story by "introducing parallel or companion narratives that often provide new perspectives, insight or clarity to the existing story" (Dowd et al. 2013, 22–24). It is a process for developing new story material inspired by the original narrative or storyworld.

The *Carmilla* series begins with Laura recording a video for her journalism assignment about missing girls in her school. The process of adaptation meant that producers were able to bring the first-person narration into a modern context through the format of video blogs (vlogs). The video blog format allows the audience to hear first-hand how Laura feels about her circumstances. In the first episode, when her roommate Betty suddenly goes missing at a college party, Laura is assigned a new roommate, Carmilla Karnstein. Laura begins an investigation, aided by her friends, to determine what happened to the missing students. The first season follows Laura, her investigation and her tumultuous relationship with her new roommate Carmilla, which evolves from antagonistic to romantic over the course of the seasons.

The series started small at first, as a single-frame show in a video blog format, but it continued to grow and eventually contained four seasons (123 episodes) over three years. In between seasons on YouTube, the producers also created Twitter accounts for the characters, publishing extra story content about the characters after the events of the season one finale. Following the first season a Christmas special aired, showing Laura, Carmilla and LaFontaine's encounter with Mrs. Claus that ends rather unpredictably. In Season 3, one of the secondary characters also transmits a podcast (thirteen episodes). The KindaTV YouTube channel also added "extras" that ranged from interviews with the actors and the actors participating in online challenges. Following the success of the web series it was announced that a full-length movie and a book deal was in the works. The contemporary *Carmilla* transmedia storyworld, then, includes the web series, a feature film, social media, and novel, showing elements of character and world-building through expansion and extension practices.

The Carmilla Movie (2017) is a feature-length film set five years after the series ends. The story picks up with Laura and Carmilla living together. Laura begins the film with her usual vlog-style presentation, but the film soon switches to a traditional film production format. The story starts with Laura feeling disenfranchised with her stagnant journalism career and experiencing lucid dreams of herself in a Victorian setting (Le Fanu novella style). Laura begins noticing supernatural happenings, most notably, that her now-human girlfriend Carmilla is becoming a vampire again. Carmilla soon realizes that Laura's dreams are actually memories from Carmilla's past and they decide to return to Styria to the Victorian mansion from Laura's dreams, and Carmilla's former residence. Once there they face the literal and metaphorical ghosts from Carmilla's past and must fight Carmilla's ex-lover in order to return Carmilla's humanity. The film brings much of Le Fanu's original novella to life, where the series did not. The characters find themselves returned to the past, in Victorian period clothing, setting, and undertakings, including a masquerade ball.

Many of the passages from Le Fanu's novella made the direct translation into the feature film. Through the dreams, Laura sees Carmilla's past, and in those scenes glimpses the love she had for her ex-lover (not Laura, as it was in the novella). In one of her dreams, Laura is lying on the bed when Victorian Carmilla slinks across the bed toward her, whispering, "You are mine, you *shall* be mine, you and I are one forever." This scene is a clear adaptation from a scene in the novella: "with gloating eyes she drew me to her, and her hot lips traveled along my cheek in kisses; and she would whisper, almost in sobs, 'You are mine, you *shall* be mine, you and I are one for ever'" (Le Fanu, Chapter 4). Instead of experiencing this first-hand, however, Laura experiences it in a dream. Le Fanu's lesbian desires are depicted here as powerful but concurrently something the narrator is ashamed of. This sentiment is echoed many times throughout the novella: "I experienced a strange tumultuous excitement that was pleasurable, ever and anon, mingled with a vague sense of fear and disgust. I had no distinct thoughts about her while such scenes lasted, but I was conscious of a love growing into adoration, and also of abhorrence. This I know is paradox, but I can make no other attempt to explain the feeling" (Le Fanu, Chapter 4). In the film adaptation however, Laura experiences no shame for the dreams, or for her feelings, as she leans forward into Carmilla, stating "I think I'm going to like this dream." *The Carmilla Movie* positively foregrounded the queer text from the original novella and omitted the shame that accompanied it. It then extended the storyline to further explore Laura and Carmilla's relationship. It expanded the storyworld by introducing new characters and giving modern audiences a glimpse into Carmilla's Victorian past.

The film was released online (and in select theaters across Canada) in October 2017, with much of the finance for the film raised in pre-sales from the fans. Natasha Negovanlis and Elise Bauman reprised their roles, and the film saw most of the supporting cast return along with some new actors/characters. The forthcoming book is scheduled for a Spring 2019 release, and will be the latest transmedial extension for *Carmilla*. The young adult book will be penned by Kim Turrisi and will offer fans another way to experience the characters they have grown to love on screen (Cornell 2018). Christina Jennings, Chairman and CEO of Shaftesbury (the production company behind *Carmilla*) remarked:

> We are thrilled to [...] expand the world of *Carmilla* and to offer fans of the series and the [...] feature film another opportunity to engage with characters who mean so much to them [...] over the past three years, we have seen the audience of *Carmilla* grow at an exponential rate and become an international phenomenon—and this phenomenon is showing no signs of slowing down. We are very excited to continue to branch out and build up this brand [Gutelle 2017].

For fans of serial projects—be it mono-media or transmedia—the following of canonical "events, characters, and settings featured in a storyworld is a central mode of engagement, with viewers striving for both narrative comprehension and deeper understanding of a fictional universe" (Mittell 2014, 256). Adaptation, extension and expansion can all contribute to a better understanding of the storyworld, its characters, and themes (Krikowa 2017, 96–97). For queer audiences, who crave stories centering on queer characters, their engagement with transmedial projects and their loyalty to the creatives (e.g., writers and actors) is quite pronounced.

Queering Carmilla—*Successful Audience Engagement*

Queer audiences gravitated to the *Carmilla* series as queer women remain underrepresented in mainstream television, particularly in leading roles (see GLAAD's most recent *Where We Are on TV* report). As a result, the web series format continues to reel in audiences seeking stories that represent themselves and their queer communities. *Carmilla* includes characters who were unapologetically themselves and queer. Laura Hollis was gay without having to "come out." In the first episode, her roommate entices her to a college party by hinting that the cute TA, Danny, would be there; in the following episode, Danny is shown to be a woman, with no further commentary. Laura never experiences any shame for her sexual orientation or her attractions to women. Her two love interests, Danny and Carmilla, are both queer women with distinct personalities that define them beyond their sexualities.

The exploration of the romantic relationship between Carmilla and Laura is nothing like the cautionary tale depicted in Le Fanu's novella. The powerfully erotic language Carmilla uses to seduce Laura in the original has provided the basis for many antipatriarchal readings. Nina Auerbach, Tamar Heller, Angela Tumini and William Veeder, among others, explain the peculiarly female and/or feminine threat Carmilla presents to patriarchal and heterosexual systems of identity, knowledge, and affective exchange (Lee 2006, 27). This once-cautionary tale has now become an iconic queer story. In the new series, Carmilla and Laura fall in love, and although their relationship is strained and tested at times, it is treated as "normal." The lesbian vampire, Carmilla, remains seductive, sexy and dangerous like her novella predecessor—she is still the object of Victorian patriarchal fear found in literary history, and the object of desire found in cinema history. Haefele-Thomas suggests that "Like 'vampire,' 'queer' and 'half-breed' connote a liminal existence, Queers [...] move within literal and metaphoric geographies, across continents, traversing and re-inventing languages and places, disturbing the 'natural' order" (2012, 100). This "outsider" or marginalized position is reiterated in the industry itself, as even within the media of storytelling, queers exist in liminal spaces, relegated to the fringes of independent production. Karen Hollinger suggests that the reason for the lack of lesbian representation in Hollywood film relates to marketing strategies, as lesbian films are perceived as having limited appeal and are considered too risky. She also highlights how open portrayals of lesbian relationships pose a significant threat to the "heterosexist, patriarchal status quo" as they "provide an alternative to the patriarchal heterosexual couple and challenge female dependence on men for romantic and sexual fulfillment" (1999, 11). As Shameem Kabir states, "the position of the lesbian spectator of mainstream film is one where we are usually denied any direct representation of lesbian desire" (1998, 185). This is often due to the lack of queer female representation, notably the representation of love or sex between two female characters.

Portrayals of queer female relationships represent a complex but rewarding part of feminist film study, however these portrayals need to be "placed within the history of lesbian and gay cinematic representation and theories of the potential threat these films pose to the patriarchal, heterosexist status quo" (Hollinger 1998, 3). Due to the film having lesbian protagonists and being based on a central lesbian romance, it is unlikely this film would have been produced and distributed within the Hollywood studio system. Karen Hollinger discusses how "until very recently, lesbianism was either barred from mainstream cinema entirely or, when it was infrequently represented... it was portrayed as sordid, depressing, and deviant behavior resulting either from congenital deformity, arrested psychic development, or pathological gender reversal" (1998, 9–10). Hollinger goes on to claim that "lesbian characters were, and in too many cases still are, presented as sinister villains, victims of mental illness, cultural freaks, or pornographic sexual turn-ons for a male audience" (Hollinger 1998, 10). Had the adaptation of Le Fanu's novella been a more literal translation then this trend would have continued.

The actors brought their own life experiences as queer women to the film and this manifests in how the characters relate to one another, with their single love scene portrayed as tasteful, sensual, emotional, and necessary for both plot and character development. Since the beginning of the series both actors have come out as queer women, with Bauman speaking about her own bisexuality at a fan convention in 2017 and Negovanlis discussing her pansexuality in many interviews online and in award acceptance speeches. The pair's acting in the film makes it stand out as one of the better queer female feature films as their connection is palpable—there is a specific queer female gaze held between the two women. Carmilla and Laura, as Hollinger would describe them, are the "coupled lesbian protagonists of the film, each of whom is simultaneously both subject and object of the look and consequently of female desire" (Hollinger 1998, 12). This active desire is then carried to the film's queer female spectator, who are subsequently empowered as an active desiring female subject. What results is a feeling of acceptance and celebration of queer female sexuality. Just as Laura leans in to her feelings for Carmilla and is rewarded for doing so by their enduring relationship, the audience in reciprocity also leans forward into their identity. Arguably, this is what resonated with the queer audience and made the modern *Carmilla* adaptation successful.

Conclusion

It has been 147 years since Le Fanu's groundbreaking novella was published, and *Carmilla* is now being reimagined in a time when the sexuality that was once disdained is now approbated. At its heart, the modern transmedia series is a romance story; Shari McNally, writing for *Medium*, described *Carmilla* as "a queerly fractured fairy tale" (McNally 2018), and this is particularly fitting. *Carmilla* is the antithesis of the heteronormative and male-centered world which vampires were relegated to after *Dracula*. Given the historical Victorian context, it is not surprising that Le Fanu's novella, with its not-so-subtle Sapphic subtext, did not gain much attention when it was initially written.

The iconic stature of *Carmilla* within lesbian culture persists, suggesting that a queer readership remains comfortable with "reading between the ambiguities to find something positive to take away" (Haefele-Thomas 2012, 107). Of the main cast, three are lesbians, and one is non-binary. Their sexuality is not treated as something that needs to be declared or discussed within the narrative, but rather the characters' attraction to one another leaves no doubt about their feelings or intentions. All the characters are fun: Laura is a dork with a heart of gold, and Carmilla is finally given her due as a complex female vampire heroine struggling with her own morality. The female relationships explored throughout the series are complex and authentic. There is no male-gaze forced upon the female characters, no lesbian out to destroy the morality and purity of young virgins, and no male love interest swooping in to save the day.

The web series gathered a young queer audience, who were then further engaged through social media narrative extensions, and who, in return, funded a feature length film, which would never have been made, were it not for the fans. With the young adult novel due out in Spring of 2019, and rumors of a primetime television show in development, the *Carmilla* transmedia experience shows no signs of slowing down, and the lesbian vampire, in her new positive presentation, might pave the way for more respectful and positive representations of queer identity and love.

Éternelle Colonization

The Figure of the Vampire as Colonizing Factor in 21st-Century Québec

Maureen-C. LaPerrière *and* Julien Drainville

> The colonized does not seek merely to enrich himself with the colonizer's virtues. In the name of what he hopes to become, he sets his mind on impoverishing himself, tearing himself away from his true self. The crushing of the colonized is included among the colonizer's values. As soon as the colonized adopts those values, he similarly adopts his own condemnation. In order to free himself, at least so he believes, he agrees to destroy himself.
> —Albert Memmi, *The Colonizer and the Colonized*, 121

The figure of the vampire has been a steadily evolving metaphor for many centuries. The vampire-as-revenant was a terrifying figure in most of the world's cultures until the advent of medical science, when the fear and superstition that surrounded him somewhat abated. Indeed, although the word "vampire" itself is relatively modern (most accounts trace the word in English to the late 17th century), the creature who causes fear and trembling in entire villages has been recognized for millennia in various forms and incarnations worldwide. After the Enlightenment (especially in the Americas and Western Europe) finally laid to rest the possibility of the vampire's rising from the grave to assail his victims, his persona was nonetheless resuscitated to serve in a new capacity. The Romantic vampire, warming up in the early 19th century from the pen of authors such as Polidori, Coleridge, or Byron, gained acceptance to respectable society in the 20th century through popular culture. This vintage of vampire proliferated in response to the clamoring for more of his ilk that came to life in film and fiction. It was inevitable then, that the vampire would quickly become culturally ubiquitous in certain societies where his parasitic nature became the perfect metaphor for inequitable situations and endophytic conditions.

Shifting political and economic situations and categories, however, demanded a figure that would accommodate the romance/horror of a given state of affairs and, as Mark Neocleous points out,

> Like the monster in general, the vampire is the "harbinger of category crisis," resisting easy categorization in the order of things. As a form of monster, the vampire disrupts the usual rules of interaction, occupying an essential fluid site, where, despite its otherness, it cannot be entirely separated form nature and man. As simultaneously inside and outside, the monster disrupts the politics of identity and the security of borders [Neocleous 2003, 673].

In post–Romantic vampire fiction, it is customary that the vampire be the metaphor for the oppressed, the "other." In contradistinction to this generally accepted metaphor, however, is Karl Marx' use of the term "vampire" in his *Capital*, the most notable and enduring citation being: "Capital is dead labor which, vampire-like, lives only by sucking living labor, and lives the more, the more labor it sucks" (Marx 1867/1976, 342). There is in *Capital*, however, a plethora of references to vampiric functions and the parasitic nature of the "ruling classes," rife with historical, philosophical and literary allusions, the most interesting to our cause being that which references the spectral or even the monstrous. Robert Paul Wolff posits that:

> Marx invokes religious images, Mephistophelean images, political images.... He swings with baffling speed from the most abstruse metaphysical reflections to vividly sensual evocations of the sufferings and struggles of English workers against the oppression of their bosses. At the next, he is a pedant, calling down authorities in six languages from twenty centuries to confirm his etymological tracings and analytical speculations [Wolff 1988, 13].

It is against a backdrop correlative to Wolff's appreciation of Marx's prose that we are introduced to William Liebenberg and Federico Sanchez's 2004 horror film, *Éternelle*, which features Caroline Néron, a stunningly beautiful Québécoise actor who is presented in a sumptuous and unapologetically sexualized setting. The establishing shot is "Slovakia, two years ago." This reference to Eastern Europe will doubtless strike a familiar chord with Fans of the horror genre who will doubtless recognize the historical Elizabeth Báthory of Hungary, who has been reincarnated into the protagonist of many horror films and novels. Countess Báthory was believed to have tortured and exsanguinated young girls so as to bathe in their blood in order to maintain her youth. Her crimes occurred over the turn of the 16th century, and she was believed to have been responsible for the disappearance of over 650 young women and girls.

Although the Countess' name is referenced by Liebenberg and Sanchez in the portrayal of their own villain, her practice of drinking human blood (as opposed to only bathing in it, as the real countess seems to have been wont to do) clearly situates her as a vampire. The identity of the vampire as blood-drinker, here, is necessary in order to evoke both the political dimension the vampire has attained, as well as the Marxist appropriation of the term. The next setting, however, is a manor in Montreal, Québec, Canada, more specifically in the neighborhood of Westmount, which most Québecois will recognize as the province's most upscale, elite neighborhood, and essentially its most significant bastion of English culture and ostentatious wealth. It is in this haven of the privileged that Liebenberg and Sanchez have chosen to showcase Erszebet Báthory, their main predator.

The vampire has matured over the centuries from dreadful revenant to pulchritudinous creature of the night, not wasting a single occasion to display its finest physical attributes and indicators of privilege. In considering the historical vampire, however, it is important that we remember the creature's understated sexuality, described by some as metaphysical, by others as latent. The vampire's 21st century audacious, undisguised sexuality is showcased here not only to put on display the actor's physical beauty, but to unabashedly equate the vampire's obsessive need to exsanguinate her victims not only as a means of survival but as desperation to maintain her status as a figure of power and wealth and in so doing, calling upon what is usually a generative process, now morphed into a horrifying manner of dealing death. The sexual nature of vampiric blood-drinking here is made not only explicit, but perverse and terrifying in a way that instills an inescapable, pervasive horror. The first type of fear that the vampire evokes is a visceral, guttural fear of what is different, ugly, and repulsive to our sensibilities—the expected response to the Nosferatu-type vampire. Second, the vampire's victims suffer the fear of being physically maimed by the monster, of having their throat ripped open, of having their bodily boundaries transgressed. Third, the blood-sucker's victims are subjected to the far more complex (and significant) fear of having their cerebral/emotional/spiritual selves in thrall to the vampire after the physical assault. This last fear is by far the worst as it makes no allowance for free will and offers no chance of succor. This is the fear of annihilation, of being physically, emotionally, and psychologically powerless. It is little wonder, then, that the members of the provincial movement for an independent Québec, suffering very similar fears, might recruit the figure of the vampire. Who better, after all, to personify what is perceived to be the excessive depletion of Québec's resources and the erosion of its language and values in a way that would convincingly transmit the horror and irreversibility of the insidious changes in Québecois society?

It might be tempting to shoehorn the imperial domination of Québecois society by the British colonial empire into the critical discourse of postcolonialism in film. However, to even entertain the possibility of a postcolonial reading of *Éternelle*, it is necessary to show if, and precisely how, the Québecois people can be considered "colonized." Mary Jean Green explains that New France (the original name of the French North American colony) was essentially a "white settler colony," hence labeling Québecois society either "colonized" or "colonizer" can be problematic (Green 2009, 251). Green points out that several scholars, like Linda Hutcheon ("Circling the Downspout of Empire"), have completely rejected the "colonized" label for the Québecois people, while others, like Maurie Vautier (1998) have contested relegating Québec to a "colonizer" society on account of British domination (Green 2009, 252). In the 1960s, several intellectuals from the Québec independence movement embraced the idea of the Québecois as a colonized subject, thus situating it unreservedly within the worldwide decolonization process (Green 2009, 251).

This ambiguity surrounding Québec's status as a colonizer state is not new. Albert Memmi, one of the early intellectuals to tackle the dynamics between colonizer and colonized (*The Colonizer and the Colonized*), was reluctant to unreservedly declare the Québecois people a "colonized" one, preferring the label "dominated one" (*dominé*) (Green 2009, 249). Québec's history sheds some light on the issue. Before 1763 and the conclusion of the Seven Years' War—what is known as the Conquest (*la Conquête*) in Québec—French settlers undoubtedly were colonizers. However, during British rule, French-Canadians arguably became much more economically and politically marginalized. To complicate things further, during the Quiet Revolution, a period ranging roughly from the 1960s to the late 1970s, Québecois people achieved a relatively successful emancipation in the spheres of culture, politics and economics. The term *Québécois* itself stems from such a liberating impetus (Green 2009, 251). The Québec independence movement never succeeded in its goal of full political sovereignty for Québec, but the Quiet Revolution radically changed the composition of the province's elites, which now includes French-speaking Québecers.[1]

Québec's complex relationship with colonialism has had a fundamental impact on the way Québecers perceive their own situation and their art. For Green, Québec's peculiar relationship with colonialism (and postcolonialism) has engendered three distinct "colonial moments" in which Québec intellectuals and artists' works are framed ideologically. First, following the British conquest of Québec in 1763 and the failed Patriots' Rebellion of 1837–1838, a "colonized" mentality develops in French-Canadian society. The colonized

French-Canadian subject turns from ideas of revolt against British rule and toward "an ideology of *survivance*" (Green 2009, 253) which is characterized by what Memmi defines as a retreat into "refuge-values,"[2] namely those of the Catholic Church. Second, with the 1960s and the Quiet Revolution, "Québec writers targeted the 'colonized' mentality itself, regarding 'refuge-values' as a hindrance" (Green 2009, 254). Still resisting assimilation, and now firmly claiming their *Québécois* identity, authors embraced the contemporary values of the larger western world.

Revolting against a perceived "colonized" status, the themes they tackled helped bring forth a cultural revolution which went hand-in-hand with significant political gains for the protection of the French language, easier access to higher economical echelons for French-speaking Québecers, and increased autonomy for the province (Green 2009, 253). Third, after the Quiet Revolution, Québec writers and intellectuals began to turn their attention toward other forms of domination within their society. As Green notes, "freed from the need to articulate issues now being attended to by politicians, many Québec writers of the 1980s continued to explore more complex forms of domination in texts [...] They also began to analyze the effects of domination produced by Québec's own project of cultural self-definition" (Green 2009, 255). This new awareness of Québecois artists and intellectuals for those "others," so far excluded from the public debate by the omnipresence of the opposition between English-Canadian and Québecois, constitutes the third "colonial moment" identified by Green (Green 2009, 255–257). This third "moment" is characterized by a "focus on the multilayered critiques of forms of subalternity and hybridity that characterize Québec texts of the 1980s and beyond" (Green 2009, 257).

While all three "colonial moments" and their associated frame of thought are relevant for a critique of *Éternelle*, Liebenberg and Sanchez's movie clearly positions itself within the third, and most recent, way of critically approaching Québec's relationship with colonialism. One need only compare the main antagonist, Erszebet, to the main protagonist, Raymond Pope, to understand that the underlying colonial theme of domination escapes the simple binary conflict between British-colonizer and Québecois-colonized. Erszebet is ostensibly of old aristocratic European stock. As such, she displays economically and culturally dominant traits. She shows a mastery of both French and English, which sets her apart from her victims, while enabling her to condescend into communicating with her lessers. Erszebet also owns real estate in Westmount and Venice, appears to have significant financial means, and displays strong charisma. Plainly put, Erszebet is the incarnation of Montreal's old elites, both British and French. Pope, however, is excluded from such elite groups. While a native English speaker, Pope does not appear to be fluent in French, whereas the two characters who hold the most power over Pope, Erszebet and Captain Gérard (detective Pope's superior officer), speak French. As a police detective, Pope is not a part of the English-speaking Montreal elite either, but rather a middle-class citizen.

The character of Erszebet clearly signifies the figure of the colonizer, taken to its extreme manifestation of licentiousness. Her victims, especially the young women she lures to her mansion, go there of their own volition; heeding the vampire's call seems to be a great idea at first, promising excitement and even, for some, the promise of eternal life. It is therefore easy to make the leap to perceiving the victims, shedding their lifeblood and energy to enrich the countess, as the classic colonized subjects. Where Marx has posited his perception of the vampire as the one who drains the very lifeblood of a people and "lives the more, the more labor it sucks," the film now makes the usually metaphorically implicit, explicit. Erszebet's victims are truly completely exsanguinated, depleted, their bodies effectively vampirized. The colonizer's domination and consumption is mirrored in the countess' horrific, voracious sexual appetite and power over her compliant, unresisting subjects.

The horror genre, a genre to which the vampire clearly belongs, has morphed into a sophisticated form, no longer serving up only regular monstrous fare. Much ink has been spilled in charting the cultural trends and anxieties with which the vampire has been contemporaneous. He has served remarkably as, at first, the vilified antagonist and more recently as the misunderstood "other." Québecois sensibilities have long dealt with the issue of otherness in its many incarnations. There is no doubt that the connection between politics and popular culture in *Éternelle*, at first seemingly tenuous, is clearly an opulently illustrated representation of an enduring dialectic in Quebecois society. The vampire does, indeed, stand in for social conflicts and malaises in Québec, but he also provides a locus for resistance in the people's popular creation. Liebenberg and Sanchez have joined the titillating to the terrifying in a manner that refreshes the Québecois collective imagination through the medium of film. We can now control who we perceive to be the oppressor, by foisting Québecois anxieties onto Erszebet the vampire *qua* colonizer.

The meeting of both parties in the colonial encounter is not a simple negotiation between oppressor and oppressed. This is where the intersection of film horror and post-colonial theory finds its cinematographic expression. The relationship between the vampire and her victim is mirrored in the association between colonizer and the colonized. The vampire genre allows for multiple types of identification, not shying away from the representation of masochistic identification rather than that of sadistic control. In the film, the aptly named Raymond Pope, police detective and husband of Erszebet's victim, is first introduced in the midst of a sexual encounter, bound to his mistress' bed while she caresses his face and head with the detective's own gun. It is Pope's quest for his absent wife, however, which pulls the thread which eventually unravels Erszebet's appropriation of Montreal as a feeding ground. Pope's masochistic tendencies and arousal at the suggestion of impending death (as evidenced by the scene with the gun) manifest themselves again and again in his relentless pursuit of Erszebet, even as he bemoans his wife's departure. Pope is clearly situated in a position where he slides between identities in an instability representative of the repetition compulsion in horror as well as in colonial theory; Pope is in what Diane M. Nelson has described as "a terrible place full of bloody colonial domination and peopled with the 'terrible family' of vampiric capitalists, oversexed women, ghostly hidden labor, revolting natives and desecrated burial grounds" (Nelson 1997). Empire, says Nelson, is not "elsewhere"; like Pope and the victims who have entered the vampire's lair, the monster is, indeed, in the house.

This idea is brilliantly summed up by Anne McClintock. She says,

> If postcolonial theory has sought to challenge the grand march of Western historicism and entourage of binaries (self-other, metropolis-colony, center-periphery, etc.), the term post-colonialism nonetheless reorients the globe once more around a single, binary opposition: colonial-postcolonial.... The postcolonial scene occurs in an entranced suspension of history, as if the definitive historical events have preceded our time and are not now in the making.... Colonialism returns at the moment of its disappearance [McClintock 1995, 10].

McClintock insists (and rightly so) that colonizer/colonized (in our case, vampire/victim) cannot be assessed as a diametrically opposed binary. The one is not all evil and the other all purity and goodness. Raymond Pope is clearly a "bad husband"; he is having an affair with his partner's wife, neither loyal to his spouse nor to his brother in blue. As an emblem of loyalty and fealty, Ray Pope falls short. The woman to whom he eventually succumbs, the countess herself, is also attracted to him and engages in a coital encounter, into which she enters without pursuing bloody sustenance. The clear-cut duality of vampire and victim is blurred here; by definition, the sexual encounter between vampire and lover usually serves as, primarily, a quest for sustenance, and is usually rife with blood imagery, but the sexual union between Pope and the countess is not merely utilitarian and it moves beyond the bounds of the usual vampire/victim association.

The relationship between the countess and Pope, however, is clearly not one of equals. Erszebet is wealthy and powerful in similar measures; the material fortune she has amassed by virtue of her rank and its accompanying prosperity provides her with the means to seek out her source of physical strength, vitality, and the beauty that follows. Should the countess be pursued by the Law of whatever land she inhabits, she can choose to flee from this location and use her prodigious means to re-establish her occupancy, and to continue to ply her trade in procuring death. Detective Pope, on the other hand, has neither Erszebet's physical might nor her riches. The power which he possesses as a police detective gives him the right to regulate and control the behavior of others of his own social standing, but, as we are shown when Pope is suspected of having committed the murders perpetrated by Erszebet's minion, he is questioned by his own police chief and is clearly subjected to the law of his own organization, a law which manifestly sanctions him in the same way that he is empowered to sanction others under his jurisdiction. This Law, ironically, prevents him from pursuing Erszebet in the vampire's erstwhile violation of the women he is supposed to have protected, a group to which his wife belongs.

It might be useful, at this point, to hark to the futility of designating temporality to the development of relationships within a colonizing structure, to situate the actors along a temporal x-axis of ongoing power relations. Plotting a relationship within this Cartesian framework does little to elucidate the power dialectic (in this case, between the vampire/vampirized, and/or the colonizer/colonized) and the way this relationship is maintained. The simple temporal correlate renders the intricacy of the dynamics that unfold much more difficult to visualize, and perplexing to theorize. The metaphor I suggest to illustrate the relationship between the colonizer and the colonized is that of a web emanating from a locus of power, where we find the countess Erszebet holding court over those she lures to her, and then whom she drains of vitality.

This tentacular imagery effectively mirrors the ongoing preoccupation with oppression in Québecois culture. This situation is not tidily circumscribed by dates or plotted punctually on a timeline. The considerations alluded to in Québec/Canada relations are certainly not the stuff of spy intrigue and military bravado. Rather, as McClintock insists, it is the power of the dominant culture "to command the flows of capital, research, consumer goods and media information around the world can exert a coercive power as great as any colonial gunboat. It is precisely the greater subtlety, innovation and variety of these forms of imperialism that make the historical rupture implied by the term post-colonial especially unwarranted" (McClintock 1995, 13).

What follows from this is that no social category exists in privileged isolation. No matter how powerful the countess is, bodily and monetarily, she cannot afford to live in isolation from those she effectively colonizes and literally siphons of their lifeblood. This is indeed the manner in which the Québecois independence movement perceives those who would drain Québec of its vitality and resources and alter its language and customs.

Popular culture can express this political reality by moving beyond the didactic and around the overtly political. The term "post-colonial" is not simply temporal, or a suggestion that a truce has been reached. Indeed, popular culture has indeed taken on the task of explicating and resisting the impact and continued influence of a colonizing power. It is often the medium through which one will be introduced to, and will experience, foundational and folk myths and the characters that bring these myths to life. One such character, the vampire, mirrors the displacement of real interpersonal and social relations onto page and film so that we may analyze and perhaps question what may have been accepted as "normal" for so long. In the role of antagonist, the vampire as paradigm of evil makes her serviceable to the exploration and denunciation of what Liebenberg and Sanchez perceive the role of "colonizer" to be.

The representation of the Countess Erszebet Báthory, the vampire, does not follow the popular trend which personifies the undead as misunderstood creatures who need to survive amongst mortals. Because of their immortality, these vampires have travelled the world and gleaned its secrets over time and distance. Because they occasionally need sustenance, they feed in myriad ways. When vampires are "bad" monsters, they commit what is clearly seen as murder, and very little is made of the act of vampirization itself, except for the focus on the villainy of the act. When they are "good" vampires, the act of feeding takes on a ritualistic, intimate function. Authors who create their vampires to be mysterious, seductive and a little dangerous follow quite nicely in the footsteps of the Romantic authors who wanted to elucidate their particular take on the position of the "other" in their sociocultural milieu. The romance and intimacy generated in the wake of the exchange of blood between the vampire and his lover is a popular topos in popular culture. Liebenberg and Sanchez's vampire, however, has reverted back to the original figure of death and destruction, wrapped in the countenance of sexual beauty and unlimited power. The use of overt carnality in *Éternelle*, in opposition to the practice followed by the creators of the first Romantic vampires, sublimates the political context, and packages the suggestion of possession and control by denoting its lurid visual appeal while connoting its insidious evil.

Viewers of *Éternelle* are invited to unpack its political context from the overarching sexual theme. Whereas more standard vampire lore may ask of the viewer to suspend not only their disbelief but their trepidation in encountering the vampire, *Éternelle* proffers an ostentatiously sexual encounter so as to evoke the spectator's revulsion at the display of the countess' hunger. There is no life in the vampire, first, obviously, because she is one of the undead, but second, and most importantly, because Erszebet has no fondness for humans or even fleeting nostalgia for the humanity she has clearly left behind in both its literal and metaphorical sense. Erszebet has no qualms about the lives she takes in her quest to stay not only alive but beautiful. The melding of the vampire and the victim/lover, a unit defined and described as the *raison-d'être* of much vampire fiction is not to be found in *Éternelle*. Sex is not a goal; it is a tool. The carnal activity which Erszebet engages in is a means to an end. The blood-play usually involved in sexual communion with the vampire is glaringly absent from her encounter with Raymond Pope. There is no true communion between vampire and victim, no shedding or sharing of blood, just a very clear indication that Raymond Pope, like all of Erszebet's hapless victims, will continue to be in thrall to her, for in a particularly ironic twist for Pope (and for the entire vampire genre as a whole), it is not the detective's blood that revitalizes Erszebet, but rather his semen. Through their sexual encounter, the countess obtains the product of Pope's orgasm to plant on Lisa, Pope's babysitter, a woman who has been exsanguinated by Erszebet's minion, Irina. Pope will be accused of rape and murder, thereby alienating his colleagues and cutting him off from his connection with the Law, the only empowerment he could lay claim to in bringing down the vampire.

The copulation between the countess and the cop is the closest to an act resembling a sexual situation in the usual sense of the word. The act by which Erszebet gains sustenance from her other victims blatantly signifies that she is not engaging in erotic communion and exchange. While the most riveting image of all vampire fiction is the moment at which the vampire orally penetrates his lover in all its metaphorical glory, this practice is horrifically subverted to a dreadful and terrifying act of murder via bloodletting. Once the purview of classic vampire lore and the much-feared/awaited moment where the vampire lays claim to his lover, this act is reduced to a utilitarian process with no possibility of sexual salvation or promise of everlasting life. The visually and metaphorically compelling image of the vampire's mouth, penetrative and consumptive, as a tool of possession and pleasure, is replaced by an instrument which is more evocative of torture than of sex. Although it is certainly phallic in shape, there is no mistaking the purpose of this tool: to slit the throat of Erszebet's victims so that she can siphon, feed upon and bathe in their blood. The act is inorganic, purposeful and murderous. The countess is not seeking to embrace, understand or inherit anything from her victim other than the life-giving blood. Whereas this moment of concupiscence between vampire and lover is usually one of exploration of the other (whether the other is considered to be the vampire or the lover), a freedom from hunger (for the vampire) and freedom from the shackles of earthly strife for the lover, *Éternelle* very clearly establishes the vampiric act as one of predation and possession. Much like the colonized land, the colonized body will never experience the hoped for and coveted communion and exchange, only sacrifice and theft of vitality.

This departure from the classic vampiric symbiosis is not, however, gratuitous or misplaced. The unwillingness of the countess to bond with her victims is necessary so as to maintain secrecy in her quest for sustenance. We learn that the countess regularly moves to locations where sustenance is plentiful, areas which she occupies, seducing its inhabitants, and eventually controls by using her sexual wiles and, ultimately, the force needed to obtain nourishment in the form of the life-giving blood.

    The countess' actions metaphorically mirror those of the colonizer very closely, usually adhering to the classic vampire genre, only deviating from it to pursue Liebenberg and Sanchez' political agenda of drawing a parallel with the colonizer/colonized relationship. It is obviously necessary to give priority to the traditional genre in order to situate the viewer within the paradigm of the vampire tale so as to evoke the elements of horror and revulsion inherent in the classic genre. Liebenberg and Sanchez make use of the characteristics typically associated with the vampire tale: the predatory vampire, the victim (both willing and unwilling), the sumptuous locale reminiscent of the opulence of the vampire's halcyon days, and, of course, the practice of blood-letting and blood-consumption. Erszebet even "keeps," in the traditional manner, her familiar, Irina, who slavishly does Erszebet's bidding and clearly thirsts after her mistress' favor, while she waits for the vampire to bestow eternal life upon her. The sentiment surrounding the transmission of the "gift" is conjured up in their exchange:

> IRINA: Why won't you let me kill girls?
> ERSZEBET: It's not about killing; it's about seducing your prey. She must want you, desire you. You cannot take an unwilling soul. The blood must be pure.

This directive is particularly illustrative of the need for the vampire to be invited into someone's home/territory, where proper acceptance into the victims' society leaves the door open for the appropriation of their lifeblood. Even vampires must follow an appropriate code of conduct. The well-established premises of the vampire genre allow viewers to understand that the Law must be obeyed by the vampire, flouting of which has grave consequences. There is a pivotal moment of disobedience (mentioned above), when Irina, the countess' minion, visits Lisa, Pope's babysitter, is refused access into Lisa's home but enters nonetheless. She kills Lisa and drinks her blood, going against Erszebet's very explicit orders. In order to have Irina exonerated for this crime, Erszebet intervenes by appropriating Pope's organic production, his semen, planting it on Lisa's dead body, incriminating the detective. Erszebet is able to control his freedom to move about freely in his own homeland, effectively establishing dominion over him.

    Of course, there is another break with the classic vampire genre, which purists will criticize: Irina, not having received the gift of eternal life and all of its trappings from Erszebet, must fashion crude "fangs" out of what appears to be bone, but which are more reminiscent of the teeth of a wild, carnivorous animal, a representation which is not only beastly, but crude and revolting, harking back to a retrograde image of the vampire as predatory monster. Use of these ersatz "fangs" distances Liebenberg and Sanchez's vampire even further from the post–Romantic representation as benevolent steward and protector of the fledgling. Indeed, in *Éternelle*, the vampire is not the near-transcendent creature we encounter in representations of the modern vampire. The discontinuity between *Éternelle* and classic vampire fiction is not caused so much by the fact that the instruments of vampirization are not organically grown by the aspiring vampire herself, but that the instrument which pierces, connects and possibly bestows eternal life is no longer phallic in practice or sexual in nature. There is no communion in the merging of bodies, no partaking of the vitality of the lover, or the wisdom of the custodian, or the care of the parent, relationships which the vampiric union makes possible. The vampire in *Éternelle* moves in on her victims to literally suck them dry of whatever they have to offer so that she may flourish and thrive, not unlike the leech, the parasite or the colonizer.

In *Éternelle*, the horror film's depiction of the countess and her victims is distinctly framed by the Québecois context from which it emerged. The film's depiction of Montreal, Québec, Canada associates its most ostentatiously wealthy and privileged elements with old European aristocracy. Therefore, Erszebet stands as an asynchronous symbol of colonial and capitalistic vampire-like predation. The countess symbolizes an elite from the old world who refuses to die and would not think twice about murdering to "stay young," thus preserving her position of privilege. In this sense, Erszebet represents what Mary Jean Green describes as the first "colonial moment" in Québec's literary and intellectual history, the "ideology of *survivance*." However, given that Erszebet is portrayed as possessing traits from *both* of Québec's historical colonial elites, *Éternelle* escapes the typical dialectic opposition between British colonizer and French-Canadian "colonized" in favor of a multilayered critique of Québec's power dynamics, which fits right in with what Green perceives as the third "colonial moment" in Québecois literary thought.

The "economics of oppression" presented in the *Éternelle* are blurry and ambiguous, in that no single ethnocultural group can be assigned the role of sole "colonizer." The role of "colonized/victim" however, falls upon the individuals who stand outside the recognized dominant cultural groups (and are therefore considered "other"). In Liebenberg and Sanchez's film, Countess Erszebet Báthory's victims are lured by the promise of being granted boons (whether sexual, cultural, economic, or supernatural). In this sense, her handmaid, Irina, is also one of her victims. The young woman is seduced into acting as an accomplice to Erszebet's murders in the vain hope that her mistress will one day impart the secret of eternal youth upon her. However, Irina is consistently denied by Erszebet. There, one cannot help but draw a parallel with Memmi's description of the impossibility of true assimilation for the colonized. Memmi writes that "the first ambition of the colonized is to become equal to that splendid model and to resemble him to the point of disappearing in him" (Memmi 1985, 123–124), but "in order to be assimilated, it is not enough to leave one's group, but one must enter another; now he meets with the colonizer's rejection" (Memmi 1985, 123–124). Furthermore, the metal claw the vampire Erszebet uses to draw blood from her victims also lacks the intimacy of the classical vampiric bite, thus denying her victims even the slightest form of compensatory fulfillment in the act. This completely one-sided exchange between vampire and victim is strongly reminiscent of Memmi's description of the relationship between colonizer and colonized. Most importantly, detective Raymond Pope shows a desire to become assimilated by the elite by succumbing to his lust for Erszebet. Therefore, Pope fits well into the figure of the colonized policeman as understood by Albert Memmi:

> The representatives of the authorities, cadres, policemen, etc., recruited from among the colonized, form a category of the colonized which attempts to escape from its political and social condition. But in so doing, by choosing to place themselves in the colonizer's service to protect his interests exclusively, they end up by adopting his ideology, even with regard to their own values and their own lives [Memmi 1985, 16].

Perhaps this explains why, for some viewers, it might be difficult to empathize with a doomed protagonist like Pope, whose lust drives him to want to succumb to the vampiric colonizer. In *Éternelle*, there is no saving grace for any of the main characters. Each is trapped within their role in this allegorical "colonial" situation. Erszebet must maintain her parasitic yet powerful position as a vampire and "colonial" master. Therefore, she has an absolute need for her "colonized" victims. The victims themselves also cannot hope to escape their situation, as even a desire for assimilation is ultimately met with rejection from Erszebet. Liebenberg and Sanchez' horrific portrayal of Montreal becomes increasingly sclerotic as the film wears on. The old British and French elites rule, while everyone who falls outside these groups must serve.

Characters, true to the nature of their social position, remain static. By the end of *Éternelle*, one is left with the impression that nothing has truly changed. As a result of Pope's relentless pursuit and eventual capture of Erszebet, the countess finds herself in a makeshift prison, a medieval church, in relative comfort. Even behind bars, the countess is able to seduce Pope; although he is warned by Inspector Thurzo, the wizened and wise voice of experience, not to accept anything from Erszebet, Pope pays no heed to the old cop's warning and takes a glass of wine from the countess, only to discover that she has transubstantiated the wine into blood. Pope, the viewer feels, must always be alert to the possibility that he may be far too easily seduced by the offering of riches which show themselves to be an even deeper trap. Robbed of any satisfying conclusion, the film's viewer is left frustrated and, perhaps, wondering what could have been done differently for the film to be a more fulfilling experience. This is perhaps the true value of this unique Québecois take on the vampire myth. As an extended metaphor for colonialism, *Éternelle* confronts the viewer with the need to find a way out of such an unsettling and discomfiting experience.

NOTES

1. For a more detailed description of the unique position of Québec in colonial and postcolonial studies, see Green 2009.
2. A concept which Mary Jean Green, paraphrasing Memmi, defines as "the tendency of colonized peoples to retreat to traditional sources of value, like religion and the family, as a refuge from colonial oppression" (Green 2009, 250).

Europe and the Mediterranean

"The creatures of the night, what bad jokes they make!"
Racism, "True" Humor and the Nationalistic Vampire on Film

Simon Bacon

Humor, as Mary Douglas has noted, is used to create both a sense of inclusivity as well as exclusion, in that getting a joke exemplifies a form of insider knowledge and even superiority over those that do not (Douglas 2001, 146–164). Though this can be a fairly innocuous or reassuring phenomena in smaller contexts, when considered in terms of nationalism and national identity, it can quickly become a means of intimidation and vilification. This present study will examine three films that feature such a use of humor to create a sense of nationalism that also exemplify a construction of inclusion and exclusion through the body of the vampire: *Modern Vampires* (Elfman: 1998), *Vampires* (Lannoo: 2010), and *Kołysanka* (Machulski: 2010), which are from America, Belgium, and Poland respectively. All the narratives feature lead, undead characters that are highly representative of the nations that produced them and that find themselves in positions that question and threaten their identity as being American, Belgian, and Polish vampires respectively. In defining themselves, they all have recourse to certain levels of ethnic or racist humor in regard to individuals or groups around them, both as a means to differentiate themselves from them but also as a way to configure national identity.

Introduction

This study will pinpoint the ways in which the humor of each film can "either confirm or subvert bigoted opinions and perceptions of others"

(Lockyer and Pickering 2009, 3) or, as asserted by Christie Davies, can even enact forms of protest against "the members of a dominant ethnic majority [that] unthinkingly and effortlessly regard their own way of life as normal" (Davies 1996, 317).

Sigmund Freud, as noted by John Carey, speculated that "jokes, like dreams, come from the unconscious," being an expression of wishes and desires that cannot be fulfilled or revealed to the conscious mind (Freud 2002, viii). Jokes, like dreams and indeed vampires, act as a release valve for psychic excess with their "work" being undertaken in ways which seem to mirror each other. Freud describes the psychological work undertaken by dreams and jokes as follows, "dream predominantly serves to spare ourselves unpleasure, the joke to gain pleasure" (Freud 2002, 175). Such release, or avoidance, ensures that a measure of equilibrium is achieved from the successful handling of excessive feelings and/or emotions that have been repressed. However, as the term repression suggests, the hidden parts of jokes and dreams cannot be shown explicitly, and appear in forms that mask their true meaning as a way "to trick the censorship" of the conscious mind (Freud 2002, viii). This is clearly seen when the psychic excess is at its most extreme. For humor, this would be the case of what Freud termed "tendentious" jokes and are produced to "satisfy aggressive instincts" and which are not individually or socially acceptable (Freud 2002, viii). For the dream, this would be the nightmare which, according to Ernest Jones, "is a form of *Angst* attack, that ... is essentially due to an intense mental conflict centering around a repressed component of the psycho-sexual instinct" (Jones 1951, 54).

Jones uses this to indicate the essential sexual nature of the vampire, and this is something used in many psychoanalytical readings of the vampire in general; it can also be linked to other traumatic rifts in identity construction. So if the nightmare configures the release of the repressed psychic ambivalence of one's relationship to one's family, or where one comes from, the vampire can be seen as a way of negotiating this rift or of bringing it out into the daylight. This is something the vampire and the joke also share in expressing the hidden while also maintaining the air of something secret, which is particularly useful when looking at jokes made by nationalistic vampires, as they may seem very straightforward statements of identity but there is always something hidden below the surface. Elaine Showalter's observation captures something of this indeterminacy: "Dracula lives in Transylvania 'on the borders of three states,' which we might read as states of living, dead, and undead" (Showalter 2001, 179). While the vampire appears to be at home in one place, it actually belongs only to itself, intimating what Michael Billig sees at the core of Freud's vision of society, and humor, "that there was a fundamental conflict between individual desire and social order" (Billig 2005, 56).

Vampires and humor not only provide an outlet for psychic excess, but they also facilitate a maintenance of the established social order. So both humor and vampires allow us to release the tensions that would otherwise result in socially unacceptable behavior. This can be seen not just in the vampire's sexual mores, but often in its positioning within the social hierarchy. Moretti uses this framework to note that Dracula exemplifies an undead aristocracy that sucks off the working classes beneath him (Moretti 1988, 91). The vampire here becomes a monstrous caricature of the upper classes and their historical and unearned privilege and power. However, as seen in many vampire narratives, those seen as lower in the social hierarchy, often rise up and kill the undead monster so that the last laugh belongs the ones that were formerly considered to be inferior. This reveals as much about the relationship between different groups as it does about the nature of the group that is laughing. In this way humor and offensiveness relate to "social divisions and structures of power in society" strongly linking humor to notions of superiority (Lockyer and Pickering 2009, 17). By making a joke about another person, or group of people, one shows one's superiority over them. This can include jokes regarding another's class or sexuality, but often is aimed at nationality and ethnicity.

Such humor can be as multivalent as the figure of the vampire itself and, as Critchley comments, can be "a form of cultural insider knowledge, and might, indeed, be said to function like a linguistic defense mechanism" exampling "cultural distinctiveness," yet can simultaneously be "the Hobbesian laughter of superiority or sudden glory at our eminence and the other's stupidity" (Critchley 2002, 67–70). For Critchley, this immediately raises the connection between, what he calls, ethnicity and ethicity, and which "must be recognized and not simply sidestepped" (Critchley 2002, 70). Though theorists like Christie Davies side-step this problem and posit, "people do not necessarily dislike those whom they disesteem, and the throwers of custard pies do not regard their targets in the same way that those that hurl rocks or grenades do" (Davies 1996, 323). While this seems a somewhat black and white interpretation of the various shades of grey that are inevitably involved here, Christie does make earlier an important observation, in that: "the members of a dominant ethnic majority unthinkingly and effortlessly regard their own way of life as normal, reasonable, a pattern for others to imitate, whereas the members of a subordinate or marginal ethnic group must, at the very least, take serious account of the mores of the dominant group" (Christie 1996, 317). As such what Critchley describes as true humor in regard to ethnicity might work as a process of recognition. Although Christie highlights this in terms of a group that has little option in doing otherwise, i.e., a marginal group more obviously recognizes itself as being marginal, and thus also intimates that this can be opened up to a wider process of inter-group recognition. Subsequently, Critchley sees true humor as being able to tell us "something about who we are and the sort of place we live in, and perhaps indicating to us how it might be changed" (Critchley 2002, 11). This necessarily includes recognition of parts of ourselves, and the societal relations we construct and maintain, that "can reveal us to be persons [and a group] that, frankly, we would really rather not be" (Critchley 2002, 12). Re-integrating the earlier Freudian motifs, true humor in this context should reveal that which one would prefer to repress about oneself and one's society, and its expression performs something of an ethical release which, is not so much a confessional to restore a moral equilibrium, but has the potential to become something of a space of possibility and change. To see just how this might work in relation to specific vampire narratives in their portrayals of nationhood and nationality, it is necessary to examine the first of the films under consideration, *Modern Vampires* (Elfman: 1998).

America

The film begins with Dallas, an exiled vampire, returning to a group of friends in Los Angeles, a city run by Count Dracula, who acts as something of an undead Mafia boss. However, a rogue vampire, known as the "Hollywood Slasher," is drawing attention to the undead community, and is being tracked down by the mobster Count and his men. Dallas finds the out of control vampire, realizes that she was sired by him, and decides to educate her into the ways of modern vampires in the hope of persuading Dracula not to destroy her. Dr. Frederick Van Helsing arrives in town on a mission to kill Dallas, as he was responsible for turning the vampire slayer's son, Hans, into one of the undead. Much of the story echoes *My Fair Lady* (Cukor: 1964, Newman 2011, 349) with Dallas teaching vampire etiquette to Nico, the rogue vampire, but what it also does is establish the difference between the American and European characters. Los Angeles under Dracula, as noted by one character, "has become something of a mecca for our type," which could as easily mean Europeans as it does vampires. Indeed, Dallas' friends are all European: Richard is English; Ulrike and Vincent are German; and Panthia is Russian. The Count appears to be part Romanian and part Italian, and all the vampires under his control are shown to be European as well. Only the hired human henchmen are American. Even Van Helsing is Viennese and is variously shown as a Nazi sympathizer who worked in the concentration camps, though he "only experimented on vampires."

The Europeans are constructed as a group of outsiders who have moved to a new country to control and exploit it. As such, Los Angeles is portrayed as a processing factory, it even has a cleanup service for vampire kills, which looks like a well-run English/German/European city. That is until it is interrupted by the individualistic and chaotic Americans. This coincidentally echoes the nationalistic stereotypes as pointed out by Davies where ethnic humor between America and England is reliant on

> the clash between the easy, informal democratic manners of the former and the stiff, hierarchal status-conscious approach to life of the English. These jokes rely for their humor on the American's ignorance of and often contempt for the rules of etiquette that characterize the more snobbish and formal social life of England ... the American's behavior is either refreshingly informal or crassly vulgar [Davies 1996, 244–245].

While this specifically cites the Anglo-American relationship, within Elfman's film it works equally well for Europe as a whole. Nico, in her positioning as white trailer trash, fills the role of the crass American who, through "jokes" releases the repressed feelings of her fellow, more controlled, countrymen/women. When Dallas asks his friends to hide the sudden appearance of Nico from Dracula by saying "she's just visiting from Europe," Ulrike points out the impossibility of this when she replies condescendingly: "that little white trash thing?" Nico responds in kind saying: "Your friends are snobs. That motherfuckin' wetback with her big ass words, telling an American citizen what to do." As the narrative develops, she continues in similar vein, and as Dallas warns her of the dangers of confronting Dracula, she says: "I'm an American citizen, no foreign bag of shit is gonna run me out of my own goddamn country."

Dallas, as the film's "first" American vampire—Dallas invited Dracula and his associates over after World War II—tries to calm her down by explaining: "you have no history; that's why you're not afraid of anything." This echoes an oft cited criticism of the New World by the Old, while also hinting at a positive characteristic of American identity, a point which is reinforced by Nico's response to Dallas: "What you see, that's me OK? Of you don't like it then too fucking bad!" Although Dallas' job is to educate Nico to be more sophisticated, more European, she equally teaches him that it is more important to be American first. This is highlighted by the other American vampires in the film—the African American gang members that work for Van Helsing.

Upon arriving in Los Angeles Van Helsing soon realized there are more vampires there than he thought, and so he hires some help. The first person to reply to his advertisement is a gang member called Time Bomb. Like Nico, Time Bomb, as a member of the infamous Los Angeles gang the Crips, is shown as coming from the national underclass, yet is somehow more authentically American for that. Time Bomb's status as such is confirmed when Van Helsing says to him: "I don't understand. You're telling me you don't believe in vampires yet you're willing to drive a stake through someone's heart?" To which he replies, "Yo, I need this job." This is reinforced later when Time Bomb recruits other gang members to help hunt down vampires. Van Helsing tries to explain to them how serious their work is and tells them: "These are people who live off human blood, people who destroy things. I'm talking about bad, bad, people," to which one of their number replies: "You were just talking about us, right?" The positioning of the African American characters becomes complicated as they too become vampires. The gang members, not unlike Nico herself, in their underclass status, are shown to be already feeding off of society in some way and living a vampiric existence in relation to the larger United States. Simultaneously, however, they are also shown to be fighting for both their own identity and that of the nation itself. They join Dallas and Nico in the fight against Dracula, which results in all the European vampires being killed. As the film ends, Nico looks at the Crips/vampires and says "L.A. belongs to them" as she, Dallas and Rachel leave for New York.

Consequently, the film would be better titled as *American Vampires*, because it is very much about the future belonging to the United States, warts and all, rather than the outdated, snobbish and collective mind of Old World Europe. While the humor utilized here can be seen to come under the umbrella of a home nation defending itself against outsiders, the ethnic makeup of America makes this positioning difficult at best. The film also infers, if tongue-in-cheek, that the future belongs to white trailer trash and African American gang bangers. The humor here, particularly in reference to the Crips, is highly problematic as it constructs them as rapists and killers that do anything for money, implying that this is something that all African Americans do. This is reinforced by the fact that even the sympathetically portrayed Time Bomb joins in with the rape of Ulrike. Such complications divide as much as they unite the nation. Which is also true in the Belgian film, *Vampires*.

Belgium

Vampires (Lannoo: 2010), as was Elfman's film, is about the undead negotiating life in a modern metropolis. The relationship between the vampire and its urban environment, as Abbot notes, sees "the vampire redefining its mythology to suit its landscape, but also enter[ing] a dialogue with the newly constituted representation of the city" (Abbott 2007, 194). Lannoo, shows that this is equally true of 21st century Belgium, though through a narrative that is as internally divisive as *Modern Vampires*. If Elfman's film can be read as a critique of L.A. rather than America, *Vampires* can only be about the French-speaking Walloon community in Belgium. The region is known for documentary-style filming and producing "politicized ... socially conscious ... texts and performances focusing on Walloon society and history including the regions constituent subcultures," (Mosley 2013, 28) and Lannoo does just that.

From the start the film uses, or critiques, the notions of social realism and subcultures as a voiceover explains how Belgium's vampire community invited a team of documentary film makers to record their lifestyle. Two film crews and two years later, a third film crew goes in, and are invited into the home of George Saint Germain and his family; his wife, Bertha, and two children, Samson and Grace. The film crew are also introduced to a young girl, known only as "The Meat" who is something of a maid, or familiar, to the vampire family, and takes care of any chores and housework that needs doing during the daylight hours (the undead here are vaporized by sunlight). She is also a source of food for the family, particularly on special occasions, and is well fed so that her blood is rich and full of flavor.

As she explains to the film crew, "I'm luxury meat." It is this knowing relationship between the vampires and the humans in the local community that begins to define the politicized nature of the film because the undead are supported by a large service industry. As such the vampires form part of a well-run society and the local police make "food" deliveries directly to their doorstep. One such delivery is shown where a police officer arrives with an immigrant from Mali. The policeman says: "I brought your sausage!" George smiles at the distressed looking immigrant and calms him, saying: "Don't worry, we're here to help," and takes him out into the garden and locks him in the "coop," a large cage they keep their food in. George speaks frankly to the film crew, explaining both the vampires' place in the community as well as why they stay there:

> Everything is possible here. Organized crime, terrorism. We have illegal aliens delivered to our door ... we fulfill a social service in Belgium ... certain people encourage us to act as a sort of clean-up business for the undesirables. At the moment we're having a wave of black Malians.... Delicious ... every Monday someone comes and picks up the corpses that are laying around.

Subsequently, the vampires are constructed as an implicit part of the region's political system and become something of a manifestation of its inherent corruption and repressed bigotry. The crude humor of immigrants being brought to the home of vampires mimics the repressed feelings about illegal aliens themselves, being seen as vampires that suck the life out of the nation.

George introduces more and more members of the community, and it is discovered that they are forced to live in strict accordance to the Vampire Code, handed down to them by Count Dracula, and which is, probably not coincidentally, similar to the one imposed by Dracula in *Modern Vampires*. The undead are free to do what they like, but are not allowed to create new vampires without the knowledge of their leader, nor are they allowed sexual relations with the "wife" of the head vampire. Samson manages to do both, and is sentenced to death. George sends Samson to appeal to the King vampire in the Romanian Embassy in London—which we assume is Dracula himself. Samson travels with "The Meat," a form of vampire packed lunch, and manages to get his death sentence commuted to exile to Canada. Consequently, George and his family are forced to leave their home in Belgium, and move to Montreal to join the vampire community there. This throws up one of the other main themes within the film, namely the place of French-speaking Belgians in regard to the larger Francophile world.

Four months later the film crew follow them, and find that most of the family members are deeply unhappy. George is forced to work and must "deserve" the humans they eat, while Bertha is so depressed that she refuses to leave the house. Grace has become so disaffected that she has returned to being human again. However, Samson is reveling in his new surroundings and has a new girlfriend who is human, and who, as Samson freely admits, speaks a language, French Canadian, that he does not understand—She is called Sharon, yet he insists on calling her Sherman. This mirrors the beginning of the film when no one can understand the Malian French of the immigrant brought to George's house. This hints at something more than people being separated by speaking the same language, as seen in the relationship between George's family and their neighbors.

When in Belgium, George and his family lived in the above ground part of their house, while they had neighbors, Elizabeth and Bienvenu lived in the cellar. Although George explains it thus: "When vampires don't have children, they don't get houses. So you have to live in the houses of other vampires"; the film also suggests that it is because they are French. The neighbors were both "turned" or born as vampires in France. How they came to Belgium is never told, but they consider their hosts as "retrograde," or as Bienvenu explains: "It's terrible what goes on up there. There are no boundaries, no rules, nothing. And proper well behaved people like us are trapped in the cellar like savages." Their reactions to George very much reflect Elfman's film where Americans are seen as uncouth—but also what Davies cites in relation to a dominant language and those that are seen peripheral or unpure speakers of that tongue:

> Jokes about stupidity are also told about ethnic groups who live on the interface of two major or prestigious languages whose attempts to speak either one of the languages are likely to contain fragments of the other in a way that those in command of the "pure" language of the center are likely to find comic. Today's French and Dutch ethnic jokes about "stupid Belgians" are the descendants of dialect stories and satires

based on the occurrence of odd bits of Dutch in Walloon French and of French in Flemish [Davies 1996, 59].

What is shown in the family is a reversal of this, and while the true French see George as backwards in some ways, he sees them as inferior, indeed like all other non–Belgian-French speakers. Oddly mirroring Bienvenu, when George arrives in Montreal, he calls their behavior "retrograde," and finds them deeply unsophisticated. The film then posits both the insularity of Belgium's French speakers, while also highlights the ways in which the status of its language as being peripheral or special is used to denigrate others that speak the same tongue.

Poland

Language is touched upon in *Kołysanka* (Machulski: 2010), but it is the all-consuming nature of vampirism in society that permeates Juliusz Machulski's film. The family of vampires that feature in the narrative seem to come from nowhere and yet, simultaneously, appear to have been always present. The opening shots of the film show various drawings and tableaux from history that feature the vampire family standing in the background, intimating that these are not new or modern vampires but part of the very fabric of the past. The family is led by Michał Makerewicz, his pregnant wife, Bożena, and their four children, Wojtek, Marysia, Ola, and baby Kuba, and Grandpa. Their timeless quality is further emphasized by musical intermissions throughout the film where the family comes together playing classical pieces of music and their normal poor peasant clothes change into far more grand attire, reminiscent of apparel worn by royals and courtiers in the 17th century. Like George in *Vampires*, no specific dates are given for the vampires birthing, though Grandpa is 550 years old, yet they seem to be constantly on the move looking for a new home. This quest for home basically forms the main drive of the film's storyline, and, subsequently, the narrative opens with them finding their latest choice of residence. From nowhere they materialize on the doorstep of Roman Łapszow, who lives on a remote former farm on the edges of the village of Odlotowo, in Masuria, North East Poland, and they take it over for themselves. They quickly receive visits from various individuals, such as the local postman; a social worker; a German, who wishes to buy the house, and his interpreter; and a Priest with his Acolyte.

Unsurprisingly, they all soon vanish without a trace. As news spreads of the mysterious disappearances, a film crew from Polish national television, TVP, is sent to investigate the "Masurian Triangle." Unsurprisingly, the film crew also disappears. The vampires have not killed them, but are keeping them, strapped to tables in their barn, so that they can feed off them.

During this the buyer who purchased arts and craft souvenirs from Roman has visited the vampires but rather than putting him in the barn with the others, they accept the money that he pays them and start making the items themselves. It is at this point that is becomes apparent that almost everyone in the film is a metaphorical vampire of some sort: the Postman and the Social Worker feed off the bureaucratic system that employs them as well as prying into and feeding off the information garnered through their work; the German represents those that came back to Poland and buy cheaply the land that used to belong to their ancestors before the Second World War, as well as wealthy investors exploiting their poorer neighbors; the Priest represents the church that is seen to have been feeding off the people for centuries; and the film crew are purposely set up to reflect the kind of investigative reporting that feeds off the pain and tragedy of others. The vampires then become a form of Everyman, or Every-family, that represents simple village folks that are only trying to do the best they can for their children and relatives. As such, while the film is set in contemporary times, it also intimates that these are roles that have been acted out throughout time. This notion of timelessness or eternal repetition is integral to the vampires, but also with the "prisoners" in the barn who lose track of time and feel as though they are caught in an endless loop. Lannoo's *Vampires* highlights a similar quality to the Belgian French community. Equally, while both *Modern Vampires* and *Vampires* show a certain level of collusion between the powers that be and the undead community, in *Kołysanka* this is not the case. Oddly, the police, which feature quite extensively throughout the film are not really viewed as vampires but just stupid and ineffective, although one of them does end up in the barn alongside the Postman and the Social Worker.

While Machulski's tongue is very firmly in his cheek when ridiculing the society around him, unlike Lannoo or Elfman, his focus remains very internally directed, though it potentially goes outwards when it comes to the topic of German-Polish relations. This is obviously shown in the figure of Mr. Steinbach, who is in his fifties but has a much younger Polish interpreter/girlfriend. They arrive at the farm that the family owns, wanting to buy it, because, as Mr. Steinbach explains: "My grandma was born here. I'll build the hotel, one, two. You have to invest here. Money." Any emotional or hereditary ties to the land that the German has is superseded by thoughts of money and financial return. In this way, Germany is seen as something of a vampire from the new world that is returning to the old one to suck it dry.

As the film draws to a close, the vampire family realize they will be unable to remain anonymous and so decide to leave the village and move to Warsaw: this is something that Bożena has wanted and is decided upon, especially when Grandpa loses his teeth and can get some cheap replacement ones from a dentist in the capital. Michał and Grandpa return all the prisoners to their previous lives, after giving them all doses of vampire blood so that they will not remember what happened to them. All of them, except the interpreter and the Acolyte, return quite happily to their former lives, unaware of the adventures that had taken place. The interpreter decides to return home and go back to college and finish her degree, while the Acolyte, who was given the wrong blood, can remember everything and hysterically runs around trying to convince everyone of what has just occurred. Meanwhile the family has arrived in Warsaw, being dragged along in a small handcart by the Priest.

They have taken the Priest with them as the baby, Kuba, has taken a particular liking to him and his blood is most beneficial, or as Michal explains: "after you he's rosy-cheeked, sleeps well and poos regular." As they travel, Kuba is suddenly in need of attention and so they tell the Priest to turn into the next building, which just happens to be the Presidential Palace. No one tries to stop them and so they take up residence, with Grandpa intoning: "What will we live on?" As this is the President's home, it is clearly being indicated that it will be the people that will support the needs of the new residents, and as the film closes the Priest is shown rocking Kuba in his cradle, while the rest of the family begin playing their instruments again, changing back into their true selves, and suggesting that at long last, they have finally found, or returned to, their rightful home.

Conclusion

Vampires here, as shown particularly in Lannoo's and Machulski's films, are useful signifiers of ideologies and identities that seem to remain fixed both through history and in, what might be termed, a national identity—seen in George and the Makerewicz family.

Elfman's story contains a similar notion, but more in terms of something to react against; as such, the European immigrants exemplify the Old World, and make manifest historical undead ideologies, while the new breed of American vampires usher in the new order. The Belgian film, however, slightly complicates this by indicating that the old system inevitably contains the seeds of its own downfall, again more firmly positioning the idea of undead as being neither dead, as in without life, or alive, as in constantly changing, but something different, as intimated earlier by Showalter. This idea also permeates a consideration of the idea of true and how it relates to ethnicity and humor.

All the films considered use the idea of ethnicity, and indeed national identity, to show who belongs and who does not. In *Modern Vampires* the gang members and the new, White trash vampires are shown to be of the same category due to their reaction to the European outsiders and in their respective self-recognition as being American; in *Vampires,* this is shown largely as linguistic difference and those that can be understood by the form of French they speak being othered by those that cannot, or will not, understand them. *Kołysanka* complicates this by intimating that everyone is a form of vampire in some way, and that the only difference is in whether you recognize yourself as a vampire or not.

Indicative of these varying degrees of otherness within and outside national identity is the ways in which racism can be seen to be employed in each of the films. Elfman's film is the most worrying in this way as it portrays the African American gang members as already being vampires, even before their transformation, and unlike Machulski's film, the joking quality behind this feels far more negative, which is reinforced when they gang-rape Ulrike to become real vampires. Lannoo's film depicts one African character, the Malian illegal immigrant, but this is used to highlight the insularity of the French Belgian community, in that they cannot understand the form of French he speaks, as well satirize the local authorities' opinions of such outsiders who send them, via police escort, to the vampire's front door. Machulski's film reflects Poland's lack of a colonial past and only features one outsider, Mr. Steinbach, who somewhat represents a colonizer from the past rather than the reverse colonization which features in Lannoo's film.

It is worth mentioning one of Freud's observations here in relation to self-criticism within humor. Although Freud examples this in relation to Jewish jokes about Jews, it has wider applications and he explains it as follows when the intended criticism of protest is directed against one's self, or, to put it more circumspectly, against a person in whom that self has a share, a collective person, that is, one's own people (Freud 2002, 108). Here the joke becomes both a form of self-protection but also a recognition of oneself as an individual and/or a group. It is quite easy to extend this into Critchley's idea of true, if one can be seen to use this in a way to not only accept one's limitations and faults, but possibly as a way to critique and facilitate change.

Looking at *Modern Vampires* in this light, while it extols the traditional American virtues of individuality and self-expression, it rather allows itself to portray these as largely negative characteristics when left uncontrolled or in the hands of undesirable groups (one could almost say lower classes). As such, it intimates that the true identity of America is in the hands of its under classes and the disenfranchised, but not in a way that it sees as being good—hence why they are portrayed as vampires. *Vampires* takes a different tack, and specifically uses humor, and ethnic humor in particular, to reveal the insularity of contemporary Belgium; the tongue it sticks out at other nations is shown to be reflected back at the French Belgian community itself. Similarly, *Kołysanka* laughs constantly at itself, with its sharpest quips aimed at the most serious of national institutions. Even when directed at their German neighbors, the humor suggests that both sides are complicit the many misunderstandings that arise between them. In this way, the films by Lanoo and Machulski contain much true humor, in that it is true to the peoples that it depicts and in its intentions toward them. The use of the vampire within these two films reveals not the monstrosity of the people depicted, but the undead traditions and biases that live within them.

Humor here allows the undead parts of us all to be seen in the light of day and to be reflected back at us; to be seen, recognized and changed. In this way, the final words of Adelard, the leader of the Montreal Vampire community, are rather apt and reflect the potential of true humor: "It's for little miracles like these that I do my work. When you come back next year, this family will be completely integrated ... there will be colors all over."

Amid and Beyond Gender(s)
The Vampire as a Locus of Gender Neutrality in John Ajvide Lindqvist's Let the Right One In

Marie Levesque

Vampirism always and ever implies something which goes above and beyond the immanent world. The immortality inherent to the figure of the vampire places blood drinking creatures in an in-between realm since they "live" both in and outside society. This liminal status therefore creates a neutral space, making the vampire a potent figuration of the concept of neutrality. In the same vein, the figure of the vampire challenges ideals of identity, especially in terms of gender and sexuality. By encompassing a conception of neutrality, the blood drinker becomes a neutral ground through which any identity, any gender and sexuality, can be explored. Indeed, the correlation between neutrality and gender and sexual identities further strengthens the claim that gender and sexual orientations are fluid and not set at one specific end of the spectrum, i.e., either masculine or feminine, or either heterosexual or homosexual. Gender and sexual identities are thus performative and utterly fluid, as it has been defined by Judith Butler. Also, by understanding gender as a large fluid spectrum, the idea of binaries becomes irrelevant. Gender and sexual fluidity require an erasure of binarial systems; in other words, the deconstruction of binaries equates to the fact that norms must be challenged and questioned. Simply by being undead—i.e., being neither dead nor alive—the vampire is utterly non-normative, but this norm deconstruction goes even further since the vampire also does not adhere to set gender and sexual identities. In other words, by performing their gender and sexualities as they see fit, vampires deconstruct binaries and promote fluidity, which then leads to neutrality. Indeed, by being neutral, the figure of the vampire paves the way for the erasure of binarial systems, which, in turn, allows gender and sexual fluidity to fully take form. John Ajvide Lindqvist's novel *Let the Right One In* (2004) not only cements the coherence between vampires and gender and sexuality, but also provides a literary space in which more recent gender and sexual identities, such as genderqueer and pansexuality, can be explored. Eli, a 12-year-old "female" vampire, befriends her neighbor Oskar during a cold winter night. Eli is eventually revealed to be Elias, a boy who was castrated and turned into a vampire by a sadistic blood drinking creature. Since he(/she)[1] has no genital reproductive organs, Eli(as)[2] therefore literally performs both male and female gender identities, but more importantly also represents the concept of neutrality. In basic terms, gender performativity, as defined by Judith Butler, demands a constant stylized repetition of acts. Gender identities and expressions need to be repeated to become effective and hopefully, accepted by society. More significantly, vampiric blood consumption is also a stylized, and even ritualized, repetition of acts. Therefore, an undeniable correlation exists between gender performativity and vampirism. Eli(as)'s character in *Let the Right One In* utterly embodies the stylized—and sometimes *ritualized*—repetition of acts inherent to gender performativity because of his(/her) vampire countenance, but also because of his(/her) castrated status. Ultimately, Eli(as)'s relationship with Oskar illustrates multiple gender performances because Eli(as) can be considered a genderqueer[3] vampire.

Due to its[4] undead status, the figure of the vampire is the most potent vehicle through which the concept of neutrality can fully expand. From an etymological standpoint, the term "neutrality" comes from the Latin *neuter*[5] which means "not one or the other." It can therefore be stated that which is neutral undoubtedly goes above and beyond binaries, as binaries are always "either one or the other." Therefore, the undeadness inherent to the vampire becomes a fertile gateway into the realm of the neutral. Indeed, vampires transcend normative binaries since they are both in and outside society, human and non-human; they are always and forever in a chiasm. This in-between status gives blood drinking creatures the ability to go beyond socially created binaries, which strengthens their neutral countenance since they literally become "not one or the other." By transcending said binaries, the vampire can also go beyond gender and sexual categorizations. However, neutrality obviously goes further than simply being "neither one nor the other."

Indeed, many philosophers have tried to define the concept of neutrality in a more complex manner. As French writer Claude Stéphane Perrin states in his book *Le neutre et la pensée*, "that which is neutral takes the form of a chiasm," an in-between that "can neither be grasped nor un-grasped" (Perrin 2009, 11). In other words, neutrality goes beyond categorizations and precedes multiple significations (Perrin 2009, 31). Due to their undead countenance, vampires do transcend categorizations—and binaries—and they also do precede multiple significations because of their immortality. By being neither present nor absent and by living forever, vampires do precede various meanings since no ontological premises can be used to describe them. Ontological premises, in this case, refer to metaphysical explanations of what being human is, or what it can be.

Vampires, being forever trapped in an in-between status, cannot follow these specific premises since they are neither completely human nor utterly other. Following the same logic in terms of gender and sexuality, vampires once again precede significations and go beyond them since they cannot be defined by clear-cut gender assignments, assignments which are socially and therefore ontologically, created. Indeed, vampires are "multiple" in the sense that they encompass several gender identifications at once, but they cannot be quantified in human social terms since their neutral countenance does not firmly anchor them in the human experience. For instance, the fact that vampires bite or transform both men and women is representative of multiple gender spectrum identifications.[6]

Moreover, Claude Stéphane Perrin defines the Eternal—or that which can be considered eternal—as follows: "The Eternal becomes neutral: neither inside nor outside, neither present nor absent. It would nonetheless remain eternal like an infinite mark [...] always active, always repeated [...]." The vampire is a significant embodiment of this definition. Indeed, the vampire is neither inside nor outside society. It does live in society to a certain extent, using human beings for nourishment and company, but it cannot impact society as much as it could before the victim was transformed into a vampire. In that sense, the blood drinker is also neither present nor absent, having no tangible social impact on its environment. The most significant aspect of Perrin's definition of the Eternal relates to the idea that what is neutral will forever remain as an "infinite mark" that is always repeated. The vampiric act of drinking blood undeniably correlates with this conceptualization of neutrality. Indeed, when vampires drink blood from their victims, they do physically mark their prey's flesh when the fangs penetrate it. Also, this "infinite mark" is always repeated because vampires need to feed on blood to survive.

From that perspective, the mark perpetrated by the penetrating fangs will forever be repeated for the rest of the vampire's existence. Therefore, the immortality inherent to vampirism is representative of Claude Stéphane Perrin's theorization of the Eternal as neutral, making blood drinkers true figurations[7] of the concept of neutrality.

Neutrality and vampirism also go hand in hand in terms of transgression. Indeed, Perrin states that which is neutral can be an illustration of "the feeling of transgression one feels when in contact with the impossible." Obviously, vampires are narrative beings; they do not refer to a real entity. Therefore, in fictional worlds, the vampire is often seen as a supernatural being that cannot possibly exist. From this stems a feeling of transgression, of going against set societal boundaries. For instance, the relationship between Eli and Oskar feels like a transgressive one for Oskar at the beginning as he must deal with and accept who and what Eli is[8] before going further. Following a similar logic, French philosopher and literary theorist Roland Barthes defines the neutral as that which annuls and/or blurs, as that which evades the paradigm (Barthes 2002, 31). By blurring the lines of what is considered socially normal and acceptable, the figure of the vampire does evade paradigms and therefore transcends them, making blood drinkers potent vehicles of gender fluidity and other unorthodox cultural groups.

Claude Stéphane Perrin alludes to such a conceptualization of neutrality when he states that that thinking processes pertaining to neutrality do deconstruct binary categorizations, but "[do] not deny the *nuanced differences* which animate the multiple appearances of the real." In that sense, the vampire fits into the "multiple appearances of the real," as it always remains in the in-between realm inherent to its undead countenance. By being human and non-human, present and absent, the fictional blood drinker can vicariously provide nuanced differences which may not be easy to grasp and comprehend otherwise. For instance, Anne Rice's *The Vampire Chronicles* book series (1967–2018) did—and still does—change the American literary landscape of the 1970s. Even though the Civil Rights Movement and the sexual liberation movement had been impacting the population for a few years, some political issues were not utterly accepted by the general public. In such cases, art in all its forms becomes an incredible driving force because it is able to make its way into people's lives through characters which, perhaps, ease a necessary transition. Rice's novels provided that vicarious need to open up discussions about good and evil, yes, but also about gender and sexual fluidity. Indeed, the vampires in Rice's universe have always been sexually open, making no gender discrepancies when it comes to their partner and/or victim choices. From that standpoint, the figure of the vampire possesses the necessary assets to animate the nuanced differences of the real brought forward by Perrin. However, the figure of the blood drinker emulates an even more intricate conceptualization of neutrality.

French intellectual Maurice Blanchot, in his seminal work *Infinite Conversation* (1969),[9] states that the neutral is that which "cannot be distributed in any genre: the generic, the non-generic as well as the non-particular." It also is neither qualified as a subject nor as an object. According to Blanchot, this supposes another relationship, a relationship which does not adhere to objective conditions or subjective dispositions (Blanchot 1969, 440). The vampire fits into this theorization of neutrality as the blood drinker, by virtue of being undead, indeed cannot adhere to objective conditions.

Neutrality presupposes a fluidity which cannot be stopped, and that is why the figure of the vampire is such a potent representation of it. In the same vein, vampiric subjective dispositions do exist,[10] but they are not the exact same dispositions that human beings feel. The vampire therefore becomes the outsider, especially due to the fact that it lives in a neutral realm which presupposes an unusual way of experiencing the world. From that point of view, the figure of the vampire completely embodies Maurice Blanchot's conceptualization of neutrality.

Blanchot pushes his theorization of the neutral further by stating that "the neutral questions, by the act of neutralizing, [...] always further the limit from which the neutral might still stem from." In other words, neutrality is, to use Blanchot's terms, a *limit-experience*. In its most basic definition, a *limit-experience* breaks a subject from itself, and therefore pushes said subject in an unknown in-between. Indeed, the *limit-experience* inherent to vampirism also falls in line with Blanchot's definition of the unknown. For Blanchot, the unknown is "a neutral which supposes an unfamiliar *rapport* to any identity and unity requirements [...]." Furthermore, referring to a neutral thought process undeniably relates to thinking outside the box, "away from that which is visible or invisible, that is [thinking] in terms which do not stem out from what is possible." In other words, vampirism presupposes an intrinsic in-between status, a status which, in some way, stipulates that the vampire forever remains neither visible nor completely invisible by virtue of being in and outside society. From a similar approach, the undead status of vampires indeed supposes an *unknown rapport* to identity and unity, as well as to presence, since vampires are atemporal and are therefore neither completely inside nor completely outside (societal) time. To that effect, Blanchot also states that "the neutral is often shown in a position of quasi-absence, of both effect and non-effect." The atemporal nature of vampires can therefore be defined as a quasi-absent state. Indeed, by being in and outside society and its time, the vampire is once again a significant representation of neutrality. Neutrality has been thoroughly defined not only to illustrate the complexity and scope of the concept, but most importantly to anchor it firmly to the figure of the vampire. However, even though the vampire has a neutral countenance, this state also strongly relates to the performance of gender(s) and/or sexual orientations.

In *Gender Trouble: Feminism and the Subversion of Identity* (1990), American philosopher Judith Butler defines gender performativity as a means to deconstruct social norms relevant to heteronormativity and phallogocentrism. In doing so, she also strives to expand gender and sexual horizons, regardless of one's biological sex assignment. Gender does include a biological aspect that cannot be denied—sexual genitalia does exist—but Butler stipulates that the performance of gender is what makes said gender(s) and sexual orientation(s) viable in a social context. Indeed, one's choice of gender expression(s), be it through clothes, makeup, language use, etc., reflects one's gender identity more than one's biological sex assignment does. Gender is primarily a performative act. As Butler states in *Gender Trouble*, the most potent example of gender performativity is that of drag queens (Butler 2006, 186). Indeed, drag queens often literally perform their gender identities in social contexts, allowing them to fully experience and assert their sense of belonging to the female sex.[11] In addition to performing their gender identities, drag queens—and kings—also enact their gender expressions. In the case of drag queens, they often perform in overt female disguises, on stage and/or in intimate settings, as a way of completely expressing their true gender identities. Gender performance(s) therefore imply "[g]estures, acts, enactments [that] are performative [...] fabrications manufactured and sustained through corporeal signs and other discursive means." In other words, gender performance(s) must be repeated and sustained through bodily acts, language, etc., to become socially impactful. The social predispositions pertaining to gender performativity are especially significant since gender, in and of itself, relates to how one situates oneself toward others.

In addition to gender fabrications and their inherent individual and collective performances, Judith Butler also differentiates three aspects intrinsic to corporeal gender acts, i.e., "[...] anatomical sex, gender identity, and gender performance." Furthermore, gender performativity demands "[...] not to be construed as a stable identity or locus of agency from which various acts follow; rather, is an identity tenuously constituted in time, instituted in an exterior space through a *stylized repetition of acts*." The figure of the vampire represents all three contingent dimensions of corporeality,[12] while also being a strong embodiment of the stylized repetition of acts inherent to gender performance(s), since they always need to indulge in blood drinking, either for survival or transformative purposes. In addition to these three contingent dimensions of corporeality, Butler states that "[...] within the inherited discourse of the metaphysics of substance, gender proves to be performative—that is, constituting the identity it is purported to be. In this sense, gender is always a doing [...]." Since gender is performative, it is nonbinary, as it defies fixed gender categorizations. Gender is therefore never statically defined, just as neutrality is never definitive.[13] Moreover, as Butler describes, the "[...] perpetual displacement [of the production of gender] constitutes a fluidity of identities that suggests an openness to resignification and recontextualization [...]." This resignification and recontextualization is undoubtedly taken into consideration when the figure of the vampire is concerned.

Indeed, John Ajvide Lindqvist's novel *Let the Right One In* and its representation of the figure of the vampire not only exemplifies Judith Butler's concept of gender as a performance, but it also shows that the vampire is the most potent cultural vehicle through which various gender and sexual spectrum positions can take form. Gender performances can vary—or are bound to vary—since the large spectrums of gender and sexuality possess multiple positions and inclinations. In other words, gender must not be construed as a simple binary—(heterosexual) male or female—but rather as something fluid which goes above and beyond said male/female binary. For instance, in terms of sexual orientations, some people can identify as being fully heterosexual or fully homosexual, while some others may, for example, identify as bisexual to varying degrees on the sexual scale(s).[14] Transgender identities and transsexuality also fit into these sexual orientation measurements. Eli(as), the main vampire in Lindqvist's novel, is a literal representation of genderqueer identities and expressions,[15] inasmuch as even his(/her) name is a manifestation of these gender performances.

Indeed, writing Elias' name as "Eli(as)" throughout this essay actually solidifies Eli(as)'s genderqueer countenance. From an etymological standpoint, the term "as" comes from the Old English term "*alswā*," which means "similarly." "As" can also be defined as "expressing identity [and] likeness." In this sense, putting the "as" part of Elias' name in between brackets reinforces his(/her) genderqueer countenance. Indeed, Eli(as) acts, performs *as* a girl despite him(/her) being a boy, biologically speaking. This demonstrates that Judith Butler's theorization of gender performativity is not only still extremely relevant, but also that gender and sexual orientations are indeed part of a fluid and ever-changing spectrum. Furthermore, physically, Eli possesses "feminine"[16] attributes such as long hair and delicate features. Her(/his) choice of clothes follows the same pattern—she(/he) often wears a pink sweater, for example.[17] At one point in the narrative, Eli confides in Oskar and reveals her(/his) vampiric identity to him, which ultimately leads to the revelation that Eli's real name is Elias, and that he was castrated and transformed into a vampire 200 years prior. Therefore, Elias chooses to perform his gender identity as a female to blend in socially, especially since he is a child vampire with no genital organs. This gender identity and its performance is, like most gender and sexual spectrum positions, undeniably fluid and ever-changing. Eli(as)'s name and pronouns—his(/her), etc.—will be written that way to further solidify the fluid inclination of gender. More significantly, in the original Swedish text, Lindqvist never uses pronouns when referring to Elias' character.[18] He(/she) is always referred to by his(/her) first name or the diminutive Eli. The only instances where a pronoun may be used to talk about Eli(as) is when other characters address or talk about him(/her). These characters always use feminine pronouns in those cases, believing that Eli(as) is actually a young girl. The author's work is noteworthy as it utterly solidifies Eli(as)'s genderqueer identity and performance, while showing how society attempts to put people into pre-set categorizations. This grammatical choice therefore becomes a powerful manner through which the conceptual basis of this essay can fully expand and exist.

Furthermore, Eli(as)'s undead countenance is what ultimately allows the existence of a fluid gender and sexual space in which he(/she) can perform multiple gender identities and expressions at once, without any norm restrictions. Indeed, Eli(as)'s physical appearance—long hair, feminine clothing— may be first perceived as being normatively feminine. Eli(as) therefore transcends his biological male gender identity by performing his(/her) gender through more "feminine"-inclined attributes.[19] However, Eli(as) could also be defined as both genderqueer and as a transsexual "boy/girl" since he(/she) has no genital organs to speak of, due to the sadistic phallic castration he(/she) went through. In this sense, Eli(as) exemplifies a true neutral countenance in terms of sexual genitalia.

In addition, Eli(as)'s pre-pubescent looking physique plays an important part in his(/her) gender performance. Pre-puberty is significant in this case, especially when it comes to the embodiment and representation of gender neutrality. Indeed, a pre-pubescent state presupposes physical changes on the verge of becoming, a neutrality which will become significantly altered once the process has been completed. However, in the case of the vampire and its inherent undead status, pre-puberty becomes increasingly important. Pre-puberty supposes a neutral state, being neither completely a boy nor utterly a girl if sexual organs are foregone. In other words, this puberty in becoming is therefore somewhat of a neutral terrain. Furthermore, the immortality inherent to vampirism adds an interesting viewpoint when considering pre-puberty as a neutral ground. Indeed, since no biological sexual markers will ever develop—Eli(as) will possess pre-pubescent physical attributes forever due to his(/her) undead countenance—he(/she) can perform gender as he(/she) desires. In that sense, Eli(as) truly adheres to the definition of "genderqueer" as a representation of a gender-neutral being, among other possible gender and sexual identities.

Moreover, Eli(as)'s pre-pubescent countenance is touched upon a few times in the novel. For instance, when Eli(as) visits Oskar in his bedroom, Oskar first sees "the contour of a little head on the other side of the glass." On a basic level, the description of Eli(as)'s head shows that he(/she) is indeed pre-pubescent looking, which ultimately allows him(/her) to perform a neutral gender identity. The fact that Oskar can only see the contour of Eli(as)'s head also plays the same role, as said contours ultimately represent Eli(as)'s blurry bodily and gender features. This blurriness represents both Eli(as)'s gender neutrality and pre-pubescent body. This unidentifiable countenance undoubtedly correlates with the undead state of the vampire as this eternal in-between is what forces the blood drinker to remain in limbo forever.

Without this feature, the vampire's body would evolve and obviously age, which would make it impossible for Eli(as) to remain in a pre-pubescent body for all eternity. From that standpoint, it cannot be denied that the figure of the vampire is all indicated to represent neutrality, both in terms of gender and sexuality, but also in terms of physicality. Eli(as) him/herself believes he/she is neutral when sharing a first physical encounter with Oskar.

Indeed, Eli(as) asks Oskar if he(/she) can come in through the latter's bedroom window. Once granted permission, Eli(as) gets under the covers with Oskar and takes off his(/her) clothes. After they have begun to cuddle, Eli(as) eventually admits to Oskar that he(/she) is not actually a girl: "'I'm not a girl.' 'What do you mean? You're a *guy*?' [...] 'Then what are you?' 'Nothing.' 'What do you mean, 'nothing'?' 'I'm nothing. Not a child. Not old. Not a boy. Not a girl. Nothing.'" The fact that Eli(as) insists that he(/she) is nothing, not a boy, not a girl but rather nothing, undoubtedly shows that Eli(as)'s neutrality is utterly embodied in him(/her), as even Eli(as) repeats so. Moreover, even though Eli(as) slips under the covers naked, Oskar does not see Eli(as) naked until later in the text. After taking a shower in Oskar's bathroom, Eli(as) comes out only wearing a towel around his(/her) waist, making his(/her) naked upper body visible: "The small nipples looked almost black against her pale white skin." Eli(as)'s lack of puberty markers and his(/her) "young age" reinforce Eli(as)'s genderqueer identity, while also making him(/her) a vampiric representation of gender neutrality. In addition, the fact that feminine pronouns are used throughout the entire excerpt, even though Elias is biologically a boy, reinforces Eli(as)'s gender-fluid/gender-neutral identities. This statement gains even more significance when Oskar sees Eli(as)'s entire naked body:

> Her upper body was slender, straight, and without much in the way of contours. Only the ribs stood out clearly in the sharp overhead light. Her thin arms and legs appeared unnaturally long the way they grew out of her body; a young sapling covered with human skin. Between the legs she had ... nothing. No slit, no penis. Just a smooth surface.

This description provides considerable indicators as to why the figure of the vampire, and especially Eli(as)'s character, is the most potent figure to provide an understanding of gender and sexual fluidity, as well as the importance of neutrality. Indeed, Eli(as)'s body is a blank slate, an undefined form to which any gender and/or sexual orientation can be applied. His(/her) lack of corporeal contours and his(/her) genitalia being simply a smooth surface, a neutral space, also reinforce that claim. In other words, Eli(as)'s bodily countenance is irrefutably gender-neutral. From that standpoint, it can be stated that Eli(as)'s character is truly genderqueer/gender-neutral and identifies as such. However, Eli(as)'s genderqueer identification originally stems from a traumatic experience, an experience which, in its own sadistic way, further reinforces the conceptualization of (gender) neutrality brought forward in this essay.

Indeed, one of the most significant and shocking scenes in Lindqvist's novel occurs when Elias[20] gets castrated by a sadistic vampire before said vampire transforms Elias into a blood drinking creature. Here, the castration is not only a literal neutering act but the events, although extremely graphic, perfectly illustrate Eli(as)'s future genderqueer identification, while also demonstrating the possible ritualistic aspect of gender performativity. Elias' castration, which is shown to Oskar through a vivid vision[21] is described as follows in the narrative:

> *Cold fingers grasp Oskar's penis, pulling on it. He opens his mouth to scream [...] The man under the table asks something and the wig man nods without shifting his gaze from Oskar. Then the pain. A red hot iron forced into his groin, gliding up through his stomach, his chest corroded by a cylinder of fire that passes right through his body and he screams, screams so his eyes are filled with tears and his body burns. [...] ... opens his eyes and sees the blond hair unclearly, the blue eyes like distant forest pools. Sees the bowl the man is holding in his hands, the bowl he brings to his mouth and how he drinks. How the man shuts his eyes, finally shuts them and drinks.... More time.... Endless time. Imprisoned. The man bites. And drinks. Bites. And drinks.* [emphases original].

The phallic castration is what transforms Elias into Eli/Eli(as), which, in turn, opens up a bodily space in which Eli(as)'s genderqueer/gender-neutral identity can fully develop.

Obviously, a castration equates to a literal neutralization and is thus a factual illustration of the concept of neutrality. The removal of the phallus is also what ultimately pushes Elias to change his name to the gender-fluid "Eli" diminutive, as it can be applied to any gender identity. This diminutive also strengthens Eli(as)'s position as a gender neutral/non-binary being. More importantly, as Judith Butler defends, gender performativity is achieved through a stylized repetition of acts. Vampirically speaking, the transformative blood exchange is also a stylized repetition of acts. Indeed, a human being's blood is first drunk by the vampire, and the victim will, in turn, drink his/her sire's blood to complete the vampiric change.[22] The act of blood drinking perpetrated by the newborn vampire is therefore a literal duplication of the master-vampire's initial bite.[23] In other words, vampiric blood consumption is a true stylized repetition of acts. More importantly, blood drinking and/or exchanges are so spiritually intense that they can sometimes be associated with religious rituals. The phallic castration in *Let the Right One In* follows this logic. Indeed, the removal of Elias' penis and the fact that it is placed inside a bowl from which the vampire can drink undeniably confirms that vampiric fluid consumption not only implies a stylized repetition of acts, but that this stylization can even morph into a *ritualized* repetition of acts. Indeed, the bowl into which Elias' penis and phallic blood falls can be likened to the Christian chalice.

In *Undoing Gender* (2004), Judith Butler relates the act of psychoanalytic confession to bodily acts, which, expectedly, imply the presence of others so that one's confession can be heard. This is especially significant since gender performativity also requires a social component.[24] Butler's definition of the act of confession can also be correlated with the relationship between vampirism and gender/sexual identities. Butler describes the act of confession as follows: "In confession we show that we are not truly repressed, since we bring the hidden content out into the open." The vampire is indeed a figurative representation of the psychoanalytic act of confession since blood drinking creatures literally bring hidden content out in the open, whether through multiple gender and sexual inclinations, incest, pedophilia,[25] perverse behaviors, gender-neutral manifestations, etc. More significantly, the "vampiric act of confession," which can be correlated to the highly intimate and sexual bond which blossoms during the transformative blood exchange, is reminiscent of the Christian Eucharist. Indeed, the stylized repetition of acts inherent to gender performance is *ritualized* in Lindqvist's novel. Elias' phallic castration and the way in which the vampire eats the penis and drinks its blood from a bowl can be correlated to both the Eucharistic sharing of the Host and the drinking of the wine in the chalice. Consequently, the figure of the vampire is not only a representation of the stylized repetition of gender and sexual performances, but the act of blood drinking also entails a *ritualized* repetition of acts. Elias's phallic castration transforms him into a gender-neutral being, but it also shows that the figure of the vampire is the most potent manifestation of gender/sexual performativity since it embodies both *stylized* and *ritualized* repetitions of acts.

To conclude, the vampire is the most significant cultural figure to provide an understanding of gender and its multiple spectrum positions, since vampires always have provisional identities. The in-between status which stems from their undead countenance allows them to enact their multiple genders and sexualities as they see fit. Eli(as)'s character in John Ajvide Lindqvist's *Let the Right One In* is a manifestation of that statement since he(/she) utterly performs genderqueer and gender-neutral inclinations. Eli(as)'s character provides a space in which non-normative gender and sexual performances can fully expand. This proves that multiple gender and sexual inclinations do exist and should not confined to the (heteronormative) masculine/feminine binary. In addition, it shows that cultural and literary figures can be illustrations of non-binary gender paradigms. Vampires perfectly represent these non-binary inclinations through their undead status, their multiple gender/sexual identities and expressions, and also through the act of blood drinking. Indeed, by consuming blood, vampires utterly adhere to the *stylized repetition of acts* intrinsic to gender and sexual performativity, especially since this blood consumption will go on—will be repeated—as long as the vampire lives. Furthermore, the vampiric consumption of the life fluid also confers it a *ritualized* status. This ritualization is brought forward in an explicit fashion in Lindqvist's text through Elias' phallic castration. By drinking and eating the penis from a bowl, the removal of Elias' phallus is reminiscent of the Eucharistic ritual of drinking the blood of Christ from the chalice and ingesting a part of His body through the sharing of the Host. Therefore, the vampiric chalice in *Let the Right One In* undeniably illustrates the fact that gender/sexual performances undoubtedly require *stylized/ritualized* repetitions of acts.

Ultimately, the correlation between gender and vampirism not only solidifies Judith Butler's gender and queer theories as still being relevant today, but it also proves that cultural figures can help better understand human nature. Indeed, cultural and literary figurations ultimately provide spaces in which concepts and practices inherent to human nature and human experience can be put forward. Complex concepts such as gender, sexual, and queer issues can thus be defined and challenged through figurative vehicles. The figure of the vampire is malleable enough as to embody multiple gender and sexual positions, but it can also further the understanding of issues pertaining to gender and queerness, by putting more recent gender identities such genderqueerness and gender neutrality at the forefront, for instance. This is highly significant since the concept of gender, in and of itself, ultimately relates to how one situates oneself toward others. By performing multiple gender and sexual identities, Eli(as)'s character in *Let the Right One In* is not only a potent illustration of the several gender and sexual spectrum positions which can be performed in real LGBTQIA2+ circles, but it also strives to open up closed social spaces and broaden societal views concerning different genders and sexualities. Therefore, the figure of the vampire is more than a simple cultural figure; it is a social tool capable of providing a safe space to further comprehend and, hopefully, change gender and queer issues for the better.

NOTES

1. Both the masculine and feminine subject pronouns will be used when referring to Elias' character in this paper as he(/she) encompasses both masculine and feminine gender identities. However, it is important to note that this stylistic choice is in no way meant to disrespect any member of the LGBTQIA2+ community. In the case of Elias' character, the use of both pronouns is there to reinforce his(/her) gender and sexual fluidity, especially due to his(/her) castrated status.

2. Eli(as)'s name will be written as such when referring to his genderqueer and gender-neutral identities throughout the essay.

3. "[...] People who identify as genderqueer understand that gender is not fixed, but

rather something fluid that can change from day to day and even minute to minute. Many genderqueer people feel more masculine or more feminine depending on the day; some feel like both at the same time; others don't feel our current concept of gender adequately covers their experience" ("Genderqueer." Pride.com, August 15, 2018, https://www.pride.com/genderqueer).

4. The pronoun "it"—unless grammatically inaccurate—is used throughout this essay when referring to the figure of the vampire. This grammatical choice strengthens the neutral natu re of the blood drinker.

5. From a more straightforward perspective, "neuter" also relates to the act of castration. This will become significant when analyzing Lindqvist's work.

6. For a more developed take on the subject, I recommend reading Christopher Craft's essay "Kiss Me with Those Red Lips: Gender and Inversion in Bram Stoker's *Dracula*," 1984.

7. Here, the term "figuration" refers to figures being allegorical representations of a concept.

8. Eli is a vampire, but he/she is also transgender and genderqueer. From a similar standpoint, Eli literally transgresses gender and sexual norms.

9. *L'entretien infini* in the original French.

10. Anne Rice's works did open up the array of feelings vampires can experience. They are not simply the monsters that need to be vanquished, they rather become sentient beings.

11. Drag queens are most often males which dress in female disguises for their performances. Females who dress in masculine clothing for their performances are called drag kings.

12. The use of anatomical sexes is seldom necessary for vampires since their fangs serve the same purpose as one's sexual organs in terms of sexual penetration. In terms of gender identity and performance, the provisional identities of vampires, and their multiple—and sometimes perverse—sexual inclinations allow them to swiftly navigate between several identities and performances without any norm restrictions.

13. Current expressions of gender may fall into a neutral category as people feel more inclined to not only navigate swiftly through various points on the spectrum but may also be willing to simply identify as a neutral human being. The common umbrella term which defines this identity is "genderqueer."

14. Several gender and sexual scales exist. The Kinsey scale was first published in 1948 and it strived to illustrate various sexual orientation choices in a scale from 0 (exclusively heterosexual) to 6 (exclusively homosexual) ("The Kinsey Scale.," Kinsey Institute, 2 Dec. 2016, https://kinseyinstitute.org/research/publications/kinsey-scale.php). The Kinsey scale has been criticized for measuring only two sexual orientations, i.e., homosexuality and heterosexuality. More contemporary scales, such as the Klein Sexual Orientation Grid (KSOG), try to address the issues of the Kinsey scale by proposing a multidimensional grid, with questions ranging from sexual attraction to behaviors and fantasies, emotional, lifestyle, and social preferences and, finally, self-identification ("The Klein Sexual Orientation Grid.," American Institute of Bisexuality, 2 Dec. 2016, http://www.americaninstituteofbisexuality.org/thekleingrid/). Judith Butler's concept of gender performativity is a social representation of multidimensional scales, and the figure of the vampire is the cultural figuration of this statement. It is also important to note that sexual orientations are not only limited to heterosexuality, homosexuality and bisexuality, but also to pansexuality, asexuality or any other orientation one feels comfortable identifying with.

15. One's gender identity can be defined as how one identifies in one's body, sexually and gender wise. For example, a transgender male was born a girl, as was dictated by her anatomical female sex assignment, but feels more like a man on the inside. Gender expression, on the other hand, is another term for Judith Butler's "gender performance," meaning that said transgender male might choose to dress in "masculine" clothing—quotation marks are used to signify the non-binary inclination which I believe is inherent to gender as a concept—to perform his preferred gender identity in a social context.

16. Once again, the term "feminine" is put between quotation marks to signify the arbitrary nature of identity.

17. The reference to Eli(as)'s pink sweater is not insignificant here since gender is typ-

ically and normatively gendered from the start. One example of these automatic categorizations is the "blue for baby boys" and "pink for baby girls" binary. Therefore, the fact that Eli(as) wears a pink shirt while performing her(/his) feminine gender identity is relevant, since she(/he) will be automatically perceived as a girl by others, which is what Eli(as) desires in this case, performatively speaking.

18. In the English translation by Ebba Segerberg, Eli(as)'s neutrality is shown through interchanging masculine and feminine pronouns, most often in one single excerpt or from sentence to sentence.

19. "Feminine" attributes as per the societal norm. Judith Butler's concept of gender performativity strives to deconstruct these binarial gender norms, and so does the figure of the vampire.

20. Elias' name will be written in its formal spelling when referring to his castration as he was neither gender-neutral nor a vampire when the events occurred.

21. Eli(as) and Oskar kiss for the first time and it triggers the vision. Oskar literally becomes Elias while experiencing the latter's castration.

22. The way in which I have described the vampiric transformation is not the same in every vampire-centric narrative. The blood exchange between a vampire and a victim was mostly popularized by Bram Stoker's *Dracula* and Anne Rice's *The Vampire Chronicles*. Other narratives such as the television series *True Blood* have also reprised it. Novels such as Octavia Butler's *Fledgling* and Stephenie Meyer's *Twilight Saga* rather use venom to induce the vampiric transformation.

23. Drinking human blood—and/or animal blood in certain narratives—is also what enables vampires to survive. The act of blood drinking will therefore always be perpetrated by the vampire. This eternal reiteration once again proves that vampiric blood consumption is indeed a stylized repetition of acts.

24. Once again, this proves that gender—and its performativity—undeniably relates to how one situates oneself toward others.

25. Eli(as)'s blood provider, Håkan, actually is a pedophile. He has agreed to help Eli(as) find victims to feed off on in exchange for sexual favors. These scenes are also extremely explicit in the text.

The Economic Miracle and the Italian Undead in *Tempi duri per i vampiri*

FERNANDO GABRIEL PAGNONI BERNS

Rather than being just hollow escapism, popular culture is the site for negotiation of national anxieties. Michael Billig argues that academia should stretch the term "nationalism" to include "the ideological means by which nation-states are reproduced" (1995, 6) through the use of the term "banal nationalism." Billig suggests that vernacular issues can be interpreted and interrogated everyday through popular cultural artifacts such as films or television. In the course of the repetitive ideological (re)presentation of vernacular forms of identity through media, nation-states *legitimate* both a sense of belonging and a mundane sense of nationhood. Cultural identity is, in Stuart Hall's words, a matter of "'becoming' as well as of 'being'" (1990, 225).

To some extent, popular culture could become the locus of national identity. Film genres, like horror and comedy, resonate with social and cultural meanings and were highly successful forms of mass entertainment. As Judith Hess Wright notes, genre films "came into being and were financially successful because they temporarily relieved the fears aroused by a recognition of social and political conflicts" (2012, 60).

Arguably, this is the case with the Italian film *Tempi duri per i vampiri* (*Hard Times for Vampires*, Steno, 1959), a horror-comedy that explores national anxieties using the figure of the vampire as the perfect vehicle. Because he owes back huge amounts of money in taxes, Baron Osvaldo Lambertenghi (Renato Rascel) is forced to sell his family's castle. The new owners turn the gothic castle into a sunny hotel and hire Osvaldo as a bellboy. Osvaldo receives a letter telling him that an uncle who he has never met, Baron Roderico da

Frankurten will come to visit the castle. The uncle turns out to be an eternal vampire who tries to spread vampirism through the hotel/castle. Between his victims is his unattractive nephew, who becomes a "real Italian stud" after been bitten in the neck.

The film opened in Italy at a time filled with cultural and social anxieties regarding the future of the country. After years of staleness, Italy opened to progress, industrialization and seaside tourism from the 1950s onward. This progress during the 1950s has been described widely as "miraculous." Indeed, 1958 marks the beginning of Italy's economic development, just a year away from the opening of Steno's film. Italy was beginning a process of developing as never before, but Italians were mostly anxious about the fact that their beloved country was rapidly changing before their eyes. The economic boom and subsequent opening to the world, for some, were causes for concern. Previously fixed roles were destined to change, paralleling the ideological, geographical and cultural shifts that the country was undergoing.

Traditional masculinity was slowly becoming unstable, as the previously deeply religious and conservative country was flooded by emancipated young female tourists, pop music, feminism, Americanization and cosmopolitanism. Conservative forms of "masculinism"—privileging family, a culture of the male body and a work ethic—faced a crisis when the modern ethos favored the atomized, mobile, and consumerist society. As a result, "images of vulnerable, passive men feature prominently in Italian cinema throughout much of the post-war period" (Rigoletto 2014, 4). In this scenario, it is not by chance that Osvaldo defends the status quo against a changing backdrop in a twofold way: first, recuperating a set of normative beliefs in *machismo*; second, through a sharp contrast with an outmoded Europe (U.K.), the latter embodied in the old vampire. Neither is coincidence that the legendary vampire uncle is none other than British Christopher Lee, who was not only famous for his role in Terence Fisher's *Dracula* (1956) but also tall, dark and sexy, in clear contrast to short Italian comedy actor Renato Rascel.

Through a complex play between old Europe and new Europe and old vampires and new ones, *Tempi duri per i vampiri* manages to illustrate a shifting landscape from which Italy comes out *better*. In this essay, I point to the ways in which the film negotiates with the social and cultural anxieties of its era and the clash between two depictions of Europe using as vehicle the figure of the transnational vampire.

Changing Italy, Changing Mentalities

Italy is currently well known for its horror cinema. When the first Italian horror films opened, however, the country lacked a tradition on fantastic cinema (Bondanella 2009, 306). The Italians showed "a lack of interest in horror and only a passing interest in science fiction" (Shipka 2011, 31), so serious Italian genre cinema began late in contrast with other European nations such as Germany or the UK. The first ventures into horror were mostly ignored by audiences who saw with suspicious eyes Italian names in the cast credits and in the director chair. For Italian audiences, Italian horror films probably could not be very good, so they mostly turned them down.

The first horror film was *I vampiri* (Riccardo Freda, 1956—with auteur Mario Bava taking the reins after Freda fled the production). But the popular cycle of Italian Gothic/horror films did not properly begin until *La maschera del demonio* (Mario Bava, 1960). Before this groundbreaking movie, Italian horror films were mostly horror/comedy hybrids lead by vampires and filled with scantily clad ladies in various stages of undress. Films such as *L'amante del vampire* (Renato Polselli, 1960) or *L'ultima preda del vampire* (Piero Regnoli, 1960) blend together strip-tease girls and vampires in gothic landscapes. "By watering down the elements of terror with well-known and popular forms of entertainment in Italy, whether comedy or sex, Italian filmmakers showed their unwillingness to commit to true horror pictures. As mentioned before, the reason can probably be traced to the Italian population's still reeling from the atrocities of World War II" (Shipka 2011, 31). These films were never really popular among Italian audiences, thus preventing the development of a strong horror cycle until the 1960s. The utilization of vampirism can be understood as a commercial device: vampires were the most recognizable global monsters and one of the most economically available to take to the screens, since, unlike werewolves or aliens, their human appearance saved some money in special effects.

For some, however, there was a more complex reason in the use of vampires in the first Italian horror films. The undead could be interpreted as a response to the changing landscapes of Italy: vampires were metaphors of the nobility and aristocracy feeding from the lowest classes (Shipka 2011, 28). Thus, the first vampires in done the cape and fangs in Italian incipient horror cinema could be read as symbols of a stagnate past desperately trying to survive in a country which, almost in the blink of an eye, shifted from feudal-like agriculture and farming to industrial labor in what had been called the "economic miracle" (Sorlin 1996, 115).

The Italian economic miracle of postwar refers to the striking (in terms of quality and speed) reconstruction of Italy after the years of Second World War and the fascist regime of Benito Mussolini. This period, roughly encompassing 1958–63 (even if the period of high economic growth ran right from the early 1950s up to the first years of the 1970s), was possible in part thanks to the contribution of funds from the Marshall Aid program, which supported

Italian economic policies. Italy made good use of these funds, especially making investments in the most underdeveloped region, the southern area. "Italy became an industrialized nation, at least in parts of the north and centre, and centuries-old social categories—the rural day-laborer, the sharecropper—all but disappeared across much of the country" (Sorlin 1996, 115), thus changing the social traditional landscape. This shift from a (mostly) agricultural country to industrialization brought urbanization as never before which, in turn, produced massive internal migration (circa 10 million Italians moved from the rural areas to the urbanized centers). Further, the Italian miracle was part of a global "golden age" of capitalism, "which created a new world market for consumer goods and forced Italians into a modern, industrial world" (Foot 2003, 138).

The increasing prosperity brought a new consumerist society, a real novelty at the moment; many Italians (at least, those belonging to the middle-class) were able to acquire consumer goods such as cars or home appliances like fridges, televisions or washing machines (Foot 2003, 138). Schooling and an increasing in secularism, together with urbanization and industrialization, transformed the Italian landscapes, producing "a shift of power away from the traditional 'structures in dominance'—that is, the essentially regionalist bourgeoisie and intellectual class—toward the 'emergent structure' centered on the technocrats," the latter a new class whose essential features were "a new mobility across the national space" (Restivo 2002, 46). Furthering the presence of Italy in the global scenario, vernacular cinema contributed to the country's international fame: Italian cinema "was extraordinarily robust, and the art films that defined the Italian cinema internationally were only a part of its flourishing and robust film industry" (Restivo 2002, 8–9). The neorealist movement of filmmaking was embraced in film festivals and the art house circuit, and accepted by general audiences as well.

A consequence of this economic and cultural boom, Italy became a well renowned destiny for global tourism, which accumulated political and economic importance in the country steadily over the course of the 20th century, coming to a peak in the years following the late 1950s. The European postwar era, rife with trends in international leisure and traveling, influenced Italy, emphasizing socio-cultural and economic shifts to new levels which, in turn, enhanced consumer's society. The country was literally "transformed by highways and tourism" (Hendrix 2003, 35) and the invasion of hundreds of tourists from the entire globe brought to Italy new anxieties concerning the rapidly changing social, cultural and geographical landscapes. Even if the changes were for good, many Italians, arguably, were anxious about what the future of their country was within this highly fluid scenery.

Tempi duri per i vampiri reflects on this new Italian status trough vampirism, humor and nationalism. The film is a complicated amalgam of comic traditions and different types of Italian *commedias*. Probably for the inclusion of the supernatural and elements of horror such as the fanged vampire—an image that circulated widely thanks to the Dracula version made by the British Hammer Studios—the film resists the classifications made by Andrea Bini in his excellent book *Male Anxiety and Psychopathology in Film* (2015): Steno's film does not belong to the *neorealismo rosa*—the film is, indeed, filmed in real locations and is framed with optimistic nuances and interest in marriage; it lacks, however, the non-professional actors that populated this cycle, according Bini (2015, 42–3)—nor to fascist comedy—since Steno's film lacks the exaltation of the Italian male body so dear to fascist vernacular cinema (Bini 2015, 46). *Tempi duri per i vampiri* can hardly being described as part of the *rivista* (Italian versions of the old vaudeville lead by stars such as Renato Rascel and composed by a series of autonomous comic sketches with very little coherence in terms of plot: Steno's film is, certainly, lead by Rascel but has a linear plot) or the renowned and well received *commedia all'italiana*, characterized by a lack of both, closure and a happy ending (*Tempi duri per i vampiri* has a concrete closure that gives no space to ambiguity).

Steno's film seems to defy any attempt at pigeonholing it into any kind of recognizable cycle or sub-genre of Italian film comedy. It can be argued that this is the case because *Tempi duri per i vampiri* should be read as a horror film rather than a comedy, even if the film is actually more of the latter. Robin Wood writes that the horror genre is "the struggle for recognition of all that our civilization represses or oppresses, its reemergence dramatized, as in our nightmares, as an object of horror" (Wood 2004, 113). Margaret Tarrat follows this same formulation in science fiction films, arguing that the battles against extraterrestrial monsters are fantastic materializations of civilized persons' conflict with their id, the site of repressed desires (2003, 348). These repressed desires are incompatible with the moral codes of civilization, so they rise up in the form of monstrosity. Monstrosity and the horrific in films, thus, are embodiments of societal and individual repressed tensions, especially those of a sexual nature. The vampire in Steno's film is the embodiment of fears deeply repressed within the fabric of cosmopolitan, modern Italy. His presence triggers deep seated anxieties concerning Italian nationhood amidst an increasingly globalized world.

Italian comedy, however, can also be space for the critical exploration of societal anxieties the same way that horror cinema is. According Bondanella, *commedia all'italiana* "lays bare an undercurrent of social malaise and the powerful contradictions of a culture in rapid transformation" (Bondanella 2007, 145); clearly, this "social malaise" is a topic that gives substance to *Tempi duri per i vampiri*.

Hard Times for Vampires, Sweet Life for Italy

Tempi duri per i vampiri begins with the downgrading of two Barons: the first one is Roderico da Frankurten (Christopher Lee), who must abandon his castle in the Carpathians minutes before his home is destroyed by explosives placed to clear the area for the installation of a nuclear power plant. Unlike what happens in classical horror films, the castle that serves as a shelter for the vampire is not destroyed by a horde of angry villagers holding torches and pitchforks, but by modern architects wearing modern clothes, who blow-up the old building to give space to a new symbol of modernity: nuclear power. Italy started to produce nuclear energy in the early 1960s; arguably, plans to produce a nuclear power program were discussed in the last years of the 1950s. Thus, the reference to a nuclear power plant indicated a country well aware of its new status after becoming part of the modern world. Even if the action of this first scene takes place in the Carpathians, there is an unmistakably relation between the destruction of old landscapes and architecture (Italy is famous for its numerous amazing medieval castles) and the coming of a new modern era. This shift toward modernity is the reason that causes the vampire to flee his place of residence in old Europe in search of better places to (un)live. He escapes in a chariot driven by the only servant he has left, an image that conjures poverty and nobility decay. There is an unmistakable loss of power by the old aristocracy in this new, groovy world of nuclear energy and transnational tourism.

The other downgraded Baron is Roderico's nephew, Osvaldo Lambertenghi (Rascel), who, residing in Italy, is forced to sell his castle to settle debts he has with the national treasury. Without a penny in his pocket, his only economic output is to accept being downgraded to bellboy in his own castle, which has been turned into a hotel by the new owners. It is possible to establish a play of mirrors: if the castle in the Carpathians gives way to modernity in the form of a nuclear power plant, the Italian castle is converted, in the flux of international capital, into a hotel for tourists. There is another parallel: the old castle that the vampire hastily flees from is mirrored by Osvaldo's aristocratic castle. After the prologue in the Carpathians, the film cuts to the paradisiacal landscapes of modern Mediterranean Italy, populated with beaches and crystal-clear waters showed in lovely aerial shots. Osvaldo is watching the scenery through a window; after a sad sigh, he leaves to sell his castle to the new authorities. Osvaldo's castle is filled with medieval items such as armors and blazons, thus coding the place as a reliquary lifted from old times long dead.

In the beginning of the film, then, both Barons are degraded in their status due to the arrival of new times. Much of the film's humor ensues from the humiliating situation of Osvaldo, a man of nobility now reduced to being a servant in his own castle, victim to the caprices and bad manners of rich, bored tourists. Most of all, Osvaldo regrets no longer being able to financially support his gardener, Lellina (Kai Fischer), with whom he is secretly in love. Meanwhile, the tourists are composed by people who represent modern times and the new Italian citizenship; they are consumerist middle-class travelers looking for leisure time in the Mediterranean coast. There are still traditional families and Italian conservative parents among the tourists visiting the castle/hotel, but now with slight variations: the daughter Carla (Sylva Koscina) despises travelling with her old-fashioned parents as she dreams of spending her summer vacation with the man she loves, a popular American pop singer—a signpost of the Americanization sweeping Italy.

Vampire Roderico is downgraded too, converted to a refugee from another era and place in a hotel filled with tourists who love sun, tanning and superficiality. Roderico arrives at the hotel with the explicit idea of turning the castle into his ultimate sanctuary, now that his shelter in the Carpathians is lost. Great is his surprise when he finds his nephew turned bellboy and the castle turned hotel, a surprise that paralleled the shock that many Italians suffered at the changes that their country underwent in just a few years. Many of the humorous scenes come from this clash between what has been and what it is now. Roderico worries about the existence of a crypt located at the basement of the castle. He fears that the crypt, his last refugee, had been destroyed with the modifications. The crypt still exists, but is now turned into the hotel's bar. The shifts between the old nobility and its symbols now converted into forms of entertainment for tourists is one of the devices that the narration uses to create humor and tap into the cultural anxieties pervading Italy.

Still, the main contrast is given through the clash between the disparate masculinities embodied by Roderico and his nephew. The dark side of the economic miracle seems to be a crisis of identity, the dissolution of the social fabric and alienation, all the above causing a psychological crisis on men whom saw themselves unable to cope with the new realities of sexual freedom, female emancipation (the film's official poster depicts female lead Koscina gigantized against the small figure of Renato Rascel. She even holds him in her enormous grip, with Lee's face covering the background as a past time still casting shadows on the present) and a complete lack of a patriarchal figure as Mussolini was in previous years. Osvaldo is an example of the mature man living amidst a changing Italy, "who experienced the traumatic failure of Fascist-nationalist discourse and now is incapable of finding his place in the new country" (Bini 2015, 87). As a former member of the Italian nobility and as orphan of the ideology of cosmopolitanism, Osvaldo is unable to content himself within the old-fashioned scenario of traditional values embodied by the undead father figure of his uncle while the new pop society, which reduces him to bellboy, remains foreign to him.

When Osvaldo realizes that his uncle is, in fact, a vampire who wants to feed on the female tourist population, a clash of wills begin between the old, traditional—even if slightly outmoded—Europe represented in both the figure of the ancient powerful vampire and Lee's Britishness and the new, fresh, joyful—even if slightly emasculated—Europe depicted in the figure of Osvaldo and Italy.

The two Barons may have lost their status, but Roderico still has a card in his sleeve to save his tainted masculinity after the loss of his country and position: he is a vampire, a supernatural creature who can, through hypnosis, control other people, including his nephew. The old school of nobility seems to prevail over the cosmopolitanism of Italy that produces an emasculated man such as Osvaldo. After all, Roderico, if a fugitive, still embodies respectability, while Osvaldo is ridiculed in his new role of bellboy, at whom everybody shouts. The power relations seem to be maintained. The strong contrast between the charismatic, commanding, hypnotic seducer who offered "forbidden eroticism" (Spicer 2001, 202) with *piccoletto* Rascel sustains the hierarchy that places the old British vampire at the peak. Lee, still fresh from his success with Fisher's *Dracula* (Lee even wears the same type of red-lined cape and clothes that he used in *Dracula* for the Hammer Studios, thus cementing his role as the master of the vampires), was a "hyper-masculine" vampire (Weinstock 2012, 29) thanks to his handsome, erotically charged figure; his supernatural powers and "prerogative of penetration" (Stephanou 2014, 34) turned him into a type of traditional, hegemonic masculinity that seemingly did not exist anymore in modern Italy. Osvaldo is emasculated, not only through the downplaying of his economic status, but also in his inability to contend with his vampiric, hyper-masculine, sex-starved uncle who wants to penetrate and vampirize all the beautiful women residing at the hotel.

After Osvaldo realizes the undead nature of his uncle, he tries, first and foremost, to protect the tourists residing at the hotel—and especially among them, his beloved Lellina, who does not understand why the former Baron Lambertenghi insists on covering her home with lots of garlic. All of Osvaldo's attempts to protect the people living at the hotel and around it from the thirst of his uncle end with the former even more ridiculed, as these attempts are always interpreted as efforts to escape from his obligations as a bellboy. The old Europe seems to impose itself upon Italian modernity since Osvaldo can do nothing against the supernatural power of the old vampire.

Moreover, Roderico does not exhibit humor himself (except for one scene in which Roderico continually delays the main point of the story that he is telling to his nephew), so the old vampiric Baron keeps his imposing presence while Osvaldo is diminished in his futile attempts to destroy his uncle. The camera frames both Roderico and Osvaldo in wide shots that highlight the difference in sizes of both men. Osvaldo mentions that his bed would be short for Roderico even if it is large for him. In this scene, Osvaldo becomes the *inept* that, according Jacqueline Reich, constitutes the most prominent male category in Italian cinema. According to the author, the inept is a reminder of the struggles of the social and cultural shifts through which Italian men lived. Reich explains that the inept articulates "the traditional binary opposite of the masculine, as it is constructed in Italian culture and society, and as it relates to sexuality: the cuckold, the impotent and feminized man" (Reich 2004, 135). Rascel/Osvaldo embodies the characteristics of this masculine type in opposition to the hyper-masculine distinctiveness of his powerful undead uncle.

Looking to punish his nephew for his attempts to curtail his uncle's nightly visitations, Roderico bites Osvaldo: immediately after, the humble, inept bellboy becomes a vampire and the power relations begin to shift. Osvaldo becomes a super-human who uses his newfound powers not to spread horror, but to save Italian masculinity. The main difference is that, rather than being *undead*, Osvaldo seems to become *powered*, inexplicably having all the advantages that popular culture attributed to vampirism but none of its disadvantages.

First, Osvaldo starts to address the audience, speaking to invisible listeners while looking straight at the camera. This narrative device, never used up to this point, explicitly marks the empowerment that the clumsy bellboy now has: he can escape the diegetic world and become the main narrator, the leading voice. Second, he gets back his lost status, at least, in masculine terms. Osvaldo was emasculated after the loss of his titles of nobility. His position as an employee challenges his role as master of the house and he is constantly dwarfed when carrying the big suitcases brought by the different tourists. Osvaldo also lost his position as the protector of Lellina, who has been fired by the new owners of the castle/hotel. As a short, plain middle-age man, Osvaldo needs economic power as a way to secure a hierarchical relationship with a beautiful young woman like Lellina. Unlike the male vampire, historically coded (at least, in cinema) as a master of sensuality, Osvaldo has nothing without money. His vampirization brings back some of his lost masculinity, replacing economic power with supernatural status.

As he explains in a monologue addressed to the audiences, vampirization has not brought a curse on him but a solution: "I'm happy with the transformation. My hair is now larger, my coat is long, my fangs too. [...] *Everything is larger now.*" While not explicitly mentioned (after all, this is Italy in the 1950s), Osvaldo has earned a new manhood in this transformation. The phallic teeth are complemented with an augmented masculinity and genitality that renders him as hyper-masculine. Hyper-masculinity is the exacerbation of attributes naturalized as masculine (power, aggression, psychical prowess, genitality, etc.) and the exaggeration of male "macho" behavior, all the above in sharp contrast with equally culturally constructed notions of femininity. Thus, hypermasculine is "always hyper *not* feminine" (Schroeder 2004, 418. Emphasis in the original). Osvaldo's emasculation ends with his conversion to vampirism, a creature of the night who even surpasses his uncle in terms of manhood.

Indeed, Roderico, as a vampire of the old school, is unable to cope with modern Italy. There is always some situation (including, sometimes, his nephew) who interrupts the nightly visitations that the old Baron makes to the female guests of the hotel. Even if a powerful vampire, Roderico seems out of place in this cosmopolitan landscape. Unlike the classical scenario in vampiric tales, the young ladies of the hotel seem to always be bathing at the sun, completely awake at night, or visiting with men in their bedrooms, making Roderico's ventures into the night completely futile.

Osvaldo, as a vampire, succeeds where Roderico fails. The immediate scene after Osvaldo's transformation into a creature of the night informs the viewer that the new vampire has spent the whole night visiting, hour after hour, many of the female tourists, biting them in their necks with his "long teeth." The next morning, all women in the hotel wake up relaxed and in a newfound, conciliatory mood. Unlike traditional tales of vampirism, they are not turned into vampires themselves, but, surprisingly, into women with liberal ideas who now embrace modernity: thus, the morning after Osvaldo's visitation, the mother who despises Carla's boyfriend finds the relationship good enough. There is an implication that, unlike the vampires of old, Osvaldo's vampirism is closer to the ideal of the "Italian stud" who insatiably satisfies all women. The "sickness" that Osvaldo pass between the female guests is love for modernity and a *joie de vivre*, rather than pale skin and haunted eyes.

This way, the delicate power play between the old Baron who arrived from an aging Europe and the young Italian stud finds a new equilibrium. Osvaldo succeeds where Roderico has failed as a (undead) man. Unlike Roderico, Osvaldo can walk through the day without further explanation. It seems that Mediterranean vampirism comes with advantages that the undead of the old Europe can only dream of. As a vampire, Osvaldo saves Italy's pride through a powerful (hyper)masculinity which allows him to spend whole nights visiting women, whom he fully satisfies. Moreover, women who have been bitten at night have, during the day, a remnant and unexplained strong attraction to Osvaldo (who does not remember during the day his adventures as a vampire at night, a good way to slip out of male responsibilities in the ever *macho* Italy), a novelty in vampire fiction that turns the Italian man into a true sex symbol. He will only stop at Lellina, as she represents the chaste "future wife" who must arrive virgin at marriage; the latter marks a return to traditional values still shaping Italy.

Osvaldo resists his vampirism to preserve Lellina's virginity up to the point of overcoming his vampiric condition. In this sense, using strong willpower and Mediterranean manhood, Osvaldo surpasses Roderico and put the old Baron to shame. In the last scene, Osvaldo recounts that he has been named director of the hotel (without further elaboration), thus recuperating his economic status but with a sharp difference: the excessive pride that comes with nobility has been supplanted with the capitalist riches that comes with transnational venture. But, more importantly, Osvaldo has surpassed any crisis of masculinity by not only reinstating the myth of the "Italian stud" but by crawling out of the shadow of the hypermasculine, strong-willed and imperial UK now completely defeated and dismantled as *passé*. In this battle between vampires, Mediterranean cosmopolitanism wins over outdated forms of masculinity, here conflated with vampirism.

Conclusions

Tempi duri per i vampiri was a cultural product made using a nascent genre (horror) mixed with a popular one (comedy), produced within the borders of a nascent cosmopolitanism. The mirror that Italy chooses to reflect itself upon is that of the UK, a colonizing, imperialistic nation with a renowned tradition of horror film and with a strong presence in the global scene. Christopher Lee was the tall, sexy, hypermasculine vampire who fed on others, an adequate metaphor for the UK as a whole. Italy, in turn, only has Renato Rascel, an actor only known within Italy, a star lifted from dated forms of Italian *commedia*. While Lee embodies all them—Dracula, the powerful Hammer Studios (at its peak in the late 1950s) and Great Britain—Rascel only has cosmopolitan Italy at his side. Still, it is Rascel who wins in the battle between nations and between modernity and old Europe. While Italy was passing through its own conversion to modernity, prosperity, cosmopolitanism and globalization, some argue that the UK "never passed through such a stage" and that the British 1930s "lasted until the 1960s," being the coming of The Beatles the event that ended "a kind of long Victorian age" in Great Britain (Vinen 2011, 14). Even if exaggerated, it is undeniable that the UK did not project a modern image to the world right up until the 1960s. On one hand, the economy boomed in the British 1950s; on the other, the UK was seen as frozen in time, while the process of decolonization accelerated through the decade as colonies fought to end their dependence on Great Britain. Italy, in turn, was flourishing, its modern vampires a far cry from the disempowered creatures of the night that the UK had to offer. Italians prevail and the vernacular masculinity is recuperated, establishing that "macho" Italy outshines weak, passé, emasculated old Europe.

As Joke Hermes argues, "it is in the conjunction of local circumstance, international media genres, and situated production of meaning that we can see unfold how popular culture mirrors widely shared underlying concerns and allows for the concretizing of these concerns in ways deemed fitting by local users" (Hermes 2005, 15). Italy was making a stand, asking for its right in calling the world's attention. Even Roderico is won by the Mediterranean landscape and ethos. The film ends with the Baron Roderico da Frankurten staying in Italy, walking away with two beautiful Italian women backed with the tunes of the song "Dracula Cha-Cha-Cha," an explicit statement that says that better than fighting modern Italy is embracing it.

"Time is an abyss"
The Role of History in Werner Herzog's Nosferatu *(1979)*

Thomas Prasch

In Werner Herzog's *Nosferatu* (1979), a melancholy, philosophical vampire tells Jonathan Harker: "I don't attach importance to sunshine anymore, or to glittering fountains, which youth is so fond of. I love the darkness and the shadows, when I can be alone with my thoughts. I am the descendant of an old family. Time in an abyss, profound as a thousand nights. Centuries come and go. To be unable to grow old is terrible. That is not the worst. There are things more horrible than that. Can you imagine, enduring centuries, experiencing each day the same futile things?" Harker appears uncertain what to make of Dracula's soliloquy, but he can be forgiven that; he is only there to sell a house, after all, and cinema vampires are seldom so garrulous.

Herzog repeatedly insisted his *Nosferatu* was not just a "remake" of F.W. Murnau's same-titled silent classic (1922): "I never thought of my film *Nosferatu* as being a remake. It stands on its own feet as an entirely new version" (Cronin 2002, 151; see also Blume, 1979; Kawin 1980, 45; Walker 1978, 202). Lotte Eisner put it even more forcefully after a visit to the set: "The film is not being remade, it is being reborn" (Andrews 1978, 33). That rebirth not only made the Dracula story into a typical Herzog film—featuring the isolated protagonist, engagement with nature, fascination with the breakdown of civilization, and quirky sidenotes typical of his oeuvre—but also allows Herzog to unpack the historical context of his source material.

To understand what Herzog intended with his reimagining of Murnau, we can begin by isolating the ways in which the two films differ. Then we can outline Herzog's complex engagement with German history: both the deeper cultural tradition upon which both he and Murnau drew, and the historical rupture Nazism constitutes. But such engagement with German historical traditions carries its own dangers, and it is with the ambiguities in Herzog's work that we can close.

Divergences

The distinctions between Herzog's *Nosferatu* and Murnau's are made clear early in Herzog's film, even before we meet the vampiric count (Orlock in Murnau's film, Dracula in Herzog's[1]). The first significant divergence occurs at the inn where Harker stops, just shy of the count's castle. The narrative structure closely follows Murnau, but Herzog makes a key shift. The people at the inn in Murnau are village folk, while in Herzog they are Roma. Beverly Walker recalled: "True to his penchant for people scarred by society's neglect, Herzog had become fascinated by the gypsies upon his arrival in the Tatra, and had himself fetched them from their village especially for the scene" (Walker 1978, 203; see also Prawer 2004, 54–56). The Roma are typical Herzog exotics, but he also plays up their links to the supernatural. The innkeeper tells Harker, "The gypsies. Some of them have been to the other side. They know." So when one Rom warns Harker of the "great chasm" that "swallows the unwary," it has a distinctive resonance. The innkeeper translates another warning: "The gypsies here have been saying that no such castle exists, except maybe in the imagination of men. It's just a ruin, they say, a ghost castle. A traveler who enters that land of phantoms is lost." The Roma have one further, darker range of resonance in the film: they were among the groups targeted for extermination by the Nazi regime.

In Murnau's film, Hutter catches a carriage in the morning, but it drops him off at the pass. "Pay whatever you like! We are not going any further!" the coachman tells him, "The other side of the pass is haunted!"[2] But Hutter only crosses a bridge before another, more mysterious carriage arrives, with a silent and uncanny driver, and the trip grows stranger. Hutter is "seized by … sinister visions," and a portion of the journey is through forest projected in negative: "**Coach drives at top speed through a *white* forest**" (Eisner 1973, 242; boldface and italic in original). Herzog jettisons this eerie ride. In Herzog's version, when Harker cannot get a carriage in the morning, he stubbornly proclaims, "Well, then, I'll have to walk."

Harker's day-long walk (five full minutes of screen time) from foothills through forests to mountain top, accompanied till near the end by the haunting music of Popol Vuh, offers a Romantic interlude of a solitary man engaging with nature; Harker is silent, but his interior monologue might echo Johann Goethe's *Italian Journey*, as he hiked in the Alps or on Sicily's mountains. As S.S. Prawer notes, such extended hiking has deep roots in German literary culture, from the *Fussreise* of Romantic literature to "the *Wandervogel* movement of idealistic young people in the 1920s and early '30s—hijacked, in the end, along with so much else, by the Nazi youth organizations."[3] The tradition ends with Leni Riefenstahl's tent city of *Hitlerjugend* in *Triumph of the Will* (1935).

The engagement with the landscape intensifies as Harker climbs. Roger Ebert catches the Romantic sublime in the sequence: "There is something fearful and awesome in Herzog's depiction of nature. It is not uplifting so much as remorseless.... Peaks tower in intimidation. Shadows hint at horrors" (Ebert 2001). Ebert earlier wrote in similarly elegiac terms of "tenuous cloud layers that drift a little too fast, as if God were sucking in his breath" (Ebert 1979). Brad Prager notes another Romantic connection: "Many of Herzog's shots are composed in a style that resonates with [Caspar David] Friedrich's paintings" (Prager 2007, 84). The mountain sequence also hearkens to the prewar *Bergfilm* (mountain film) tradition, with which Herzog's work has also been associated.[4] But *Bergfilme* were where Riefenstahl got her start, and, like the *Wandervogel*, the genre was appropriated by the Nazi regime (Kracauer 1947, 257–60; see also Rentschler 1986, esp. 170–171; Wahl 2012, 247–48). Herzog has spoken of his interest in rescuing the *Bergfilm* from the taint of Nazism (Cronin 2002, 222–223). But that connection is instead reinforced with the musical shift when, as Harker's reaches the mountaintop and glimpses the castle's ruins, we hear Richard Wagner's *Rheingold*.

The differences between Murnau and Herzog become clearer still once we meet the count. In Murnau's version, Orlock has only a handful of brief lines, all spoken in the two days at the castle; he is silent for the rest of the film. In comparison, Herzog's Dracula seems downright loquacious. He extends upon Lugosi's line: "Listen, listen, the children of the night make their music. Aye, young man, you are like the villagers, who cannot place themselves in the soul of the hunter." He soliloquizes on "time's abyss." Late in the film, in two sequences without equivalents in Murnau, Dracula has a conference with Renfrew and an extended tête-à-tête with Lucy, in which they talk of love and salvation.

Given the significant differences between the two films, Herzog's insistence that his was not a remake should be superfluous. Yet Leslie Halliwell opines: "Werner Herzog produced a crude, almost scene for scene, revamping of *Nosferatu*" (Halliwell 1988, 94). Similarly, Morris Dickstein describes it as taking "the form of a tribute, scene by scene," to Murnau (Dickstein 2004, 50), and Tom Huddleston insists that "Herzog brings little of his own personality to the proceedings: the story is largely unchanged" (Huddleston 2013). Such fundamental misreading stands at one end of an incredibly wide critical spectrum of responses to the film. John Sandford asserted: "even Kinski's magnificent performance does not redeem the film of its inherent weaknesses" (Sandford 1980, 62) In contrast, Prawer declares: "His *Nosferatu* deserves a place, in any history of the cinema, as a milestone on the road travelled by a gifted writer-director who drew on the heritage of Expressionism and Romanticism to take us onto a mysterious journey into his, and our, inner world" (Prawer 2004, 79); Vincent Canby sought a middle ground, lamenting that *Nosferatu* offered "something less than the voyage of self-discovery that each of Mr. Herzog's earlier, very original films has been." But Canby had little sympathy with the subject: "Dracula, after all, is not Hamlet or Othello or Macbeth. He's not some profoundly complex character" (Canby 1979). The critical range reflects the extent to which commentators appreciated, or not, the aims of Herzog's project.

Herzog and German Tradition

Among the descriptors that haunt Herzog criticism—mystic, visionary, and the rest—"Romantic" has been among the most frequent (see Johnson 2016, Prager 2007, 11–14; Prawer 2004, 18; Calhoon 2012, 102–104; Johnson 2012). Laurie Ruth Johnson suggests: "Herzog's films re-envision overlooked aspects of romanticism, animating in particular romantic understandings of relation between reason and passion, civilization and wild nature, and knowledge and belief" (Johnson 2016, 2; 173–75). Thus the regular figuring of Romantic tropes—specific citations like paintings by Friedrich or texts like Georg Büchner's *Woyzeck*,[5] shared themes like the doppelganger (see Casper and Linville 1991, 17–18, 20), or common sensibilities about nature, outsiders, and the limits of Enlightenment thought—in the discussions of Herzog by critics.

Herzog himself bridles at the label: "Please have a look at what I said to Les Blank about the jungle? [That 'nature here is vile and base,' that there 'is no harmony in the universe'] Anyone who understands romanticism will know that those were not the words of a romanticist" (Cronin 2002, 135–36, 151–52 n. 2). And yet, in practically the next breath, he says: "There are works of literature of which I can only speak in awe ... like Büchner's *Woyzeck*, Kleist's short stories, Holderlin's poetry" (Cronin 2002, 136), an entirely Romantic canon. He asserts that his interest in "an inner state of mind" constitutes "my real connection to Caspar David Friedrich, a man who ...wanted to explore and show inner landscapes" (Cronin 2002, 135). Looking for an analogy to his feelings when screening a film for an audience, Herzog references Kleist sending a manuscript to Goethe (Cronin 2002, 110). For someone so imbued with Romantic thought, why resist the association?

Part of the issue is the filter through which Herzog reads the Romantic tradition: not only in their own right, but as the source for Weimar cinema (see Casper and Linville 1991, 17; Johnson 2016, 173–74). But making that connection requires overcoming the fundamental rupture that separates Herzog and his contemporaries from their Weimar sources: the triumph of Nazism, and the sealing off of the German past in the immediate postwar era: "as children growing up in post-war Germany we had grandfathers but no fathers to learn from.... As a filmmaker you clearly cannot work without having some coherence with your own culture. Continuity is vital. So it was our 'grandfathers'—Lang, Murnau, Pabst, and others—who became our points of reference" (Cronin 2002, 151–52; see also Kennedy 1978, Blume 1979). Through those grandfathers, in turn, Herzog could reconnect with the great-grandfathers, the Romantics he identifies with "legitimate" culture.

This sense of the German past informs all New German Cinema, taking shape in the Oberhausen Manifesto's declaration of independence (and orphanhood) for a new generation of filmmakers in 1962. As Garrett Chaffin-Quiray summarizes: "The New German Cinema was a movement born from generational conflict. Following Germany's defeat in World War II, the coherence of its national identity was split among occupying allied powers ... and dwarfed by memories of its former status under Adolph Hitler" (Chaffin-Quray 2002). A new generation of filmmakers sought to challenge both the postwar "anomie and malaise" and the restrictions of a film-production system that stifled creativity: "the Oberhausen Manifesto aimed at disrupting then-current cinematic practice" (Chaffin-Quray 2002). John E. Davidson defines the movement as "anti-colonial": "They adopt the position of victims resisting practices that have robbed them of an indigenous tradition of film and continue to stifle their reemergence. Thus, the Nazi period becomes constructed as a colonizing agent disrupting 'native' traditions, a situation only exacerbated by the post–World War II, cultural imperialism of the occupying powers, particularly the United States" (Davidson 1996, 52). Thus, Prawer notes, by "paying tribute to Murnau," Herzog "is seeking to attach New German Cinema to a 'legitimate' tradition broken off the advent of Nazism" (Prawer 2004, 19; he makes a similar argument about Herzog's whole oeuvre in Prawer 1980, 18–19). Davidson emphasizes how "Werner Herzog creates for himself a more active role in reestablishing a tie to the past" by walking to Paris to see Eisner (Davidson 1996, 57). As Eisner provides Herzog a bridge to Weimar film, Murnau gives him a link to the Romantics.

That sense of rupture, however, exposes a second issue about Romanticism for Herzog, the trajectory of German culture since the Romantic era: "the Germans were a dignified people, the greatest philosophers, composers, writers and mathematicians. And, in the space of only ten years, they created a barbarism more terrible than had ever been seen before" (Cronin 2002, 218). Laurie Ruth Johnson suggests that Herzog denies Romanticism because he "may associate German romanticism with, at best, apolitical aestheticism, and, at worst, a proto-fascist focus on folk culture and politics," the "regressive views [that] emerged later in the nineteenth century as a quintessentially German aesthetic in Richard Wagner's idea of the 'total work of art'" (Johnson 2016, 3; see also 173, 177–78). Recall that shift to Wagner when Harker reaches the mountaintop in *Nosferatu*.

Recuperative citation of Romantic tradition, given the links to Nazism, present potential problems to contemporary filmmakers. Tom Brass asserts, in relation to the attempt to return to some form of *Heimat* (homeland) film in the 1970s: "by the mid–1970s a number of directors (Herzog, Reitz) ... [were] depicting not just a rural/historical version of grassroots discourse, and thus recycling ideological components emanating from the backward-looking agrarian myth, but in some instances also the reactionary forms linked to this" (Brass 2000, 209). Since four of the five films Brass names are Herzog's, he seems the principal target.

Eric Rentschler, also highlighting *Heimatfilm* tendencies in Herzog, pushes the analogy further. He compares Herzog to Riefenstahl: "Herzog and Riefenstahl share a romantic critique of the Enlightenment as a category-bound way of thinking.... Both celebrate individual subjects in touch with a mysterious realm.... Theirs is a cinematic art that puts aesthetics beyond morality and history" (Rentschler 1986, 170). He also identifies common ground between Herzog and Joseph Goebbels: "No doubt the visions of the future remain ... and do not fully coincide with the quite concrete utopia promulgated by National Socialism's powerful spokesman, Joseph Goebbels" (Rentschler 1986, 175, with another comparison to Goebbels on 177). Herzog has spoken of the burden of being German in the post–Nazi era: "As a German, I am even apprehensive about insecticide commercials. I know for sure that there is only one step from insecticide to genocide.... Hitler's heritage to German youth has made us hypersensitive to these things" (Kent 1977). But his referencing of past German culture, however much Herzog delimits it to that he defines as "legitimate," opens his work to such critiques.

A third problem with asserting Herzog's romanticism comes from the fact that he is, simply, post-romantic. Herzog's films consistently disrupt and undermine Romantic expectations, as Kent Casper and Susan Linville suggest: "Herzog manipulates the romantic narrative code in ways that collapse the dualistic framework of romanticism and foreground ironic reversals of the patterns he invokes" (Casper and Linville 1991, 17). This shows in Herzog's consistent refusal to reestablish disrupted forms or provide full narrative closure. Herzog notes: "I am fascinated by the idea that our civilization is like a thin layer of ice upon a deep ocean of chaos and darkness" (Cronin 2002, 2). That thin layer, once cracked, tends not to reform.

Such disruption and failed closure play a key role in *Nosferatu*. As John

Sandford noted: "the eruption of the plague of rats ... that brings a smugly comfortable bourgeois world tumbling to the ground is a further element in Herzog's continuing fascination with the fragility of a self-deluding 'civilization'" (Sandford 1980, 62). Prawer echoed the point, finding in Herzog's *Nosferatu* "a distrust of bourgeois values, a rejection of the scientific approach to life, and an ultimate pessimism, which go beyond anything in Murnau's original film" (Prawer 1980, 134).

When one of the burghers demands the arrest of von Helsing, he is told the police are "dead and gone." "Then take this man to prison," the burgher insists. "There's no one there to guard him anymore." The sociopolitical order remains in disarray. And Lucy's sacrifice—since Harker himself has become a vampire—has been for naught. Casper and Linville note: "unlike that of her counterpart, Murnau's Nina [*sic*; they mean 'Ellen'], her act does not restore the communal bourgeois order, nor does it function for the spectator as a cathartic resolution" (Casper and Linville 1991, 22). At the film's close, as Harker calls for his horse and mutters "I have much to do now," the disruption is anything but contained.

Herzog's understanding of German history shapes his distinctive reading of Murnau's *Nosferatu* and his own reconception of the work:

> Murnau's *Nosferatu* is the most visionary of all German films. It prophesied the rise of Nazism by showing the invasion of Germany by Dracula and his plague-bearing rats. And it gave a legitimacy to German cinema that was lost in the Hitler era. We are trying in our films to build a thin bridge back to that time, to legitimize our own cinema and culture. We are not remaking *Nosferatu*, but bringing it to new life and new character for a new age.[6]

That "new age" Herzog envisioned in millennial terms: "'When Dracula comes to the town,' says Herzog, 'it is almost like the coming of paradise. He is a prophet of change in a bourgeois world that must change'" (Andrews 1978, 37). Herzog's characterization of Dracula and his impact break from both Murnau and the Stoker-sourced Hollywood vampire tradition.

Making Herzog's Nosferatu

The making of Herzog's *Nosferatu* proved complicated. Working with international financing and an international cast of actors, Herzog made the film in both English and German versions (even the titles differ: *Nosferatu: The Vampyre* in English, and *Nosferatu: Phantom of the Night* for German and French audiences). Herzog has insisted that filming in English made sense because, "where we had people from sixteen countries on the set, English was the common language," but he finds the German version "the more 'culturally authentic'" (Andrews 1978, 33). Actors working outside their native languages, in combination with a deliberate echoing of silent acting styles (Prawer 1980, 265), produced a decidedly anti-naturalistic acting style that disturbed audiences. Kevin Thomas observed: "the film's antiquated declamatory style of acting of course come[s] across as outrageous camp" (Thomas 1979). Viewers had difficulty understanding Herzog's defiance of genre conventions.

Locations presented a problem: plans to shoot in Transylvania were thwarted by difficulties with the Ceauşescu regime in Romania. Herzog recalls, "I actually never received a direct refusal from the government, but got word from some friendly Romanian filmmakers.... They advised me to leave the country immediately" (Cronin 2002, 159). Czechoslovakia would have to do. Delft replaced Murnau's Bremen, but, after a successful rat-eradication campaign, the town had difficulties with Herzog's plans to herd thousands of rats through the city. After much controversy, and a violent confrontation near the farmhouse where the rats were stored—Beverley Walker recalled: "Windscreens were smashed, cars were damaged, everyone was badly beaten"—the rat scenes were filmed at nearby Schiedam (Walker 1978, 205). Kinski's hours-long make-up sessions, reproducing Murnau's grotesque vampire with Kabuki inflections, added difficulty and garnered critical scorn, as when Vincent Canby opined: "his makeup is so heavy that it seems to remove the actor from his performance as effectively as if he were hiding behind a Greek mask" (Canby 1979). Despite all the obstacles, Herzog paid homage to the original while making the film his own.

At the level of images, Herzog constructed a deeply intertextual film that cites both Murnau and a range of antecedents in German and Dutch visual arts. Kenneth Calhoon notes references to Albrecht Dürer's prints, Dutch still-life painting and *memento mori*, Rembrandt's so-called "Dr. Faustus" print, Jan Vermeer's views of Delft, compositional tactics from 18th-century cityscapes, and Friedrich's Romantic landscapes in his catalog of references (Calhoon 2012, 106–117). The technique looks back to Murnau's citations of earlier visual culture, although Herzog reorients it to reflect his thematic interests. Most central among these are: first, the humanization of Dracula (and the heightened eroticism in his relationship to Lucy); and second, the complete breakdown of civilized order, connecting to Herzog's sense of the limitations of Enlightenment thought and bourgeois civilization.

Herzog's Dracula is, above all else, that most familiar of Herzog types: the outcast, or, as Roger Ebert put it, "people living at the edge of life or at the extremes of existence" (Ebert and Herzog 1979, 7). For Herzog, such characters "are just very *pure* figures that have somehow been able to survive in a more or less pure form" who, when put "under very extreme pressure ... reveal their various natures to us" (Ebert and Herzog 1979, 6–7). In *Nosferatu*, however, the experiment gets reversed, the town rather than the vampire subjected to the experiment.

Central to Herzog's revision of Murnau's conception of the vampire is his humanization. Prawer noted: "Klaus Kinski's vampire ... for all his uncompromisingly grotesque appearance, has a pathos and a tragic dignity absent from Max Schreck's performance in Murnau's original" (Prawer 1980, 72). Prawer credited Kinski's performance, as does Herzog himself (Cronin 2002, 158), but it is there in the script as well, in Dracula's monologues early in the film and his dialog with Lucy later. As Herzog put it: "In Murnau's film the vampire is without a soul, he is like an insect, a crab. My vampire plays against his appendages—his long claws, his pointed fangs. He is so suffering, so human, so sad, so desperately longing for love that you don't see the claws and fangs any more" (Blume 1979). Kinski observed: "We both see him a little differently from Murnau's film.... We see Nosferatu more sympathetically. He *is* a kind of incarnation of evil, but he is also a man who is suffering, suffering for love. This makes the story more dramatic, more double-edged" (Andrews 1978, 34). We get a sense of this when Lucy spurns him. Dracula tells her "Dying is cruelty against the unsuspecting. But death is not everything. It's more cruel not to be able to die. I wish I could partake of the love which is between you and Jonathan." That scene, and the seduction/killing of Nosferatu that follows, depend on an erotics unparalleled in Murnau.

As critics have noted, the heightened eroticism is foretold by the name shift: from Nina to the more sexualized Lucy. The film develops that link, first in their conversation about love and eternity, and then in their final scene. Kinski observed:

> The character of Lucy is a complete departure from previous vampire films. Gradually she is attracted toward Nosferatu. She feels a fascination—as we all would, I think.... There's a sexual element in it. First she hopes to save the people of the town by sacrificing herself. But then there is a moment of transition ... suddenly her face takes on a new expression, a sexual one, and she will not let him go any more. A desire has been born. A moment like this has never been seen in a vampire picture [Andrews, 37; first ellipsis in original].

Clearly Kinski had not been keeping up with his vampire movies—after Roman Polanski's *Fearless Vampire Lovers* (1967) or Roy Ward Baker's *Vampire Lovers* (1970), such desire was hardly unprecedented—but the point remains that such shared erotic desire was absent in Murnau. If Lucy's desire for him is part of the story of that final moment, another element is Dracula's own complicity in his death. Murnau's vampire is simply surprised by the dawn; something more complicated operates in Herzog's version.

Herzog's second radical thematic shift concerns the breakdown of civilization in response to the onset of the plague, a fundamental theme throughout Herzog's oeuvre, as his "thin layer of civilization" remark suggests. For such a breakdown, Delft provides an especially rich setting.

As Andrews noted: "the choice of this genteelly beautiful Dutch town, home of china and canals and cobbled streets, is a stroke of genius. There is a sense of fragility in Delft" (Andrews 1978, 35). Herzog observes: "Delft is so tranquil, so bourgeois, so self-assured and solid and has remained unchanged for centuries.... The horror and destruction would show up very effectively in such a clean and uncontaminated town" (Cronin 2002, 156). It would shatter as easily as its precious porcelain.

In Murnau, the plague theme is secondary. We see rats in Orlock's coffins (but dozens, not thousands); coffins are paraded through the streets; the need to counter the plague informs Ellen's sacrificial act. Compare that, however, to Herzog: both the rats and the coffins multiply dramatically; parades of coffins perform an eerie dance of death in the town square; at the plague's height utter chaos rules the town, animals meandering, fires of abandoned furniture burning, with end-of-times citizens feasting, drinking, and dancing to discordant music on the square. They beckon Lucy to join them: "It's our last supper. We've all caught the plague. We must enjoy each day that's left." Against such chaos, no principles of enlightened civilization hold. Lucy tries to reach authorities, but she is told the town council is "dissolved, it exists no more." Van Helsing councils her against her belief that vampirism is at the root of the crisis: "We live in a most enlightened era. Superstitions such as you have mentioned have been refuted by science." He urges, pointlessly: "This has to be studied first. Scientifically." But for that there is no time.[7]

The collapse of civilized order reinforces the Rom's argument that the problem is entirely "in the imagination of men." Lucy wonders aloud: "Do you think it possible that we are so insane that one day we will all wake to find ourselves in strait-jackets?" And she counters Van Helsing's arguments for a scientific approach: "Faith is the amazing faculty of mankind which enables us to believe things which we know to be untrue." Against an enemy that exists in the imagination, untrammeled imagination itself—not science, not social order—must provide the solution (although, finally, since Lucy's death does not reverse Harker's vampirism, her sacrifice saves nothing).

Unresolved Issues

Andrews, discussing Kinski's make-up, observed: "The makeup is clearly influenced by Max Schreck in the Murnau original—there is the same bald, bony head, the rat teeth, the large pointed ears, the long fingernails—but it is subtly adapted to Kinski's own physiognomy and personality" (Andrews 1978, 37). Andrews fails to note, however, one significant difference between

Herzog's vampire and Murnau's: Kinski's vampire lacks the long hooked nose of the original.

Like many other cinematic horrors of the fraught Weimar era, the shadow of German nationalism and anti–Semitism haunts Murnau's *Nosferatu*. Ken Gelder underlines "the film's evocation of a foreign threat to an otherwise 'innocent' German town." He concludes: "Given the appearance of Nosferatu and the connection to Renfield ... it is, in fact, difficult *not* to see this film as anti–Semitic" (Gelder 1994, 96). It may well be the case that, as Herzog argued, Murnau's film "prophesied the rise of Nazism." But Murnau's film also participated in that onset, and by cutting off the hook on his vampire's nose, Herzog shows that he knows as much.[8]

Kinski, recall, said of his vampire: "He *is* a kind of incarnation of evil, but he is also a man who is suffering, suffering for love." But what does it mean to humanize the "incarnation of evil," especially when this particular incarnation is identified with Hitler? Leticia Kent provocatively posed the question to Herzog, in relation to his earlier film *Aguirre: The Wrath of God* (1972): "Do you feel compassion for Hitler?" Herzog deflected:

> Let's not speak of Hitler; there is too much resentment and it ill becomes a German to defend Hitler. Let me speak of Son of Sam. He has been called a mad dog. He is not a mad dog—he is a mad human being, perhaps only a step removed from the rest of us. One has to acknowledge him as a human being and to respect his dignity even in his madness. Otherwise, there is the danger that people may start to kill each other like mad dogs [Kent 1977].

While this rationalization sounds persuasive, it undermines Herzog's ostensible aim in *Nosferatu* to overcome the rupture of Nazism by building a bridge back to a "legitimate" past. And his final warning about the collapse of civilized values sounds hollow given his clear delight in portraying just such a collapse.

Herzog's film presents no clear way around this fundamental quandary. But perhaps, in a film that so resolutely refuses the restoration of order and narrative closure, such irresolution perfectly fits.

Notes

1. Seeking to evade copyright protections (and royalties) for *Dracula* (1897), Murnau and his screenwriter, Henrik Galeen, changed the names, location, time frame, and some plot points. Stoker's widow Florence was unamused and sued to suppress the film (Hughes 2009, 106–109). No longer bound by the then-expired copyright, Herzog reverts to Stoker's names (with one exception: Nina becomes Lucy, the more sexualized other woman in Stoker's novel). Some see in this Herzog's return to Stoker as a source (see Mayne 1986, 125, 127, 128–29; Prawer 2004, 47–49; Kawin 1980, 46), but it appears no more than a nod to the genre, on a par with the utterly superfluous staking at the film's conclusion (played for comic effect) or Dracula reiterating his "children of the night" line (in which, even if it is in Stoker's novel, we all hear echoes of Bela Lugosi's Dracula).

2. A complete set of title cards, and Murnau's annotated copy of the script, are included in Eisner 1973, 228–70; quotation on 229.

3. Prawer 2004, 67. Herzog's own engagement with the tradition includes, most dramatically, walking in winter from Munich to Paris in 1974, when he heard that Lotte Eisner was sick, convinced that his pilgrimage might save her. He told Roger Ebert the book constructed out of his diary from the time "I wrote during the shooting of NOSFERATU" (Ebert and Herzog 1979, 32). Nigel Andrews recalls that he "walked to his bookshelf and pulled out ... a handwritten draft" on the *Nosferatu* set (Andrews 1978, 38). Herzog tells Cronin: "When you come on foot, you come with a different intensity" (Cronin 2002, 281). See also Herzog 1980 and Isenberg 2016, Horak 1986, esp. 31–37; Cronin 2002, 281–83; Prawer 2004, 67; Davidson 1996, 57.

4. Prager 2012, 112–14; see also Wahl 2012, 147. Both Prager and Wahl focus on Herzog's *Heart of Glass* (1976). I would argue that in many ways *Heart of Glass*—with its mountain scenery, anti-naturalistic acting style (this is the film in which Herzog hypnotized his actors; see Cronin 2002, 128–30), and vampiric subplot (it is hoped that blood will provide a way to recover the lost secret of making a magical ruby glass)—works as a prequel to *Nosferatu*.

5. Herzog's own adaptation of Büchner's play was filmed on the back of *Nosferatu*, in a quick seventeen-day shoot using the same crew, Kinski again, and the same permits to film. See Ebert and Herzog 1979, 12; Cronin 2002, 159.

6. Andrews 1978, 33. That Dracula and the rats are an "invasion," however, sharply distinguishes him from Hitler, an indigenous German creation.

7. Herzog's deep distrust of Enlightenment thought shows clearly in the distinction between his Van Helsing and either the Stoker-derived type (reenacted in innumerable cinematic variations), a committed vampire killer, or Murnau's Bulwer, a "Paracelsian" whose lectures on insectivore plants at least show he read his Darwin. Herzog's Van Helsing, in contrast, does nothing except seek to dissuade Lucy from her beliefs in vampires until, converted by her sacrifice, he stakes the already-dead count.

8. Johnson notes that Wagner's place in the score similarly troubles: "Whether intentionally or not, the use of Wagner's music in *Nosferatu* functions to question the motives for and consequences of German nationalism" (Johnson 2016, 178).

There's Water Here

Cities, Safety and the Global Environment in Jim Jarmusch's Only Lovers Left Alive

Karen E. Viars

Jim Jarmusch's 2013 film *Only Lovers Left Alive* opens with a frame of stars in the black night sky, which gradually blur into a spinning record, mirrored in the homes of vampire lovers Adam and Eve. They live in different cities—she in Tangier, he in Detroit—which is a regular practice in their long and happy marriage. Adam and Eve's "love story transgresses not only generic formulae but also geographic borders in a highly transnational production" (Andreescu 2018, 93). Cities in several countries are a significant part of the lovers' history and present. The modern urban landscapes that Adam and Eve have chosen reflect their attitudes toward the dangers that the 21st century poses to their survival. While both of the lovers' choices echo an overwhelming concern for safety in a world that grows increasingly hostile, they also demonstrate how the changes in cities keep them in constant—and eventually fatal—danger. Human cities are an enormous strain on the environments that support them, particularly on clean water supplies, which are their lifeblood. *Only Lovers Left Alive* "sidestep[s] the horror and the (sexual) violence usually exploited by vampire tales" (Andreescu 2018, 92). As new interpretations of a long-lived myth and literary tradition, Adam and Eve have a unique perspective: the vampire who is "no longer a cruel mirror of mankind's worst violence, but a cultured outsider who observes and comments on this cruelty" (Senf 1988, 5). In Jarmusch's film, the cruelty is to the earth; in the environmental collapse that the lovers expect, based on their long view of history, water will be the determining factor in human survival.

As the opening shot pans back from the spinning record, the audience sees that Adam and Eve, thousands of miles apart, are both listening to music. They are poised at the beginning of the 21st century, a uniquely perilous time in their long lives. Art persists as a solace and refuge, as steady as the stars, in their increasingly unsafe lives. They both remain committed to beautiful works of art, literature, music and science from around the globe. "From the vantage point provided by their centuries-old existence among their human counterparts," Adam and Eve "advance a critique of present-day civilisation [*sic*] and embody an alternative to mass society and culture" (Andreescu 2018, 92). Andreescu traces the literary lineage of vampires from the barbarous eastern European peasant of folk tales to the 19th century fanged aristocrat (2018, 94). Adam and Eve are "articulate, eloquent, cultivated, and highly empathetic nocturnal beings, who have developed a consciousness and have started narrating their own stories" (Adreescu 2018, 95). The lovers do not feed directly from humans to avoid contaminated blood and detection.

This choice also allows them to "harness their feral energies in order to pursue aesthetic goals, either as collectors or creators of fine art" (Andreescu 2018, 96). Removing the image of them as hunters "eliminate[s] the horror" associated with their need for human blood, and helps the audience to see them as "more humane and temperate" (Senf 1988, 8; Andreescu 2018, 96). Their fangs "only [...] point to the vampire's 'otherness'" rather than elicit a feeling of menace in the audience (Senf 1988, 9). Their long lives have given them abundant time to hone an appreciation for human artistry and science; part of Adam's despair stems from his empathy. He has a litany of brilliant scientists that humans have denigrated and ignored: Pythagoras, Galileo, Copernicus, Newton, Tesla. "They're still bitching about Darwin" he tells Eve as proof positive of humanity's failures. Eve, in contrast to Adam's despair, approaches life with sanguinity born of long-term survival, having seen many sublime and brutal human events over centuries.

Despite their need for safety from humans, the lovers are themselves deeply humanized. They "obey human laws and social norms" and "protect ethical values neglected by people" (Stepien 2016, 2019). The film seeks to explore the success of their survival strategies in an interconnected, globalized environment that is itself headed toward inevitable, profound ruin.

Agriculture, Trade and Water: City Development

Compared to other significant changes in human history, according to Douglas, "the development of cities has been short-lived, but dramatic." Human communities "where a specialization of labour and some form of social hierarchy emerged, began to develop 9000 to 6000 BC" (Douglas 2013,

8). Agriculture and trade predicated the first human settlements, and "the first towns were essentially overgrown villages associated with trade routes and *water management*" (Douglas 2013, 8, emphasis mine). The availability of clean water as a form of safety comes up as a theme throughout the film, mirroring the vampiric need for blood; as vampires must drink to survive, so must humans, and water management is a vital need for human health and survival in an urban setting. These needs set up one of the major dangers for the lovers: avoiding polluted blood. Maintaining access to clean blood is a constant challenge, but Adam and Eve cannot change their circumstances. They require blood for survival, and as humans have steadily polluted the environment, contaminants have infiltrated our bodies. Blood-borne toxins are fatal to vampires; so is discovery in a world where they are creatures of legend. They must constantly balance their hunger with the danger of acquiring the blood that they need. When Eve asks, in their final on-screen conversation, whether "the water wars have started," the audience sees that the lovers know the water supply problems that humanity will face in a few (to an immortal vampire) short years.

Humanity's long history of settling near waterways, digging wells, building cisterns, and engineering aqueducts demonstrates that water is a critical consideration for human habitation. When water supplies fail, human life quickly becomes nasty, brutish and short. The Paris water shortages in the late 18th century serve as a warning and example; in 1785, the city had a population of 600,000 citizens, most living in poverty with a life expectancy of 40 years, as water availability dwindled to about a liter per person daily (Douglas 2013, 112). In 1827, radical London politician Sir Francis Burdett addressed Parliament about water safety in the West End. He described London's water supply as "charged with the contents of the great common sewers, the drainings from dunghills and laystalls, the refuse of hospitals and slaughter houses, colour [sic] lead and soap works, drug mills and manufactories, and with all sorts of decomposed animal and vegetables substances" (qtd. in Douglas 2013, 112). He argued that exposure to these contaminants "render[s] the said water offensive and destructive to health" and insisted that it "ought no longer to be taken up by any of the water companies from so foul a source" (qtd. in Douglas 2013, 112). Sir Francis omits Eve's observation that the Thames contained a host of diseased corpses, as well. Clean water allows cities to create many of their defining characteristics: "permanent settlement in dense aggregations; nonagricultural specialists; taxation and wealth accumulation; monumental public buildings; and a ruling class" (Douglas 2013, 112). These conditions create an environment where "writing techniques; predictive science; artistic expression" flourish (Douglas 2013, 7). City life is also marked by "a decline in the importance of kinship" (Douglas 2013, 7). All of these conditions are ideal for Adam and Eve.

Cities provide a multitude of the arts and sciences, which both Adam and Eve treasure. Books are stacked everywhere in Eve's Tangier apartment, and they are the only items in her luggage when she departs to go to Adam in Detroit. She lovingly selects the volumes that will travel with her from many countries and in many languages, reading them as she packs. She flies to Detroit with a passport under the name of "Fibonacci," an Italian mathematician of the Middle Ages whose work still informs mathematics in the present day. She reads Shakespeare's (or in the world of the film, Marlowe's) sonnets on the plane. Later, as the lovers flee Detroit, she gives her name as Daisy Buchanan from F. Scott Fitzgerald's famous novel *The Great Gatsby*. Adam's passport is in the name of Stephan Dedalus, the protagonist of James Joyce's *Portrait of the Artist as a Young Man*. She and Adam both easily name plant and animal species by their scientific names throughout the film. Though the characters' namesakes are the protagonists of Mark Twain's *The Diaries of Adam and Eve*, their frequent naming of flora and fauna evokes the Biblical text. When commissioning his wooden bullet, Adam names three types of trees that provide especially dense, hard wood, repeating the names as Ian, Adam's human assistant, copies them down. Eve delightedly greets a skunk in Adam's front yard, calling by its scientific name as she approaches his home. She also notices *amanita muscaria*—fly agaric mushrooms—in his basement, telling Adam "You know, this is not their season." She takes a moment to address them about her concerns regarding environmental change: "You guys shouldn't really be here. Not until the autumn." Adam adopts the name "Dr. Faust" when he visits the local hospital to collect his supply of blood, referencing the work of his friend, Marlowe, who wrote the famous play *The Tragical History of the Life and Death of Dr. Faustus*. His life in Detroit focuses on music, which has been a longtime fascination for him. Eve reminds him of the time he allowed Schubert to take credit for one of his compositions, and he continues to compose and distribute music in the present day, though he assiduously avoids all the trappings of fame. In his home, "there are a wide variety of people on his wall of portraits, from science and rock'n'roll, comedians and a few film directors"; and while "he's definitely hurt by human behavior [...] he loves these human contributions so much" (Pinkerton 54, 2014).

Cities were developing in complexity when Adam and Eve experienced their respective transformations into vampires. City dwelling in past centuries allowed them a form of anonymity and safety that modern cities, equipped with modern technologies, do not. While the film never names their ages precisely, in an interview with Nick Pinkerton, Jarmusch says, "In earlier versions of the script, we did identify their ages, and she was a 2,000-year-old druid from a matriarchal tribe, and he was only 500 or 600 years old" (Pinkerton 2014, 53). During their long lives, many cities developed into complex urban landscapes that provided an ideal vampiric hunting ground. Cities in the past faced the same public health challenges as cities today: managing refuse; removing sewage; importing food and other necessary items; and managing fires, crimes, and other hazards. Above all, cities needed water to survive. They grappled with these urban issues without the benefits of modern medicine, transportation, engineering, or fire management techniques. Coupled with the decreased focus on kinship, the high rate of mortality made disposing of a dead body without fear of eventual discovery far simpler in a city of the past.

The lovers are forcibly reminded of simpler times when Ava, Eve's "infamous" sister, carelessly kills Adam's assistant Ian. As Eve says, driving with Adam through the dark streets with Ian's body in the trunk, "I mean it's not like in the old days," recalling how easy it once was to dump bodies in the Thames. The changes in cities, including advancing technologies like forensics, an organized police force, photography, and personal identification documents make it much more difficult for a human victim simply to disappear. As Jarmusch observes, "In the 21st century, with forensic evidence and authorities, you have to be very careful" (Pinkerton 2014, 50). Better public health removes another plausible excuse for vampires, who could formerly disguise their victims' deaths as one among many in an epidemic. As cities have grown, we also cause more damage to the environment, both locally and globally. Growing urban cities affect the environments in which they exist, raising the question: "how [cities] have aggravated or produced environmental problems and how city governments and communities have endeavored to deal with these problems" (Douglas 2013, 7). All of humanity's collective efforts have not saved our environment from pollution, and the threat that it represents to human (and vampiric) survival. Adam says that humans "have succeeded in contaminating their own fucking blood, never mind their water," and he is correct. The advance of factories and industry have created new ways to pollute: the first recorded case of groundwater contamination in America happened in California in 1945, as a chemical plant released chlorinated hydrocarbons (a byproduct of an herbicide) into the water system (Douglas 2013, 132). Adam and Eve "see humans are becoming more and more fragile" (Pinkerton 2014, 50).

So This Is Your Wilderness: Detroit

As Adam and Eve mirror each other's actions in the film's opening scenes, they both look out their windows at the cities they inhabit. Adam's view is darkness and silence, punctured by the arrival of Ian, his assistant, the only other person visible. "[P]ost-industrial Detroit with its exuberant gloom and existential agony aptly illustrates the destructive effects of late capitalism" as it mirrors Adam's despair, and reinforces his perspective to the viewer (Stepien 2016, 219).

Ian is admitted to the crumbling house only after he rings the doorbell and waves at the security camera that Adam has rigged near his front door. Adam's home also displays the decay he has come to inhabit emotionally; there are patches of paint and plaster missing from the walls, and when Ian tracks in mud by accident, Adam tells him not to bother removing his shoes. Despite the succor of his music and the safety he has found in a vital supply of uncontaminated blood, he confines himself to his home, his music, and occasional trips to a local hospital. His few relationships are entirely transactional: he employs Ian as his assistant and procurer—particularly for musical supplies like vintage guitars, and a single, suicidal wooden bullet—and pays a doctor at the hospital for his blood supply. Aside from a few service workers and the doctor (notably one of the only black characters), who "acts as a drug dealer, selling Adam the 'really good stuff'—O-negative blood—on the black market," Irwin writes, "black people do not exist in the Detroit of *Only Lovers Left Alive*" (2017, 86). Though there is a classroom-sized globe in Adam's living room, his world is intensely local and as solitary as he can make it. He spends his time composing, becoming increasingly disillusioned with humans, whom "he's always dissing [...] as being zombies, saying they don't respect their imagination, that they're pathetic" (Pinkerton 2014, 54). In this way, "Jarmusch brings together onscreen the two titans of horror in contemporary cinema, the vampire and the 'zombie,'" even if the zombies are "an allusion to the decline of human individuality" rather than the brain-seeking undead (Andreescu 2018, 96). Irwin interprets the zombies as "a kind of white Other, [...] working-class Detroiters," enmeshed in the competition inherent in capitalism, which Adam himself, as an aristocrat, eschews (2017, 88). Zombies "are not capable of noticing the mechanisms of advanced capitalism, such as the technological intrusion and schizoid logics of buying that has dominated our lives and robbed us of our creative powers" (Stepien 2016, 220).

Jarmusch was highly specific in his choice of locations for the film: "Detroit [represents] post-industrial America; the decline of the American empire is seen very transparently in Detroit" (Pinkerton 2014, 52). "The apocalyptic, post-industrial Detroit landscape represented in *Only Lovers Left Alive* does not sit idly behind Adam and Eve, reflecting Adam's mood or his flight from (Western) civilization" (Irwin 2017, 82). Irwin instead argues that "Jarmusch actively constructs a landscape of social and spatial monstrosity" (2017, 82). Adam's visit to the hospital is the audience's first view of the city, a deserted urban landscape of abandoned buildings. Eisenbach explains: "In 1951, Detroit celebrated its 250th birthday during a time of expansion [...].

In 2001, Detroit celebrated its 300th birthday during a much less optimistic time" (2008, 56). By the time that Eisenbach's article was published in 2008, "much of the white community has fled from the city to the suburbs taking with them much of their wealth, leaving a city population that is predominantly African American, and impoverished. The city has a reduced population and a reduced tax base and struggles to provide services to an area that once housed a much larger number of people" (57). Irwin is even more direct: "White people who left the city accelerated Detroit's economic collapse by taking their tax dollars with them" (2017, 90). Detroit struggles with this dichotomy. While at the hospital, Adam overhears a knot of hospital employees talking about a decrease in overtime pay, the kind of self-defeating "cost-saving" measure that that a desperate city makes. Detroit has also resorted to cutting off water supplies to residents who had fallen behind in their payments. Mitchell reports in 2014 that 19,500 people were without water between March 1 and August 22, a state that resulted in a public health warning from the United Nations.

In 2006, the year that Detroit hosted two major sporting events, the Super Bowl and the World Series, McGraw, a journalist and native son of the Motor City, writes "Like most of the other 4.5 million residents of the metropolitan area, I was proud of Detroit's performances in front of a national audience and pleased to see the city receive some good press for a change" (McGraw 2007, 289). He continues, "But the idea that Detroit has recovered from its decades-long downward spiral does not ring true" (McGraw 2007, 289–290). During the nationally televised and widely praised sporting events, "[Detroit] was continuing to shrink because of its devastating financial crisis, which coincided with massive layoffs and plant closures by two of Detroit's biggest employers, General Motors Corp. and Ford Motor Co., as they fought for survival" (McGraw 2007, 290). At the same time, "City officials were laying off police officers and firefighters and closing police stations and taking fire rigs out of service." There were other cutbacks, too: more layoffs of city employees, closed recreation centers, and privatized cultural institutions like the historical museum and zoo.

For Eve's first night in the city, Adam shows her around. "Everybody left," he explains, as they drive past abandoned houses and silent, empty streets. What Jarmusch's representation of Detroit fails to include is everyone—primarily African American, and poor—who stayed. When she asks about the Packard plant as they drive past it, he says, "They once built the most beautiful cars in the world. Finished." "Packard is twentieth-century Detroit in microcosm" (McGraw 2007, 291). The headquarters and assembly plant opened in 1903, just in time for the city's auto boom. "Detroit's population leaped from 285,704 in 1900 to 993, 678 in 1920, two decades in which auto pioneers reconstructed the city into an industrialized landscape of massive factories and tool-and-die shops and parts depots" (McGraw 2007, 292). Packard ceased operations at the Detroit facility when the company was bought by Studebaker in 1956. At the time that Adam and Eve drive the uninhabited streets, the Packard complex is Detroit's largest abandoned building, "a five-storey citadel that has forty-seven connected buildings that stretch for nearly a mile and encompass 3½ million square feet of space" (McGraw 2007, 292). It is a "labyrinth of rusted steel, shattered glass, crumbling concrete, standing water, freshly dumped trash, vivid graffiti, junked cars and crud-encrusted artifacts of a bygone age" (McGraw 2007, 292). And though it is the biggest, it is one of many: "Detroit has thousands of empty buildings. It has derelict downtown skyscrapers with large trees growing from the roofs" (McGraw 2007, 293). There are also "vacant homes, churches, schools, fire stations, police precincts, libraries and armories" (McGraw 2007, 293). The lovers' tour ends at the Michigan Theater, a magnificently enormous concert and movie venue, whose fading painted ceiling now encloses a parking lot. Jarmusch paints a more complex and bleaker portrait of the city inhabited by its citizens:

> In fact, Detroit, like a lot of urban America, is a kind of apartheid, segregated, heavily.... So the black parts of Detroit, with the exceptions of a few middle-class and upper-middle-class neighborhoods, are destitute with no schools, no street lights, no roads being fixed, no policemen ever going there [Pinkerton 2014, 53].

Irwin argues that the vampire lovers "place themselves above the monstrosity of the city and its other inhabitants, which includes the hypervisible zombies of Western civilization, but also the very invisible residents of Detroit who are too poor to move or who resort to various forms of violence/savagery" (2017, 92). Though it has a thriving music scene, Adam shows Eve only one musician's house on their night-time tour of the unrealistically empty city. Jarmusch's choice to highlight Jack White rather than one of the many musicians and songwriters of color who call Detroit their hometown (among them such luminaries as Aretha Franklin, Stevie Wonder, Bebe and CeCe Winans, Berry Gordy, the Four Tops, the Temptations, the Supremes, and Smokey Robinson) reinforces Adam's incomplete view of the city.

Detroit otherwise offers few of the benefits that Adam could have in other cities, such as the company and support of his beloved wife, especially given his blindness to most of its residents. Jarmusch says that Adam is "hiding out there, hiding out from the world, in a way. It's the best city you could imagine to do that in." Adam lives on its periphery, inhabiting the margins that he has created for himself, but he has not always been consumed by despair. "You loved the music" in Tangier, Eve reminds him in their transnational phone call. She travels to him out of quietly desperate fear for his safety; the evening before she departs Tangier, Marlowe calls Adam "that suicidally romantic scoundrel," to which Eve replies, "Do you really think he is? […]

Well, let's hope he's just romantic," before attributing Adam's disillusionment with humanity to Shelley, Byron, and "those French assholes he used to hang around with." Despite Detroit's seemingly desolate nature, Eve predicts its future safety. She recognizes one of the city's greatest natural strengths: its location on the Detroit River and proximity to the Great Lakes, the largest bodies of fresh water in the United States. "When the cities in the South are burning," she predicts, "this place will bloom."

You Used to Love Tangier

In contrast with Adam's isolation and darkness, Eve's view of Tangier in the film's opening scenes shows a city lit up by night, populated streets, and audible activity as people go about their business. The city itself, illuminated in shades of cream and gold by night, is a contrast to Detroit's industrial darkness. While Adam only leaves his home in the carapace of a car to travel to the hospital, Eve walks the city's streets among humans, wrapped in a scarf the same warm color as the city's walls. Tangier is a far more ancient city than Detroit, one that remains populous and thriving, and can trace its history from a Phoenician trading post located on the Strait of Gibraltar to its current position as a major city of northern Morocco. In the interim, it was Carthaginian, Roman, Byzantine and later was colonized, invaded or administered by Spain, Portugal, England and France (or a combination of these and other countries). It has long been a site of expatriate living, and was a destination for Western writers in the 1950s and '60s, such as Tennessee Williams and William S. Burroughs. Tangier's popularity with Western authors was peaking just as Detroit's postwar industrial boom was beginning to slow. When Eve reaches her journey's end, a populated café run by Bilal, a student of Marlowe's, she greets him warmly with kisses to both cheeks. Bilal assures Eve that he will keep Marlowe's and Eve's vampiric nature a secret, clearly because of his emotional connection with them. At the conclusion of their conversation, Eve touches her hand to her heart in gratitude for his loyalty, and evidences only trust in his promise. Bilal assists an elderly Marlowe to Eve's table, where he gives her a bag filled with her blood supply, "the really good stuff from the French doctor." No money changes hands. Eve's experience is a marked contrast to Adam's strained relationships with Ian, whom he deceives about his true nature and pays handsomely to avoid contact with other humans, and the skeptical doctor whom he bribes for blood.

As a survivor of centuries, Eve has seen both the best and the worst in humanity and has retained a vital sense of wonder. In Tangier, she has developed and maintained friendships with humans and other vampires alike, continues to treasure her experience with literature, and sits outside by the harbor at night. Her openness to experience includes even those who have hurt her previously, such as her erratic sister Ava. "Eve's well-being results from the fact that she is fearless and tolerant, eager to explore the unknown and enter into a dialogue with the outside world" (Stepien 2016, 223). Though she recognizes "all the deformities [of human culture] that are despised so much by Adam," Eve retains an interest in the world (Stepien 2016, 223). As she leaves Tangier, she brings her philosophy with her to Detroit. As she tells Adam: "I'm a survivor, baby." Her previous experience colors her approach to their current dilemma; she has a sense of optimism borne from enduring some of history's great horrors. Eve explodes at Adam after her arrival in Detroit: "This self-obsession is a waste of living. It could be spend in surviving things, appreciating nature, nurturing kindness and friendship, and dancing." However, Eve's survival strategies and her continuing delight in the world are no longer enough to sustain her or Adam's existence. As advancing technology and environmental decay threaten their lives in new ways, errors that would have been manageable in the past are now lethal. "That Paris thing," as Ava dismisses the unspecified difficulty she created for Adam and Eve eighty-seven years ago, may have included the kind of murder she commits in Detroit. Regardless of her offenses, it was simpler at that time to hide the effects and to keep them all alive. Now, in the face of a dwindling safe blood supply and human advancement, it means death.

I'm Sorry, London's No Good

While Detroit and Tangier are in the foreground of the film, London fills up the margins, present in references and images from the movie's beginning. Originally, a Roman settlement on the Thames, London was burned and reconstructed for the first time in 60 CE, and has a centuries-long history of ruin and rebirth. In the past, London would have been an ideal city for vampires, replete with art, music, science, and human victims. Its periodic plagues and fires—which sometimes occurred simultaneously, as with the Great Fire and the Great Plague, both in 1666—would have made any disruption caused by vampiric activity difficult to detect. The first reference to London occurs just five minutes into the film's running time, when Adam decides to name a guitar that Ian has procured after William Lawes, a 17th century English composer. He gives a brief biography of Lawes to satisfy Ian's curiosity, focusing on his composition of funeral music and his death due to politics. Shortly afterwards, the audience sees Eve visits their friend Christopher Marlowe in Tangier. Marlowe's presence imbues the narrative with Londonian history, as it summons up his close association with the theaters which are still famous today, as well as his well-known (though apparently faked) death in Deptford, then a London suburb. She teases him about "the most outrageously delicious literary scandal in history"—that Marlowe himself authored the plays and poetry attributed to Shakespeare—and her desire to drop a few hints about it. Before Eve departs Tangier, he tells her "I wish that I had met [Adam] before I wrote Hamlet. He would have provided the most perfect role model imaginable." *Hamlet* and *Dr. Faust*—in the world of the film, both authored by Marlowe—are the only plays mentioned by name, and their tragic nature cannot be an accident. "It would cause such thrilling chaos," she says, to reveal his authorship; "the world has enough chaos to keep it going for the minute," Marlowe rejoins. He can glimpse the beginning of the end, though Eve herself has not yet begun to see it. When they return to Tangier and meet Marlowe on his deathbed, he is surrounding by his writings, and even a portrait of Shakespeare adorns the wall. He quotes Hamlet, "What is this quintessence of dust?" the second time that the Danish prince has been invoked in the film, and a reminder of Adam's melancholic nature. Marlowe is not the only British literary figure that the lovers have met; Eve asks Adam about his experiences with Byron, whom Adam declares "a pompous ass" and Mary Wollstonecraft, who he says was "delicious." Adam's admiration of Wollstonecraft, who bucked social norms and advocated for the equal education of women, fits with his pantheon of scientific heroes, who were also often ahead of their time. Adam and Eve have a strong, long-standing relationship with London, and its arts and culture.

While London may have been an ideal urban environment in the past, by the time Adam and Eve seek to flee Detroit in the wake of Ian's murder, it is no longer a safe haven. The limitations that the 21st century imposes on them become increasingly clearer to Eve as she and Adam seek a place to dispose of Ian's body in the wake of Ava's disastrous visit. She recalls the "days when we could just chuck them in the Thames alongside all the other tubercular floaters" without fear of the murder being traced back to them. Her recollection of the Thames, he critical river that enabled London's historical and present existence, reminds the viewer again that that London again is an essential city in the lovers' past. It also underscores the importance of water to survival. After Ava's forced departure, Eve, sitting on their bed surrounded by passports and credit cards, carefully orchestrates flights to avoid a London layover; any time in the city is too perilous. In addition to whatever shadows loom over London from the lovers' past, it is also one of the most heavily surveiled modern cities in the world. Lewis, writing for *The Guardian*, reports that there are 1.85 million CCTV cameras in the United Kingdom; at the time of that writing, there was one camera per thirty-two citizens. Whatever prevents Adam and Eve from revisiting their former haunt, the intense surveillance forms an additional barrier to their return.

Conclusion: Eighty-Two Percent of Human Blood Is Water

In the final moments of the film, Eve asks Adam to tell her again about Einstein's theory of entanglement, which she and Adam repeatedly call "spooky action at a distance." Adam explains: "when you separate an entwined particle and you move both parts away from the other, even at opposite ends of the universe, if you alter or affect one, the other will be identically altered or affected." This theory explains the interconnected nature of relationships in the film, especially for Eve. Her love for Adam, whom she calls, "my liege lord," is profound, arguably the definition of "entwined" after their centuries of mutual devotion. This connection is evident as they mirror each others' actions in the film's opening scenes, listening to music and drinking their humanely acquired blood in tandem. Their phone call unites them "narratively, technologically": across thousands of miles, in different countries, "there they are, together at a distance" (Hastie 64, 2014). Adam's despair moves Eve and she travels to Detroit to help him bear it, as she clearly has done in earlier depressive episodes. Ava, Eve's destructive sister, communicates her impending arrival to Eve, Adam and Marlowe through dreams. While still at a remove, she affects their emotional lives, causing dread and fury on Adam's part, and hopeful ambivalence on Eve's. When Adam contests their sisterly relationship, Eve reminds him "we are related by blood." She and Ava are also entwined.

The theory of entanglement also underscores the complex symbiotic web of the Earth's environment. Changes in any part of the environmental system affect the whole. Ecocritics William Major and Andrew McMurray write that "the course of global environmental health arcs steadily downward" despite improvements in "some charismatic environmental issues: water and air quality, recycling, local food, renewable energy" (1, 2012). The Earth faces omnipresent pollution problems, the kind that Adam has criticized indirectly throughout the film. Microplastics, minuscule pieces of plastic prevalent in water, are a clear example. Microplastic pollution is "uniquitous and persistent" and "openly threatens marine biota," with as yet undetermined effects on humans (Ivar do Sul & Costa 352, 2013). Microplastics cannot be recovered from the marine environment due to their size; they will "continue their slow, intricate paths towards the bottom of the ocean and ultimately become buried in sand and mud for centuries" (Ivar do Sul & Costa 361, 2013). Though a love story, *Only Lovers Left Alive* also functions as a cautionary tale about humans exhausting our environment, an abuse that has enabled the rise of great metropolises and industrial societies at a significant cost. "According to tradition," Senf reminds us, "vampires have no mirror reflection [...] Nonetheless, their hidden countenance is always there—a reflection of our deepest fears and desires" (16, 1988). As humanity grapples with (or chooses to ignore) our fears about the ecological problems of our own making, "the planetary tragedy plays on, and it is well into its third act" (Major and McMurray 2, 2012). The lovers cannot separate themselves from their polluted environment. The contaminated water that poisons human blood supply is already affecting the present, and will have an even greater impact in the future. In the end, Adam, ravenous and facing the prospect of attacking a young couple for blood, echoes the dilemma of humans facing our environmental disaster: "What choice do we have, really?"

Asia and Australia

From Sunnydale to Seoul
The Vampire "Fan" in Korean Dramas

Cait Coker

Popular culture has a history of articulating the anxieties that preoccupy each generation; its consumption is and always has been explicitly gendered as well. In the past twenty years, two figures of popular and cultural anxiety converged, perhaps irrevocably: that of "the vampire" and "the fangirl." This confluence reached its peak between 2009 and 2012 during the "Twi-craze," in which every American newspaper published think-pieces dwelling on the potential harms that could befall young women reading books and watching films about handsome vampires. As Nina Auerbach famously articulated in *Our Vampires, Ourselves* (1995), "vampires blend into the changing cultures they inhabit. They inhere in our most intimate relationships; they are also hideous invaders of the normal" (6). Auerbach's study focuses on the vampire in the America of the 1980s and 1990s as being specifically about the AIDS epidemic and anxieties of queerness, in which the drinking of blood in text and onscreen was sexually symbolic as well as transgressive. By the 2010s, the fear of the vampire was linked to something very different—fandom. In the introduction to their edited collection on *Fanpires: Audience Consumption of the Modern Vampire* (2011), Gareth Schott and Kirstine Moffat argue that "contemporary treatments of the vampire fulfill a similar performative role to that which has been associated with media fandom" (7), especially in terms of textual sharing and engagement. In short, massive, public anxiety was focused on the reading and writing habits of women fans online, and this cultural fear began to appear in popular culture texts themselves—including, and perhaps especially, in texts involving vampires.

Indeed, the vampire fan as depicted in American popular culture is universally derided. An early example is the episode "Lie to Me," from *Buffy the Vampire Slayer*, in which a cult of heavily made-up teenagers in goth wear who read "too much Anne Rice" are groupies out for immortality. Despite her best efforts, Buffy is unable to save many of them from either themselves or from the demonic vampires she slays on a weekly basis. A few years later, the motion picture of Anne Rice's *Queen of the Damned* (2002) mocks the same aesthetic—and the same type of fans—as vampire rock star Lestat feeds on his attractive young groupies. More contentiously, the long-running horror-fantasy television show *Supernatural* directly aped *Twilight* fandom in "Live Free or Twi-Hard," as brothers Dean and Sam Winchester investigate a series of disappearances of teenage girls. The young women are obsessed with the romance series *My Summer of Blood* and are wooed by handsome young men, who turn out to be vampires who enslave and kill their conquests, all while explicitly quoting dialogue and re-enacting scenes from the *Twilight* films. In these examples among others, the fan is a literal punchline, brutally dispatched and only occasionally rescued to acknowledge the error of their ways.

In contrast, the vampire fan in South Korean television dramas (or kdramas) is heroic, assisting and often rescuing the vampire hero himself, as in *Scholar Who Walks the Night* (2015), or protesting social prejudices, as in *Orange Marmalade* (2015).¹ This shift is all the more interesting as the vampire figure is adapted specifically from American popular culture, down to the term "vampire" (or, occasionally, "vampiru," which keeps the English term but adds Korean subject endings) rather than *gangshi*. A gangshi is the Korean folkloric term for the vampire figure (analogous to the Chinese *jiangshi* and the Japanese *kyonshi*), a corpse that hops around with its arms outstretched and which nightly consumes human *qi*, or lifeforce, rather than blood. The American interpretation of vampirism, specifically through the transmedia franchise of the *Twilight* books and films, predominates the Korean interpretations of the genre; the vampire (or vampiru) is an eternally youthful young man or woman, physically attractive and gifted with supernatural senses and strength, nobly tortured, and in love with the human protagonist. The Korean vampire fan is not a figure of contempt, nor is she punished for her romantic desires. Instead, she often becomes a hero in her own right.

A Globalized Context for Fandom

Academic study of fandom has tended to be, much like the study of the popular vampire, historically constrained to Anglo-American texts and contexts. This has created significant gaps in the scholarship as well as problematic narratives of textual migration and reception. For instance, American studies of the *Twilight* phenomenon have primarily focused on franchise development from books to films, as well as critical analyses of fan fiction and examinations of fan pilgrimages (see Leavenworth & Isaksson 2013; Aker 2016). The narrative in a Korean context is quite different, however. While the *Twilight* book series made the leap to Korea in 2007, it wasn't a financial success until the publication of new editions in 2008 and 2009, concurrent to the international release of the first films in the franchise (Han and Hwang 2012). The vampire in kdramas more generally was similarly neglected, utilized only in a single short series called *Freeze* in 2006, well after the popularity of *Buffy the Vampire Slayer* but before *Twilight* and its imitators. However, in 2011 and just at the height of Twi-fever, the popularity of the kdrama *Vampire Prosecutor* spawned what would become a popular subgenre of supernatural romances and thrillers: *Vampire Idol* (2011), *Vampire Prosecutor 2* (2012, a rare sequel), *Vampire Flower* (2014), *Blood* (2015), *Orange Marmalade* (2015), *Scholar Who Walks the Night* (2015), and *Vampire Detective* (2016).

Examining the vampire in kdramas resituates "fandom" writ large in transnational contact zones; as Lori Morimoto has written, "there is no clear line neatly dividing the transnational from the transcultural; if anything, the necessarily transcultural orientation of transnational fan studies inextricably links one to the other" (286). Thus, the kdrama vampire is very much in the mold of Benefiel's "New American Vampire," sexy and heroic, but "still an Other, still a figure who presents as the embodiment of an ideal beyond humanity, but his danger is in his very attractiveness, not in his agency of destruction" (Benefiel 11). The vampire in these kdramas thirsts for blood, often in an outright sexual fashion; he or she also feels guilty about these sexual hungers, especially since the objects of their desire are human. The media contact points between the American and Korean properties are blurred through global trade; it is difficult to define where and when exactly franchise popularity and fandom overlap beyond general patterns. For instance, the overwhelming physical beauty of the vampires portrayed in *Twilight* feeds into a popular Korean stereotype called *kkotminam*, or "flowerboy"; Han and Hwang transliterate the phrase as "a beautiful guy (minam) like a flower (kkot)" (221) and note that especially in the graphic novel adaptation that the artwork makes the connections explicitly.

The flowerboy type is seen broadly throughout Korean and Japanese culture, but its popularity in Korea has a specific cultural history stemming from the *hwarang* of the first millennium. The *hwarang* flowerboys were a military elite who possessed physical beauty, skill in the composition and recitation of poetry, and were responsible for protecting the country's northern borders. While they were not known for an equivalent to the chivalric codes for the west, they were popularized as a kind of ideal not too different from contemporary k-pop idols, especially since their modern counterparts receive celebratory public farewells and returns before and after their compulsory military service. Modern flowerboys are present in *manhwa* comics aimed at teenage girls, usually with a romantic element, boy bands, and of course, kdramas. As stock characters they are typically portrayed as fashionable, often wearing jewelry and make-up, and as the objects of desire for both women viewers and female characters in the drama. Indeed, when such characters make their entrance onscreen, the video speed slows down to highlight the men's grace of movement and physical beauty, almost always as women nearby gape in awe and admiration. It is notable that the Cullens's entrance to the high school cafeteria in *Twilight* was filmed in a very similar way to emphasize their inhuman attractiveness; though it was unlikely meant to be in imitation of kdramas or flowerboys, it does show the similarity of viewership and reception.

Having examined the transplant of American franchises and their reception in Korea, we should look at the reverse—the import of kdramas into the U.S. While Hong Kong, Chinese, and Korean films have often received limited release in art house theaters in America, television dramas from these and other Asian countries were usually limited to DVD sets. However, a variety of streaming services online have made these shows much more accessible, often with minimal fees, and sometimes with English translations available within hours of the first broadcast in their home country. Writing in the *New York Times*, Glenn Kenny noted that the import of foreign films has traditionally come to the country "through the filter of art," but the Internet has allowed for a much broader influx of popular TV (Kenny). Ease of access allows for a commensurate increase in fandom; discussion groups, gif sets of favorite scenes and actors, and fanfiction are much easier to find now than they were even five years ago.

The Pop Fan

One of the subgenres of vampiric kdramas plays off of the popularity of k-pop music and k-pop idol fandom by remaking the vampire hero in this mold. The trope also allows for the inclusion of vampire fans who contribute to the plot indirectly by cheering for the vampiric heroes. These fans also adhere to the traditional model of fandom as passive consumers; they react rather than act and play only a small role in the plot.

Vampire Idol (2011–2012) is a comical satire of both vampire dramas and music idol competitions. The show is different from the others discussed here because it is a sitcom that ran for seventy-nine half-hour episodes, in contrast to the usual drama format of sixteen to twenty-five hour-long episodes. It is also shot with (largely) stationary cameras in the flat lighting of sitcoms, emphasizing the broad comedy of the show. The characters' costumes are unusually flashy, from the Prince's faux-brocade coat to the black PVC outfits of his servants and bandmates that recall Goth clubwear from the early 2000s—a pointed counterpoint to the usually hyper-fashionable clothes worn in Korean television by way of conspicuous product placement, though they are eventually replaced by more boy band appropriate formal wear. In short, everything about the mise-en-scène is meant to play on visual stereotypes of both genre and format for laughs.

The plot revolves around vampires from another planet, Vampyrutus, who visit Earth because the young Prince wants to go to a conference headlined by his favorite band (and a girl band at that). The Prince's family has forbidden human popular culture on their planet, in shades of strict and uncool parents everywhere, so the trip becomes a secret undertaking that predictably goes wrong when their transport bubble breaks and they are separated. After a series of comical mishaps and misunderstandings, the vampires reunite, and the Prince is found out by his parents who summarily banish them from their home planet. In need of income and a place to live, they decide to enter an idol competition with the Prince as the lead of their new band, "Vampire Voice." Ensuing plots involve dealing with sketchy talent managers, hiding their true natures, and of course, dealing with their fans.

Fans are seldom shown and are largely an offscreen presence during the idol competition; they must be courted as they progress through the contest. The characters' vampiric natures are seen as a pose or gimmick for the competition, their "reality" frequently juxtaposed against vampire movies on television or otherwise present through mass culture. However, the fans are never shown in a negative light or assumed to be evil or crazy; they are also certainly not fed upon as they are in the American *Queen of the Damned* (2002).

Teenage Vampires in Love

Orange Marmalade (2015) is, in contrast, primarily a teenage melodrama, albeit one with intermittent pop performances. Indeed, in encompassing the problems of first love, bullying, sexual awakening, navigating between divorced parents and step-parents, and anxieties regarding state control, the show is distinctively different than most teen vampire romances. The show takes place in a world much like our own, but one in which vampires are present—and not only known to the general human population, but strictly policed for safety. The everyday prejudices and harassment the vampires face have clear analogues to a variety of oppressed minority groups, including immigrants (the vampires are periodically threatened with deportation), religion (there is reference to and concerns about terrorism as well as a state apparatus to combat terrorist threats), and queerness (from "coming out" as a vampire to threats of losing jobs and homes because of being a vampire).

The main character is Baek Ma Ri, a teenage girl and vampire starting high school. Like most teen girls, she's anxious about blending in, so she forces herself to eat the cafeteria lunch which she later has to throw up because vampires can't digest food; sometimes she gives up, locks herself in a bathroom stall, and drinks blood disguised as tomato juice packets. The most popular boy in school is Jung Jae Min, who has hated vampires since his mother divorced his father and remarried a vampire; a promising musician, he stopped playing after his mother's remarriage as a form of protest. When Ma Ri and Jae Min embark on a tentative romance, she has to hide her vampiric nature—which becomes increasingly difficult because of the common trope mixing blood lust with sexual lust.

Indeed, *Orange Marmalade* is unusual for its depiction of sexual desire as a part of romantic love. Because of "moral" constraints on what can be filmed or aired on Korean television, discussions and depictions of sex and nudity are minimal; in many romance comedies, for instance, adult characters will be genuinely baffled as to why they wish to interact with a specific member of the opposite sex, or occasionally, characters will make a whispered reference to people doing "that" (sex). While *Orange Marmalade* certainly never goes as far as conventional American television would in terms of teenage sex, an illustrative scene shows Jae Min dreaming of Ma Ri in a sequence reminiscent of Bella's dream of Edward in the first *Twilight* film: rather than wearing her conventional school uniform, Ma Ri wears a black mini-dress with heels, her hair styled in an attractive up-do; she approaches Jae Min with a smile, places her hand on his chest, then presses him down into a chair and kisses him seductively before leaning in to bite his neck. Jae Min awakes in shock and dismay, and then the scene cuts to him washing his boxers in the bathroom in embarrassment and disgust. While this depiction of a wet dream is comparatively chaste to most American interpretations of desire for a vampire, it does underline how the trope has been borrowed from one culture and repurposed for another. And Jae Min's embarrassment also indicates his discomfort with Ma Ri's vampirism, showing that he "knows without knowing" her true nature.

As the show continues, Ma Ri finds herself in a love triangle with Jae Min and Han Si Hoo, another boy and vampire. Si Hoo resents human oppression and urges Ma Ri to "come out," being honest with both herself and others. Frustrated herself, Ma Ri instead joins a school band with first Jae Min and another classmate and then with Si Hoo. They call themselves *Orange Marmalade* because, as Ma Ri explains, that food is something made from orange peels, which are ordinarily discarded but are here something integral to making something deliciously wonderful: "Even the orange peels destined for trash are something you need to make a good orange marmalade. To not discriminate based on differences but to make room for those who say they have no use. I hope our band can come together and make music like marmalade." This message becomes the moral of both the band and the story itself. The group joins a television competition, but when the news comes out that half of its members are vampires, they are not allowed to perform in a concert with their competitors. Instead, the band opts to perform publicly outside and upload videos of their performances online, where they quickly become a hit.

The fans of *Orange Marmalade* become an important plot element by effectively "saving" the band and their ability to perform in the competition; the television producers and record label are shamed by public disapprobation into allowing the students to compete. One scene shows Si Hoo in his after-school job where his boss is about to fire him for being a vampire—just as a group of fans come in and want Si Hoo specifically to help them buy merchandise; the uncomfortable and embarrassed boss takes back her words as it is clear that the boy's presence in the shop will bring in more business. More widely, fandom enacts social change because the popularity of the band leads to more widespread acceptance for vampires generally. In the end, a protestor tries to disrupt a live performance, but he is dragged away by cops who admonish him that "Vampires pay their taxes too, pal." The story also concludes with Jae Min apologizing to both his step-parents and to Ma Ri for his previous phobia and prejudice, with he and Ma Ri together in a happy romantic relationship.

The Fan Writer?

Scholar Who Walks the Night (2015) provides a different portrayal of fans and fandom by way of a literary context ... in the 18th century. This show also takes place in an alternate universe, one where vampires had a shadowy presence in the Korean government since the country's inception in the late fourteenth century; it is revealed that King Taejo (who ruled from 1392–1398) unified the provinces to form the nascent Goryeo with the strategic advice and supernatural assistance of the vampire Gwi. Gwi has continued to live beneath the Emperor's palace ever since and periodically receiving propitiatory sacrifices of beautiful maidens, and occasionally criminals, to feed upon.

The story starts with the human Kim Sung Yeol's friendship with the Crown Prince Junghyun, who in real life died in mysterious circumstances. In the show, Prince Junghyun had uncovered both the existence of Gwi and the vampire's ties to the monarchy, and was summarily murdered, while Kim

Sung Yeol escapes death by being reborn as a vampire who devotes his existence to vengeance for his lost friend and family. Generations later, Sung Yeol is a scholar for the Hongmungwan, the royal library and archives, searching for a lost manuscript by Junghyun that he believes contains the secret to destroying Gwi. On this search, he encounters Jo Yang Sun, a young bookseller who specializes in finding and selling antiquarian manuscripts as well as more popular novels. Yang Sun is also a young woman masquerading as a man to earn money for her poor family. As Yang Sun starts to uncover Sung Yeol's true identity while searching for Junghyun's manuscript, the ties between a corrupt government and Gwi's influence become ever more clear.

By the end of the series, both Yang Sun and Sung Yeol are actively part of a resistance movement to overthrow Gwi's government and restore the rightful crown prince, Lee Yoon, to the throne. As her contribution to the effort, Yang Sun writes and publishes popular novels in which Sung Yeol is the hero who comes to aid those in need. Sung Yeol's vampiric nature is known and accepted by the resistance fighters who see his supernatural strength and speed as assets in their fight. As Yang Sun continues to write, Sung Yeol observes that "Moonlight Rebellion [Yang Sun's nom de plume] has a bigger following than Forbidden Quest [another popular writer] now." In the same scene, Yang Sun's words on the page are translated as "The Night Scholar picked himself up with the help of the people," referring to both a literal scene in which Sung Yeol is saved by the peasants and figuratively to his redemption as a freedom fighter.

There are several notable elements of fan culture portrayed in the series. The first is that the manuscript novels that Yang Sun writes and circulates resemble fanzines with *manhwa* style illustrations in a visual departure from the other, more realistically historical books shown in the series. The illustrations are also all hand-drawn in black charcoals, rather than utilizing the woodblock prints that would be more often used during the period. Given dramas' general attention to scrupulous detail, I argue that these elements are meant to consciously and visually invoke fan publication practices rather than strictly historical manuscript practices. The second is that Yang Sun more than once draws upon her knowledge of popular novels and genre literature to solve clues and save the day—her knowledge and love of popular culture actively contributes to resistance and to victory. Effectively, Yang Sun is both a fan girl in her enthusiasm for novels as well as a *fan writer* through writing and publishing the adventures of The Night Scholar, Sung Yeol. Though she details their very real adventures, she is still writing what amounts to Real Person Fic, a genre of fan writing about real people, typically celebrities (and one that often contains romantic plots). Yang Sun's status of "fan" also complicates her romantic relationship with Sung Yeol who, in addition to the usual angst of an immortal vampire in love with a human, worries that her fannish admiration clouds her judgment of his true nature. But by the concluding episode, when evil has been defeated and the world is set right, Yang Sun is still writing....as fans do.

Conclusions: Vampiru, Not Gangshi, and Reshaping the "Problematic Fangirl"

The Korean portrayal of the popular Western vampire adapts popular American tropes to a new, transnational, and transcultural audience. While the Korean vampire acts as the familiar romantic revision of a popular figure of horror, the disdained vampire fan is revised to a positive and even heroic figure, in noted opposition to the usual American construction of fans in genre fiction. By remaking the figure of the fangirl from a problematic victim/threat to the hero to someone who actively *helps* the hero reshapes, in at least one part of the world, the relationship between consumers and producers of popular culture as well. Further, this reshaping uncovers the cultural anxieties, or rather the lack thereof, regarding fans and fandom.

American fan culture, especially where it is gendered feminine, has a very specific and problematic history. As mainstream culture, it emerged concurrent to popular films in the 1920s; magazines, photo-novels, and photographs of handsome actors for purchase and collection were more or less an acceptable outlet as a demonstration of heteronormative desire. (At the same time, purchase or collection of such materials by men was frowned upon.) By the 1960s, fandom as a subculture, especially where it involved science fiction, fantasy, and other genre material, was also inextricably bound up with countercultural movements, including feminism and in some cases lesbian separatism, the civil rights and anti-war movements, and eventually, fan fiction. Fan Studies theorist Henry Jenkins has famously labeled fan fiction as a way of "translating politics into the personal" and giving fans "a way to speak about their experiences and commitments" (264). Mass cultural anxiety regarding fans (and fan writing) is therefore as much about political desire as it is about women's sexual desires. When fixated upon the American vampire, women fans' desire is to create as well as to consume, creating a new economic nervousness for "legitimate" cultural creators, as with the controversies surrounding both *Twilight* and *Fifty Shades of Grey*.

In South Korea, fandom is a more mainstream and accepted social outlet, but it (seemingly, at least) lacks the overt politics inherent in the American subculture. While the creation and dissemination of fan writing and art is nonetheless a norm, it is not consistently portrayed as culturally transgressive. For instance, in the drama *You're Beautiful* (2009), members of a pop idol band explain fan fiction (and slash fiction), to a neophyte member; a series of vignettes show the boys in various pairings sharing tender, sexually charged moments or looking on in jealousy and spitefully vowing to "Break them [the couple] up!" This playful engagement with familiar fan tropes is amusing because of how accurately it sums up a certain kind of boy band fic, but the cheerfulness with which it is portrayed to the viewer is all but impossible to imagine in American productions.

Finally, the shift from *gangshi* to *vampiru* amplifies the revision of the stereotypical vampire. A shambling undead or hopping foot it is not; the *vampiru* can be a fearsome and evil figure like Gwi, but it is more often a sympathetic figure like Ma Ri or a hero like Sung Yeol. The *vampiru* continues a shift in the romantic exploration of a character type that began some forty years ago in American genre fiction and continues on television screens on the other side of the world.

NOTE

1. For simplicity's sake, I use English translations of Korean titles in the main text, with Hangul titles given in the Works Cited.

"Don't adjust your life to mine"

Moon Child, *Homoeroticism* and the Vampire as Multifaceted Other

MIRANDA RUTH LARSEN

> Another film adored by female BL fans throughout Asia is *Moon Child*, a transnational vampire/gangster movie directed by Takahisa Zeze (2003).... Many scenes in the film suggest a homoerotic relationship between Gackt and Hyde.
>
> These scenes were most likely the reason for the film's genesis, as its plot clearly points to an intention to appeal to BL-hungry female fans throughout transnational Asia. The film led to the production of other forms of popular media, such as a book that has become a transitional fetish item among girls throughout Asia containing 160 color photographs of the two beautiful leading actors taken during the filming of the movie.
>
> —Laura Miller, 2010

In her book *Beauty Up: Exploring Contemporary Japanese Body Aesthetics* (2006), Japan studies scholar Laura Miller reports that *Moon Child*'s (Zeze, 2003) stars, musicians Gackt and Hyde, were frequently mentioned by interview subjects as aesthetically pleasing role models and objects of desire. It is therefore unsurprising that in her later work Miller describes *Moon Child* as she does above. I quote Miller at length to emphasize *Moon Child*'s cult status transnationally; the film's stars, intriguing premise, and cache amongst fans of East Asian popular music makes it significant. The film was also screened at the Cannes Film Festival in 2003 and is a notable transnational/multilingual production, adding a layer of cinematic prestige. Aside from Miller's work, one of the few mentions of *Moon Child* academically is a quantitative study measuring student responses to the film; regardless of background, all students identified the following keywords: "human life, suffering, life, perception, confront" (Huang et al. 2006, 2119). Undoubtedly, *Moon Child* is another vampire film where "the rhetoric of the modern vampire as a creature of desire and transgression, as dynamic, demonic, uncontainable, works across a network of multiple forces" (Brown 1997, 118).

It is already well understood that "the vampire troubles the discursively constructed boundaries that define sexuality and gender, as well as sociocultural notions of what is beautiful or ugly, feminine or masculine, heroic or villainous" (Keft-Kennedy 2008, 65). This essay analyzes *Moon Child* by combining cinema studies and fan studies lenses. In doing so, I analyze how the fluidity of the vampire within the narrative and mise-en-scene connected itself readily to Gackt and Hyde's established star personas and provided copious material for transformative works. Textual analysis of the film point to the vampire as the central figure by which difference is measured within a diegesis accentuating national/linguistic/family/gang/class Otherness. The introduction of the (significantly) mute Yi-Che as a possible love interest adds sexual orientation to the list of Otherness, as Yi-Che functions as an acceptable site of rerouted homoerotic human/vampire desires. Even so, Yi-Che's presence fails to erase the wealth of elements that elevate homoerotic vampirism from subtext to text.

Moon Child *Background*

Before embarking on a solo career in 1999, Gackt found fame as the lead singer of a popular visual-kei band, Malice Mizer. Visual-kei is a sub-genre of Japanese rock music focused on concept aesthetics over uniformity of sound. Typical themes include beauty, death, love, and impermanence; band members are typically male and have elaborate costumes, hair, and makeup. During Gackt's time as vocalist the group trended toward glam-goth sounds mingled with Rococo French aesthetics. Their hit 1996 album *Voyage ~Sans Retour~*, which earned them a major record deal with Nippon Columbia, contained a song penned by Gackt called "Transylvania." The first spoken words of the track are Gackt reading lines from Anne Rice's *Interview with the Vampire*: specifically, Louis' explanation of his invitation to be released from grief and pain: "I invited it. A release from the pain of living." In the middle of the song he again quotes Louis, this time "And I said farewell to sunlight, and set out to become what I became." The song's chorus is Lestat's famous words "Drink from me and live forever." The rest of the song is sung in Japanese.[1]

Gackt left the group at the height of its popularity, likely over creative differences with one of the band's founders. He subsequently began work on his own solo career. I elaborate on Gackt's career for a specific reason: Gackt was the main screenwriter for *Moon Child*. While the film is set in and filmed in East Asia, vampirism within the film is clearly influenced by Anne Rice's work. Much of the scholarship that I will put into dialogue with a textual analysis of *Moon Child* comes from analysis of Western media. This is not an oversight on my part, but a nod to the kind of vampire Hyde portrays as written under Gackt's direction. Rather than drawing completely on more localized legendary creatures or mythos, the portrayal of vampirism (and interconnected homoeroticism) in *Moon Child* is likely tied to Gackt's previous engagement with Rice's work.

"You are not afraid?"—Kei and Sho's Story in Moon Child

Moon Child begins from the perspective of a frantic vampire, Kei (Hyde), wandering the backstreets of Shibuya in Tokyo on New Year's Eve, 1999. His companion, Luka, is exhausted of vampirism and decides to commit suicide. Kei is distraught by this decision. Luka offers the parting advice that Kei "find another 'friend'" and expresses a desire to see the ocean. Skirting the attention of partygoers, Kei agrees to go to the ocean.

Jumping to 2014, a Chinese-language news broadcast in the fictional district of Mallepa provides background: there are anti-immigration demonstrations since part of Mallepa is inhabited by poor Japanese immigrants, the "worst hit" of an East Asian economic crisis. We are shown a trio of orphan boys—Sho (Kanata Hongo), Toshi, and Shinji—who steal a suitcase of money from a local mafia boss's car, splitting up to make an escape.[2] Sho stumbles across an exhausted Kei and attempts to steal his watch, discovering that sunlight burns Kei. Sho brings him back to the orphans' hideout in an abandoned building, and tries unsuccessfully to feed him gruel. The mafia boss finds their hideout and shoots Shinji in the leg while Toshi runs off; Sho goes to retrieve Toshi but stops at a bloodcurdling scream from the hideout he just left. Shinji warns that Kei is "a monster," but Sho finds Kei drinking the mafia boss' blood. Sho accepts the vampire without fear, and they smile at each other.

A match cut transitions temporally from boyhood Sho to a young adult Sho (Gackt) in 2025 during a shootout, aided by Kei's vampiric senses.[3] Sho and Toshi set up criminals by drugging their delivery pizza and stealing their money; Kei feasts on the wounded. At Kei and Sho's home, Sho counts the latest take while Kei has a nightmare memory of Luka's suicide. Sho asks if Kei is okay afterward:

SHO: The same dream?
KEI: I'm fine.... You should get out more.
SHO: It's fine. I don't want a tan.
KEI: Let's spend time apart. [Getting up from the bed.]
SHO: [Lighting a cigarette.] What do you mean?
KEI: Don't adjust your life to mine. Enjoy yourself while you can... before you get old. Remember, I won't age—
SHO: Not this again! Mallepa is full of immigrants... different races, all coming and going, minding their own business. And that's how we get along!
KEI: I've fed on some many[4] evil men.... I'm becoming like them. I might turn on you.
SHO: As if you'd dare. Jerk.

Besides the wedge of Kei's vampirism, there are other frictions; Toshi wants to find his birth parents; Shinji is running up debt, using drugs, and suffers from a limp from being shot; local gangsters have caught on to the group's con.

Kei wanders a local park, encountering a girl painting a wall mural. Afterward he joins Sho and Toshi for another heist, where they meet and join forces with Son Tin-Chen (Wang Leehom), a young man in a similar economic position intent on taking down the same group of criminals. Son wants revenge for his mute sister Yi-Che, the girl Kei saw in the park, who the criminals raped.[5] After a bloody shootout the group patches up their wounds and heads to the beach. They take a photo together, and Son suggests they come back in the daytime. The next day Sho stops by with flowers to express his affection for Yi-Che. A montage sequence highlights the group spending time together.

Yi-Che finishes her mural. Everyone promises to attend Yi-Che's exhibition the next day, and Kei is dismayed by the sunny weather. An argument about Kei's vampirism brings Sho to tears, and Sho leaves for the exhibition. It begins pouring rain after the mural is revealed. Toshi is kidnapped by rival gang members who arrive for vengeance against Sho and Son. An emaciated Kei attempts to stop them, but he collapses. Toshi, hands bound, steps in front of Kei and is fatally shot. Sho is inconsolable, and Toshi dies in his arms. Son and Yi-Che witness Kei feeding on the gang members behind some bushes. Sho asks him to stop because Toshi is dead, but Kei continues.

The film jumps to nine years later; the mural in the park is now weathered.[6] Sho is an established gang boss in charge of a prosperous district in Mallepa; Shinji runs a bar as a front. Sho and Yi-Che are married and have a young daughter, Hana. Son has sided with Chan, the Taiwanese gang boss who called the hit on Toshi. Kei has landed himself in prison "somewhere far from Mallepa" for murdering four people, hoping to be executed.[7] Sho and Yi-Che see a news report that reveals Kei's incarceration as the "modern-day vampire." Sho immediately goes to visit Kei in prison, confessing that he married Yi-Che; he shows the vampire a picture of Hana, almost in tears as he asks Kei to look at her. They catch up about everyone, and Sho searches for a lawyer. Things escalate between the rival gangs, with some of Sho's compatriots shot in the street. Sho and Shinji argue at the funeral, as Shinji blames Sho for helping "that monster" instead of being around. Shinji tries to kill Chan on his own while high on drugs, and is killed. At the morgue, Sho confronts Son and threatens to kill him; for the first time in years Yi-Che speaks, asking them to stop and get along like they used to before Toshi's death.

A few months later, Yi-Che is dying of a brain tumor that is degrading her memory; she misidentifies Son as her father, and introduces Sho as Kei. Sho and Son exchange terse words understanding they will soon have a final confrontation. Sho calls Kei in prison:

> KEI: Hello?
> SHO: I wanted to see you. I missed you so much. A lot's happened. I can't go on alone. I need your help. Help me, Kei…. I can't go on alone.

Kei escapes during his transport for execution, appearing in the park at night watching Hana jump rope. Sho asks Kei to make Yi-Che a vampire; Kei adamantly refuses. Sho decides to go and kill Chan, telling Kei to accompany him. It seems that Sho has a death wish, refusing to take cover and acting recklessly as he eliminates Chan's lackeys. He eventually shoots out the crumbling ceiling, trapping Kei in a tiled corner of the warehouse with sunbeams. Son and Sho face each other and draw their guns on the count of three; Sho is fatally shot in the chest and collapses. Son accuses him of not firing, at which point Kei comes upon them. Furious, Kei shoots and kills Son and then cradles Sho against his chest, begging him not to leave.

Finally, the film jumps to 2045. A teenage Hana accepts accolades at a daytime reveal of her mother's mural, which she has restored. At night Hana meets Kei and thanks him for his kindness and watching over her for years. Hana leaves, planning to begin her art studies at college the next day. Kei returns to the mural, revealing Sho—now a vampire—admiring his daughter's work. Unable to let her see what he had become, Sho let Kei take care of Hana.

The two drive to the beach in Sho's open-top car and a time lapse shows the vampires waiting for sunrise. Sho's final words are "Look, Kei, here comes the sun." The song "Orenji no Taiyou" plays in the background as the empty car is revealed. Next Kei, Sho, Yi-Che, Son, and Toshi are shown at the beach taking a photo in the bright sunlight, young and healthy, possibly in the afterlife. The film ends on a freeze-frame of Kei and Sho posing for the photo together.

The Vampire as Sexual Other

Textually, *Moon Child* is almost entirely focused on Kei's relationship with Sho, connected by three motifs: blood, guns, and smoke. At their first meeting a shot-reverse-shot implies the starving vampire is fixated on young Sho's pulsating jugular vein. Later, when Sho is grown, a similar shot-reverse-shot goes from Kei's smiling face to Sho's bleeding arm and back to Kei's expression shifting, mouth falling open in desire before he excuses himself from the room. In both of these situations it's unsurprising that Kei's vampiric desire is fixated on blood, but what is surprising is that the cinematographic techniques allude to a special appeal of *Sho's blood* in particular. Right before Sho's wound is revealed, Kei is looking at Yi-Che with a smile while she bandages Son's wounded leg; the blood from Son's wound causes no distraction, and Kei's gaze at Yi-Che is clearly affectionate. Son's wounds tended to, he gets up:

> SON: She'll look at you now.
> SHO: Me?
> KEI: [Smacks Sho's shoulder, backhanded.]
> SON: Don't!
> KEI: Have her take a look.
> SON: I can smell the blood from here. [Pulling Sho to his feet.] Don't risk an infection.
> SHO: I can still walk.
> TOSHI: Quickly!
> SHO: Shut up. [Sits down at the table with Yi-Che.]
> SON: Yi-Che, look after him.
> SHO: [Lifts up his shirt sleeve.]

The reveal of Sho's wound is in extreme close up, and the next shot is Kei's smiling face changing expression quickly; his eyes widen and his mouth drops open. Another shot of the wound shows Yi-Che patiently cleaning at the dripping blood with cotton. Back to Kei intently staring, mouth agape. He sighs, turns his head, then grabs his jacket to leave.

> SON: Something wrong?
> KEI: I'm getting some fresh air.

Another shot-reverse-shot between Kei and Yi-Che suggests something unspoken, and he leaves the room, Sho looking after him.

At first glance this reads as possible jealousy over Yi-Che mingled with bloodlust, but a critical detail shifts the scene toward homoerotic jealousy. Before Sho goes across the room for Yi-Che to bandage him, he and Kei are sitting next to each other and Sho's wounded arm is clearly visible: his shirt is ripped and blood is smeared down his forearm. When Kei smacks Sho's arm to get him to go see Yi-Che, he smacks the wounded arm; he has been next to the blood source the entire time with no loss of control. Only the *undressing* of Sho's wound stirs up Kei, followed by the tender action of the cotton dabbing against Sho's skin. Only the undressing gives us any impression of Kei "dying for a drink" (Brown 1997, 114). I suggest that in this scene Kei's issue is jealousy over Sho, not Yi-Che: not only that he can't drink Sho's blood, but that he can't care for him in such moments while remaining in control. He recognizes Yi-Che as a potential rival because she is able to take care of Sho in that way. The shot-reverse-shot of Kei looking at Yi-Che before he leaves for "fresh air" is to clear his anger just as much as to stem his bloodlust. Kei realizes that he will possibly lose Sho, especially after his earlier speech telling Sho to enjoy life while he's young. Fittingly, after Kei leaves the room, Sho catches himself staring at Yi-Che longingly for the first time as she tends to his wounded arm.

The final moment following this theme is when Sho lies dying in Kei's arms, covered in his own blood and also spitting it up. Here Kei shows no desire to consume Sho's blood; he presses his hands to the bullet wounds in Sho's chest, trying to stem the flow. Eventually he clasps Sho's hand in his own, both covered in blood, when he pleads for Sho not to leave him.[8] The moment of Sho's vampiric transformation is never seen; we as the audience are not allowed to witness the "the sexualized act of siring" (Keft-Kennedy 2008, 67).[9] *Moon Child* again borrows from Rice in how vampires are created; the victim is drained of blood just before the point of death. Therefore we can infer that Kei finally gets to drink Sho's blood when he turns him.

The film's multitude of shootouts makes guns a ubiquitous component. During these scenes Kei uses his vampiric senses to often "guide" Sho; to warn him of what direction bullets are coming from, to alert him of assailants he's unaware of, and so on. During one fight Sho runs out of ammunition with a gun in each hand; a smoking Kei calls his name from behind and tosses two cartridges, which Sho loads into each gun by spinning and falling to his knees. Earlier in the same fight Kei, out of ammunition, tosses his gun aside; without even exchanging looks Sho retrieves another one from inside his jacket and tosses it aloft for Kei to catch deftly. The phallic symbol of the gun is used time and time again to highlight that Kei and Sho are intimately intuitive and aware of one another, in sync as a unit.

Finally, Kei and Sho are linked by the motif of smoke. When they first meet, Sho is given a shot-reverse-shot reaction sequence to Kei's hand smoking and burning when exposed to sunlight. The smoke is later changed to the symbol of a cigarette; their intimate intuition of one another is highlighted in Sho's ability to catch a cigarette between two fingers without even looking at Kei. During a fight scene, Sho breathlessly asks Kei to help him fight an attacker with a machete, but Kei simply offers the cigarette he is smoking to Sho for a drag and warns him the attacker is coming to get him. When Kei escapes from the prison transport after Sho calls him, he wraps a blanket around himself and runs, but the filtered sunlight still causes his body to smoke.[10]

Finally, when Kei is trapped in the tiled extension during the final firefight, he defies the sunlight—body smoking at the exposure—to reach a dying Sho. All of these moments speak to Kei and Sho's bond with one another. Kei's weakness to sunlight, especially, is consistently linked to his "weakness" for Sho.

Kei's attachment to Sho, and the homoerotic tension between them, is made especially clear in one scene: the argument in their apartment between Kei and Sho before Yi-Che's art exhibition.

> KEI: How is it?
> SHO: Perfect weather.
> KEI: Really ... perfect for Yi-Che's big day.
> SHO: Kei ... you don't drink blood these days.
> KEI: It's none of your business.
> SHO: But you're so weak—
> KEI: Should I drink yours? I live by draining the lives of others.... You know what that's like? That's my entire life. Sometimes I can't bear it. So I go without. A starvation diet. Now I'm having fun with you all ... but it's not real. You're all growing up. I'll be left behind. Sho, one day, you'll die. But I'll keep living. You think that's fun?!
> SHO: [A tear escapes as he begins to cry.]
> KEI [Approaches Sho and wipes at the tears.] You cry baby ... [Kei pulls Sho into an embrace and pets his hair.] Just like when you were a kid.
> SHO: [Sniffling.]
> KEI: So, go have fun. They'll be worried.

In this scene Kei strongly echoes Louis, as for the majority of the *Vampire Chronicles* "Louis detests what it means to be a vampire, and he fights the associated urges in order to maintain his remaining humanity" (Jackson 2012, 38). Kei finally brings up the topic of drinking Sho's blood, and their argument is played out with the intensity of a lover's spat. When Sho begins to cry he's seated with his back against the wall; when Kei approaches to comfort him, the shot is framed so a standing Kei is guiding Sho to lean forward and bend his head down. Taken out of context, still frames in this moment are reminiscent of an oral sex scene in softcore pornography, or a panel from a BL manga featuring two beautiful men engaging in foreplay.

Contrasting this, despite Sho and Yi-Che having a child together in the course of the film's narrative, their heterosexual relationship is barely present. The extent of their pre-marriage romance is the scene when Sho brings Yi-Che flowers and bumbles nervously through a lunch she's prepared, calling her "beautiful." After the time jump, the film only presents them sharing a few moments of affectionate contact. Simply put, their relationship is not the focus of the film; instead, we follow Sho from boyhood to manhood to vampire-hood to the afterlife via his relationship with Kei. Yi-Che is simply a site of rerouted desire, a catalyst that sets events into motion and interrupts the homosocial paradise.

This de-emphasis on the main heterosexual relationship of the film is compounded with Yi-Che's muteness and subsequent illness. Her muteness renders her a cypher dependent on those around her, principally her brother Son and later her husband Sho. During her phase as a mute, Yi-Che communicates only through her painting and unspoken actions. During the coda scene, presumably in an afterlife of some kind, Yi-Che says nothing and only smiles; we have no way of knowing if she has returned to her mute state. The later reveal that Yi-Che had feelings for Kei, coupled with Sho's attachment to Kei, makes it clear that the couple were essentially using one another as Kei surrogates. As Sho explains to Kei in prison:

> It's been nine years. I counted on the way here. How do I look? Look. I had a kid. She's called Hana. She's six. Kei, I married Yi-Che. She wasn't sure at first. I reckon it's because ... she really liked you. Then you left us.... I kept asking.
> Wouldn't give up. I tired myself out. She wasn't happy at first, but now things are good. Look, Kei. Please look. It's our kid. I know all Dads are proud but.... I always hoped you'd get to see her. You, above all.

Yi-Che's illness is an internal one; we infer from her refitted bedroom, hospital bed, and oxygen mask that she's unwell. This is in stark contrast to the (sometimes fatal) injuries inflicted upon *Moon Child*'s male characters; the "beautiful battered male body" that is often aligned with vampirism's appeal (Keft-Kennedy 2008, 63). Sho's decision to go on the suicide mission to kill Chan is right after Kei refuses to turn Yi-Che, which guarantees that Sho will be left without a partner; Yi-Che will die, and Kei will likely try to kill himself again. In other words, Sho's immediate decision is to either end his own life or to obtain what ultimately happens: Kei turning *him* into a vampire. His desire to end his human life and become an Other is suffused with his desire to be with Kei.

The Vampire as Refugee

While much can (and should) be made of the film's homoeroticism, another layer of Otherness attached to Kei's vampirism is his status as a refugee. Kei's name is Japanese, his primary language is Japanese, and his flashback scenes with Luka are all in Japanese. The portraying actor, Hyde, is also Japanese. We can then infer that even throughout the narrative, Kei is not only a vampire, but a *Japanese* vampire amongst a throng of Japanese refugees in another country. Since he passes as human when in the company of other humans, his body is read as a Japanese refugee male body. Mallepa is described as a "special economic zone" and home to a number of refugees.[11] The later tensions between Son and Sho settle along ethnic lines; Sho explains to Kei that Son "joined the local mafia to be with his own people." Sho, Toshi, and Shinji are presumably orphaned during whatever crisis precipitated the shift of a large Japanese population to Mallepa. These are also economic lines; Chan is behind a modernization of Mallepa, which includes knocking down the ruins where the orphaned Sho, Toshi, and Shinji lived in order to build subsidized housing for the poor.

This ties into the use of language in the film. During the Chinese-language broadcast that begins the Mallepa leg of the film, a boxy TV set in an alleyway displays information in Cantonese, Korean, Japanese, and English text simultaneously. Gangsters threatening Shinji and Sho at one point demand Sho "speak Cantonese" to them, but Sho instead switches to rude Japanese while handing over Shinji's owed money. This demand is to assert their authority and cultural dominance, not out of lack of understanding. Almost everyone in Mallepa is portrayed as functionally multilingual, with Sho speaking Japanese, Cantonese, and even English. Son is the only character that expresses linguistic confusion; when the group drives to the beach, he cannot understand Sho and Toshi's banter, leading Kei to explain it to him in Cantonese. When they reach the beach, Son looks between Toshi and Sho with a bewildered expression as they sound out the Japanese pronunciation of "romantic" for him.

Mallepa as a cityscape and ethnic melting pot, in addition to the polyglot soundscape, gives Kei perfect camouflage. Kei follows in the footsteps of the 1980s and 1990s "urban vampire," someone bred within the city space, a vampire that can "draw upon existing and emerging discourses and representations of particular urban identities to break away from the iconic Dracula image and embody the broad range of identities that define these cities" (Abbott 2003, 133). We are never told about Kei's life before becoming a vampire, or how long he's lived as a vampire when the film opens in Shibuya (the pinnacle cinematographic example of urban Tokyo). As Abbott argues, "since Stoker's novel, vampires, particularly on film, have been increasingly attracted to modern cities in which they are free to hunt amongst the crowds" (Abbott 2003, 133). While Kei spends the film oscillating between his "diet" and feeding on criminals, the chaos of the refugee population in Mallepa offers him a space to function as vampire and also pass as human. The tensions between rival gangs—homosocial spaces—also provides a space for him to be around Sho constantly.

Enduring Legacy

The first spoken words in *Moon Child* are those of a Japanese announcer excitedly introducing one of the year's hits on *Kohaku Uta Gassen*, the inescapable music program that functions as a cultural institution on New

Year's Eve in Japan.[12] While this marks a sense of realism as Kei and Luka wander Shibuya's backstreets, it also seems an odd choice given the attempt by Gackt and Hyde as actors to dissolve into their roles as Sho and Kei respectively. Bookended by Gackt and Hyde's duet version of "Orenji no Taiyou" (Orange Ocean) rolling over the end credits, we can infer that the film was meant to, in one way or another, remind the audience of Gackt and Hyde's status as active musicians in Japan's popular music scene.

Gackt's *Jougen no Tsuki* tour after the film's release included a performance of "Orenji no Taiyou"; instead of singing the duet with Hyde, Wang Leehom provided the accompanying vocals. The actors that portrayed Toshi, Yi-Che and young Sho also appeared on stage in their costumes from the film. Additionally, the music video for Gackt's song "Another World" features a similar narrative and aesthetic, minus the vampirism; we see a heist, Gackt shifting in attire and attitude from casual to sleek and gun-toting, and him driving away in the same car from the end of the film while clutching his wounded torso. Since *Moon Child*'s release, Gackt has codified the film along with a series of albums and a stage play as the Moon Saga: a string of interconnected stories dealing with themes of immortality, love, and war. By incorporating *Moon Child* as an entry into an overall mythos, Gackt continually makes intertextual references to the film. Nevertheless, his public persona has noticeably changed, and he's distanced himself from his earlier claims of vampirism.

Hyde presents the opposite case. While remaining active as the lead singer of L'arc~en~ciel, Hyde has also been the frontman for the vampire-themed band VAMPS since 2008. VAMPS' songs are written, mostly in English, from the perspective of a vampire. Frequent themes include blood, death, sex, and the passage of time. The band has gained worldwide recognition and frequently performs in the United States and South America, including on the Warped Tour. While Hyde's appearance is now different than his portrayal of the character Kei, the thematic link cannot be overlooked.

The pairing of Kei and Sho (and Gackt and Hyde) in fan fiction, doujinshi, fan art, and other transformative works is plentiful online. Due to constraints of space I am unable to elaborate about them as they deserve, but I will offer a few observations. First, a plethora of *Moon Child* transformative works attempt to fill the temporal gaps in the film, particularly the chunk of time from Kei and Sho's first meeting to the first scene depicted in 2025—in other words, Sho's adolescence—and Sho's turning to the end of the film. Secondly, the filming of *Moon Child* itself is used as a catalyst in Gackt and Hyde—known by the pairing name Gakuhai—fan fiction as a turning point in their relationship. Many works are set during the film's production, or even when the film is screened for the first time.

In sum, I believe teasing out the intricacies of *Moon Child*'s plot better explains how the film has garnered a cult following and immense fan response as mentioned in the introduction. The film's status as a multigenre and multilingual production mashing up gangsters, refugees, and vampires seems confusing at first. However, the cinematographic techniques and winding narrative repeatedly reinforce that Kei and Sho's relationship is the most important element above all. Gackt and Hyde's bodies are showcased, battered, and bloodied in the film; their voices join together to bring the song "Orenji no Taiyou" as their characters commit a lover's suicide. Influenced by Anne Rice's work, vampirism in *Moon Child* is exquisite and painful, a blessing and a curse, a force of magnetism that leads Kei to futilely chide Sho "Don't adjust your life to mine."

NOTES

1. The song is accompanied by frenetic violin eerily echoing the violin music Lestat plays on the beach in the 2002 film adaptation of Rice's *Queen of the Damned*—six years after the album's release.
2. Shinji is the oldest, followed by Sho and Toshi. Sho calls Shinji "Nii-chan," commonly used in Japanese for a younger brother to address his older brother, but the film doesn't make it clear if they are actually related by blood.
3. Sho: "Bullets can't kill you, so stay still." Kei: "They still sting, though."
4. "Some many" is likely a typo for "so many," the meaning of the words Kei says in Japanese.
5. Son later explains that Yi-Che has been mute since childhood.
6. The superimposed text says, "a few years later," but Sho specifies nine years when he visits Kei in prison.
7. According to superimposed text. Wherever he is seems to have more people of Caucasian descent, and English is used as the default language.
8. A series of sepia-toned flashbacks include scenes from earlier in the film as memories, ending on the young Sho's smile when Kei asks if he's afraid.
9. This moment is often the starting point for *Moon Child* fan fiction.
10. Kei wrapped in the blanket during his prison escape is visually similar to Gackt's appearance in his music video for the song "Oasis," released in 2000.
11. While it is never discussed explicitly in the film whether they are also refugees, Sho's gang at one point includes a Caucasian male with an Australian accent and an African American bodyguard.
12. Participating in this four-hour year-end music show is a mark of prestige in Japan; Gackt and Hyde (as L'arc~en~ciel's vocalist) have both appeared on the program five times.

Aboriginal Australian Vampires and the Politics of Transmediality

Naomi Simone Borwein

Sucking vampiric winds, cannibalistic red-skinned monsters, and demonic autophagic silhouettes and shadows exist in contemporary Aboriginal Australian horror and Gothic texts. Figures based on myth, they have names like Namorrados, Yara-ma-tha-who, Gherawhar, or Quinkan, and they bear some striking similarities to Western vampires. The fluidity of the vampiric image in Aboriginal Australia is heightened by its transformation across media and complicated by racial and cultural controversies. This essay is a transmedial analysis of the Australian Aboriginal vampire that traces its adaptations from orality to ink, and from celluloid to digitization. Both Indigenous and White Australian visions of the vampiric shape-shifter have permeated Australian narratives and media. In the 1990s, Alan McKee stated that in Australia "there is no readily accessible 'blackfella' tradition of zombies and vampires," as conventional Western figures in film (1997a, 123); this is still the case. Productions like *The Zombie Brigade* (1986) show vampiric contamination of an Indigenous community, and by proxy the continued intrusion or incorporation of classic vampires with Aboriginal myths. On page, the Aboriginal vampire is recreated by self-identifying Indigenous Australians in modern texts such as Mudrooroo's Vampire trilogy (1990–1998), D. Bruno Starrs' *That Blackfella Bloodsucka Dance!* (2011), or Raymond Gates's "The Little Red Man" (2013). It also appears in Australian vampire fiction like Jason Nahrung's Vampires in the Sunburnt Country series (2012–2016). By surveying the figure as it has filtered across media, I analyze its transformations in relation to transmediality and theories of adaptation espoused by scholars like Jens Eder and Linda Hutcheon. Significant variations in the Aboriginal vampire are visible in relation to the scientific apparatus of horror, the Antipodean footprint of Bram Stoker, and shadow and light in the Sunburnt Country. Each permutation reflects transitions in cultural context and from literary to multimedia traditions. Thus, after explicating a critical approach, this essay delineates the transformation of the Aboriginal Australian vampire in various White and Indigenous productions, taking into account the politics of transmediality. Underlying such an analysis is the issue of cultural identity and appropriation, which feeds into the metamorphic quality of Aboriginal Australian vampires in textual and digital forms.

Aboriginality, Vampirism, Transmediality: A Critical Approach to Adaptation

Aboriginal vampires have been used extensively in White Australia to describe monstrosity, cultural anxiety, and preternatural fear. Represented in many texts (film or novel), they are largely hybrid creatures constituted by both traditions. This hybridity is the result of merging two lineages: (1) the vampiric mythology of the Dreaming that has been transformed in contemporary Indigenous production of Aboriginal vampire legends, and (2) the scions of European vampires from Stoker and Joseph Sheridan Le Fanu—seen in early Australian reworking such as Rosa Praed's 1891 *The Soul of Countess Adrian*. Much like in any vampire tradition, transformation and intertextuality are a natural facet of the development of the figure in Australia. To understand its position to print and film, this analysis takes into consideration Aboriginal use of the white or Western vampire, the authorial or auteuristic perspective projected onto Aboriginal vampires, Indigenous creation of Aboriginal vampires, and the broader use of Aboriginal myth and vampiric elements in popular culture—which functions as a politicized space.

The politics of intertextuality can be defined through the process and practice of transmediality; it is wrapped up in the blatant ideological effects, as well as the commodification and economy, of images that are recycled and reused by cinematic and publishing industries, and advertising syndicates, for a variety of material, intellectual, and fiduciary reasons, creating a feedback loop between the consumer, reader, viewer/public, and the apparatus of production. Critics from Thomas Ong to Hutcheon to Eder have more explicitly explored the politics of intertextuality. Eder explicates "the political economy and ideology of transmedia practice" (2015, 67), while outlining key aspects that should impact a new model of transmediality: from the "communicative function" (representing the role of the text) to "relations between" elements, and "constellations of media" directly impacted by the politics of adaptation that relies on "core 'megatext[s]'" as "motherships"—for example, the television series *True Blood* (2008–2014). Such a model takes into account "spreadability" and distribution of texts, and notions of authorship, copyrights, and control (Eder 2015, 73, 76). Applied to a reading of the Australian Aboriginal vampire, concepts like "megatext[s]," as nexus-metatexts, "degrees of participation and co-creation," and "spreadability" (Eder 2015, 73) resonate with its adaptive state. Hutcheon characterizes the vampire in transmedial terms as "a single protean figure, culturally stereotyped yet retrofitted in ideological terms for adaptation to different times and places" (2006, 153). Within White Australian and Indigenous Australian contexts, the vampire is increasingly "retrofitted" to meet demands of contemporary urban culture, where "fluidity" as the "production-oriented elements" of adaptation visible with *Buffy the Vampire Slayer* (1996–2003), *The Twilight Saga* (2008–2012), and *True Blood* (2008–2014) is an advantage for its continued representation in non–Indigenous production, because unintended elements of antecedent vampires resurface.

Aboriginal vampires sit largely outside an Australian canon that still impacts their representation. Thomas Leitch describes a "process of adaptation" that incorporates texts "whether or not" they are "canonical"; he notes certain intertexts become canonical, while others do not, and set characteristics function as markers for images and texts that are circulated and re-adapted (2007, 302). Often the "recurrence of certain textual elements ... can be seen as a form of agenda setting" (Eder et al. 2010, 78–9). Overshadowed by Australian vampire fiction, Aboriginal vampires on page and screen are marked as postcolonial, racial, economic, "natural," and universally indigenous. In Australia, the vampire has been traditionally outsourced—to Britain or the USA. When it is developed for an international audience, Aboriginality is homogenized to a broader often magical, shamanistic, or pagan Indigenous Other. When it is represented in Australia, the Aboriginal vampire is caught up in images and ideologies of Australian fear rhetoric that implicitly fuel the home-grown Horror industry (Doig 2012, 115, 121). In a sense, Aboriginal vampires often become textual elements in the mise-en-scène as much as a destructive and predatory backdrop for Australian horrorscapes.

The Dreaming, as an ontological system or way of being for the Aborigines, is constituted by blood; it is a central symbolic and actualizing force, standing outside Western notions of time and space. Even in Dreamtime, blood often evokes lust, punishment, and violence through themes of life and death. By its very nature, it is both transformative and immutable. Vampire narratives are typically marked by transformation. Ken Gelder notes that the "fundamentally conservative" nature of the vampire is juxtaposed to its cultural adaptability "it can stand for a range of meanings and positions in culture" (1994, 141). This conservative-transformative paradox is also part of the Aboriginal vampire tradition; its mythic forms are often shape-shifters that through the metaphysics of the Dreaming are not meant to progress or change. James Craig Holte notes that vampire legends (mythologies) are expressed in a "multiplicity of forms" in various cultures "taking on different shapes and habits" (1997, xiii). Conversely, John Browning and Caroline Picart explain how pervasive the Western image of Dracula is in cultures "outside of England and America," positing "Dracula's transformation into a 'cultural body' and performance space ... wherein ideological tensions" exist (2009, x). Dreaming—as a multiplicative, telluric, ideological, and epistemological space—is often represented as vampiric, and helps constitute the Aboriginal vampire. It is a hybrid, politically charged, and codified. Gelder describes the longstanding codification of Dracula in intertextual terms, as "undercoded at times and overcoded at others" (1994, 64). He categorizes Aboriginal Australian vampires as "ethnic vampires" using the example of Van Diemen's Land (1994, 1) in a colonial framework through invader-catalyzed extinction of the Tasmanian Aborigines, replete with blood consumption (1994, 12). In any media, the Aboriginal Australian vampire is an adaptive shape-shifter, incorporating both classic Western vampire tropes and Aboriginal vampiric mythology.

The following analysis is a survey of the Aboriginal vampire from its Indigenous origin in oral tradition to print and film. The vampire of Aboriginal orality exists in Dreaming narratives as mythic and consumptive beings like the Namorrados and Yara-ma-tha-who. They are darker aspects of oral memory that have existed for tens of thousands of years. As Ong notes, "oral memory differs significantly from textual memory in that oral memory has a high somatic component" (2013, 66). He extends the idea of somatic memories to the physical embodiment of songlines and Aboriginal cultural practice (2013, 66). Indeed, Mudrooroo notes that the "ancestors of the Dreaming were artists transforming the land and using it as a page onto which to inscribe songs and stories" (1990, 39). The Aboriginal vampire represented by Indigenous authors in print is often the construction of an environment that inverts Self and Other through Dreaming metaphysics. In film, ironically, its somatic, multiplicative qualities are heightened by the replication of various vampiric images and ideologies, as well as through the orality and corporality of the medium. The somatic quality of Aboriginal myth has influenced the adaptive nature of Aboriginal vampires across an Australian milieu—which is racially and culturally politicized and polarized. Through this polarity, we find adaptive versions of the Aboriginal vampire existing concomitantly on a spectrum between more Western and more indigenized media forms and representations.

Aboriginal Vampire in Print

As a literary mode, genre has been viewed as a foreign medium in Aboriginal Australia (Mudrooroo 1990, 125–26). However, the transition from oral vampire myth to the generic vampire in print is easily identified. The image of the Aboriginal vampire created by Indigenous writers has existed in Australian adaptations since David Unaipon's 1924/1925 *Yara-ma-tha-who*. Other manifestations in print include folkloric writing, vampire encyclopaedias, children's "creature" alphabet-books, and non–Indigenous fiction—extending to digitized editions like Michael Dolf Craddock's *The Yara-ma-yha-who: An Australian Beasts Story* (2016). The "authenticity" of the Aboriginal vampire image is often lost in transmedial politics, exchanged for the mode or apparatus of production.

David Unaipon, the first published Indigenous author in Australia, translated oral Dreaming myths into English in the 1920s. Included in his volume, *Legendary Tales of the Aborigines*, is the story of the "Yara Ma Tha Who," a totemic being, which has been re-envisioned as the first Indigenous Horror story (Young 2011, 670). The tale is also considered a vampire legend. Unaipon describes the predatory, yet fangless monster that dwells in fig trees: "[He] sucks the blood from the victim [H]e does not try to suck all the blood from the body but leaves, sufficient to keep him alive.... [S]hould it happen three times ... he would become and resemble the Yara ma" (2006, 218–19). Read outside White Australian context, it is less about fear of the Other, but of the Dreaming Self. Widely cited, this story has been paratextually and intertextually used to create Indigenous vampire fiction. Unaipon wrote lesser-known myths that can be characterized as vampiric and cannibalistic. For example, the "Gherawhar" (a goanna totem), a monstrous spirit marked by transitions in ingestion and environment: "They became cannibals," and an "uncontrollable craving for flesh food took possession of them" (2006, 42–3). Another instance is the tale of the blood ritual of the "Mungingee"—which can be read in matrilineal and feminine terms.

Totemic, animistic, transformative qualities are prevalent features of Unaipon's vampires. Blood is both a part of horror, and a part of life. It incorporates contamination, but this contamination is contained within a heterogeneous Aboriginal culture (of many mobs and moieties), thus disrupting the standard foreign cultural exchange seen in Western vampires. Dark Aboriginal myths and legends spread to early settlers and colonial convicts, sometimes at the hands of Aborigines, who identified "all manner of strange skeletons, unearthly sounds from the swamp and frightening encounters as proof of the bunyips existence" (Holden and Holden 2001, 11). Vampiric Dreaming figures became adapted and incorporated into a secondary, Australian aesthetic or storytelling mode that is still practiced—a dilution of the

Dreaming. Unaipon's translation of oral myth is one source of Aboriginal vampire narratives.

When Raymond Gates wrote "The Little Red Man," he was experimenting with styles and forms of Horror (2011, Loc 4885). Marketed as an Australian vampire tale, the short story is an intertextual adaptation premised on Unaipon's Aboriginal "vampire legend" (Gates 2011, Loc 4858). In his afterward, Gates notes he found "what is reputed to be Australia's own vampire legend, Yara-ma-yha-who. I loved that this creature was so far removed from the creature of the night most of us know. Something vampiric, that doesn't fit into the stereotypical mould" (2011, Loc 4858). Gates' work is an excellent example of transmedial adaptation of the Aboriginal Australian vampiric form from Indigenous mythology. He uses the dark sun symbolism of Australian Horror tradition, which takes the place of the literary moon (or blood moon) in European vampire tales, to explore the transformation of an Aboriginal vampire (Ryan 2010, 23).

In Gates' story, the skin of the Yara-ma-tha-who is used to describe metamorphosis: Mark's "skin had taken on a pinkish hue" as if "touched by the sun," until he was "glowing like a friggin' radioactive tomato!" (2011, Loc 4544–4699). But, the sun also acts as a catalyst to transformation, again like the moon: "By the time Mark emerged, the sun had positioned itself directly above the fig tree.... Dusk had drained colour from the world.... The fig tree had taken on a sinister appearance" (2011, Loc 4694–4725)—implying the diabolical aspect of the fig totem. But, botanical descriptions of the fig by Mark, a scientist, are used to accentuate the scientific apparatus of horror. Indeed, undergoing transformation, Mark is unwell like Stoker's Lucy. The story evokes standard vampire tropes: coin-sized spots of blood ran along either side of his back. Red welts, like oversized mosquito bites, are the only evidence of the attack. Unlike Unaipon's vampire, the figure has teeth: "its mouth open to an impossible size. Mark's legs protruded from between its teeth" (2011, Loc 4784). Gates' use of repetitive, incremental acts of infection is reminiscent of Stoker, but also recalls Unaipon's three-stage transformation. Through contamination Gates gives the Yara-ma-tha-who subjectivity, highlighted by his label "The little red Mark," (2011, Loc 4818) which makes the human character both the adaptation of the Yara-ma-tha-who, the monster in the title, and a protagonist-victim. The vampire that Gates describes is an intertextual figure in a narrative that acknowledges its complex origins.

Like Gates, the vampire D. Bruno Starrs creates in his novel, *That Blackfella Bloodsucka Dance!*, is a hybrid, through paratext (intertext), medium, and content. He explores Aboriginal identity with vampire myth and metaphor in a contemporary setting, and in relation to cultural events. A cinema scholar, Starrs incorporates a filmic aesthetic. His title appears to draw from several texts: *Dracula*, the Indigenous urban Horror film *Black-*

fellas (1993), and Kim Scott's novel *That Deadman Dance!* (2010). Starrs also utilizes Dreaming narratives, and cites Unaipon's Yara-ma-tha-who (Starrs 2011, Loc 2984). He uses Gothic-parody and extensively references Stoker, yet notes that "[t]he world doesn't need any more lame Vampire fiction" (2011, Loc 3092). Western representations of vampires abound: "valiant Vampire Slayers"; "the seething mass of Vampires that were squealing and sizzling in the ankle deep Holy Water"; "the imaginary Vampire den" of the "Prince of Darkness" (2011, Loc 3149–3170). While simultaneously, the self-described "octoroon" or part-Indigenous protagonist (2011, Loc 103) transforms in an environment constructed through a female vampire's Dreaming, a figure akin to one of the wives of Dracula: "the dark elements of her fantasy would not expire, they fought for acknowledgement and supremacy" (2011, Loc 3118). Thus, Starrs plays on these two traditions in medium (form) and content. He makes the Dreaming vampiric in nature, a sempeternal and otherworldly contagion that transmits vampirism. Starrs calls this modern hybrid figure the "Aboriginal vampire," extending work by Unaipon and Mudrooroo (2014, 1, 3).

The critic and author Colin Johnson (aka Mudrooroo), who self-identifies as Aboriginal, builds a metaphor for colonialism through his Vampire Trilogy—*Undying* (1998), *Underground* (1999), and *Promised Land* (2000). To construct this vampire metaphor, he juxtaposes animistic and mythic vampiric qualities to classic tropes of the Western vampire: for example, shape-shifting totems, the "dark lord" and "Master," and a lustful, European, vampiress named Amelia. In *The Undying*, Amelia hypnotizes her Aboriginal victim to believe he is in the Dreaming. Within the trilogy, colonial bloodlust is explored through vampiric metaphor in Dreaming space, as well as political reality and Aboriginal context. But, his figure is incrementally developed with Indigenous myths of blood—seen earlier in Mudrooroo's *Kwinkan* (1993). The narrative "begins as mere reversal of dreamings," but becomes "an attempt to explore the relationship entirely" (van Toorn 1992, 110). The contemporary Aboriginal vampire is created through this process, and also reconstituted from ancient vampiric legends that exist in Dreamtime. Gerry Turcotte describes Mudrooroo's dualistic "textual metaphor" of the vampire and ghost, where colonialism is predatory and vampiric, and Indigenous figures are ghostly "absent" aspects of Terra Nullius (2005, 106).

They reinforce two reciprocal forms of the Aboriginal vampire, read through Indigenous subjectivity. Sixteenth-century Aborigines viewed Spanish whalers off the Western coast of the continent as ghostly deities. Ghosts and vampires in Mudrooroo are mirror representations of one another. The Aboriginal vampire is trapped in the fabric of the Dreaming, because the ghost metaphorically negates the Western vampire, yet mirrors it, as that ghostly deity.

Mudrooroo's novels use intertextual vampires that highlight the politics of transmediality. Within the narrative structure, "degree[s] of participation and co-creation" and the "stickiness" and "spreadability" of vampires is visible (Eder 2015, 76); colonial politics creates a forced cultural amalgam, or transcultural space, where violence necessarily happens as a result of that transgression of identity, for which the vampire is symptomatic. This is also inherently an aspect of the politics of Indigenous Australia.

Other vampires used as statements on colonialism in Indigenous texts include those in Philip McLaren's *Sweet Water, Stolen Land*. The novel is read by critics like Clark as a "Gothic-horror parody" that explores the "postcolonial vampire" (2013, 122–23). Like Mudrooroo, McLaren creates imagery reminiscent of Dracula's nautical voyage: "the wretched human cargo [that] knew little about colonies, except for terrifying rumours of black savages and strange animals that aided Satan's work in a new-fashioned hell" (McLaren 1993, 5). Conversely, Kim Scott's *Benang*, which examines the dark ravages of colonial horror, contains totemic metaphors that can be read as vampiric: for example, "a tree steeped in blood" like a wooden stake (1999, 187, 477–78). Blood is a recurrent theme in Scott's narrative. Clearly, the works of McLaren, Scott, and Mudrooroo constitute examples of transmedial adaptation of the vampiric image used as an ideological device.

In *Adapting Vampire Gothic to the Australian Landscape*, the author Jason Nahrung describes Aboriginal Australian vampirism through the "classic Gothic trope of vampire as invader," set within "stereotypes of the Australian landscape" (2007 27–32); such cliché is synonymous with Indigenous stereotype. He examines how "[e]lements of the Australian land" incorporate Aboriginal sacred sites with outback imagery "to either enhance or contrast those classic elements" of the "vampire Gothic landscape" (2007, 38). Adaptation is a key component of Australian and Aboriginal vampires. Nahrung notes, with "thoughtful adaptation, Australia can make a fitting backdrop for modern vampire stories" (2007, 40). For him, the Aborigine is still the Other of the Western or European vampire, but he also includes the Western Other as villain. Conversely, Starrs describes a transmedial, hybrid vampire in his essay "Writing Indigenous Vampires," a figure that has moved from orality to print to genre form.

Like other genres, Aboriginal vampire narratives tend to intertextually reference each other. The orality of Dreaming is a feature of the genre, incorporated as a stylistic element. It is manifested in the use of repetition, of mythic figures and tales like the Yara-ma-tha-who that have been adapted to fit a new cultural context, as well as italicized internal dialogue that usually depicts Dreaming narratives—for example, in Mudrooroo or Starrs. The Aboriginal vampire is an adaptation, and Dreamtime helps constitute the figure in print. Most critical reception to the Aboriginal vampire is entrenched in neo-colonial readings that limit the critical register of the figure, even as changing methods of publication and distribution increase the circulation of works by Indigenous Horror writers—often outside mainstream publishing. Increasingly, neo-colonialism has become an assimilated part of the Aboriginal vampire.

Vampire Adaptation in Film

In any culture, Jeffrey Weinstock states that "[t]he vampire film tradition is defined by generic hybridity," and its "films are inevitably intertextual" (2012, 16). Clearly, this is also a product of its collaborative construction between creators, critics, and consumers. The use of recurring images often sell to a viewership, or elicit a generic tradition, as echoes of past vampires and extensions based on new criteria.

The transmedial mechanisms at work in the formation of the cinematic Aboriginal vampire are similar to aspects of the structural model of characterization outlined by Eder et al. in 2010. In the production phase, big-budget films are often crafted for a foreign "target audience" (2010, 4), accentuating Western vampire tropes, amplifying clichés of supernaturalism, generalized hybridity, and exoticization of Aboriginal vampires, and homogenization of Aboriginality. At the reception phase, film critics affect how Aboriginal vampires are "understood, interpreted and experienced" (Eder et al. 2010, 4). Aboriginality itself is relegated to a set of "stylistic devices" (4) visible in the mise-en-scène that shape the figure through Romantic notions of wilderness and Otherness. Aboriginal vampires are embedded in dominant white discourse, and are broadly symptomatic of Australian "sub-cultures" that inherently politicize identity, constructed by caricatures of cultural space—like the dark side of Dreaming as dreams. At each stage, the vampire's iconography is collaboratively encoded. In filmic space, these transmedial mechanisms are often economically driven. Similarly, vampires have been commodified. Aboriginality has become a part of the myth-making faculty in the Australian Horror and vampire tradition (Strasser 1994, 4–5)—and as horrorrealism and supernaturalism, mythologized in popular culture.

Because there is no differentiated Aboriginal Australian vampire tradition in film in Australia, it is necessary to examine the white Horror and vampire tradition. Mark David Ryan notes "few" recent "horror films explore Indigenous Australian themes" (2008, 101). In "Australian Cinema's Dark Sun," Ryan summarizes the rise of the Australian Horror film genre: beginning in the 1970s, commercially backed in the 1980s, slipping into an underground movement in the 1990s, and experiencing a resurgence in the 21st century with "relative worldwide commercial success" (2010, 23–4).

Cinematic vampires have existed in Australia since the lost silent film *The Twins* (1923). There are pre-boom examples like *Thirst* (1979), *Outback Vampires* (1987), and *Bloodlust* (1992). The recent resurgence in Horror films has been "driven by intersecting international market forces, domestic financing factors and technological change," leading to "two tier" film production (Ryan 2010, 24). In 2010, Ryan describes an increase in micro-budget vampire films such as *In Blood* (2002), *Reign in Darkness* (2002), and *Bloodspit* (2008). A commensurate growth in big-budget Australian American ventures also occurred in this period, for example *Daybreakers* (2009) (31).

As Alan McKee has noted of the generic limitations of Aboriginality in Horror films, monstrous, mythic, Indigenous figures exist in Australian films like *The Last Wave* (1977), *The Howling III* (1987), *The Dreaming* (1988), *Kadaicha* (1988), *Zombie Brigade* (1988), and *Bedevil* (1993). The reason is complex. "Ozploitation films" like "'ocker' comedies, sexploitation and horror movies" (Ryan 2010, 24) readily use white clichés of Aboriginal culture to foster horror. There are few Aboriginal filmmakers and scriptwriters producing material (Smaill 2002, 141). This omission from the industry "maintain[s] exclusion of Aboriginal perspectives and realities" (2002, 141). In 2003, when Peter Krausz surveyed one hundred years of Australian film production, he found "a general avoidance of Aboriginal issues and a lack of any balanced representation of Australia's significant Indigenous population" (2003, 90). A decade later, Krausz notes an increase in the production of Aboriginal representation in Australian cinema and television (2013, 34). However, a lack is still apparent in Horror and vampire genres. Ryan notes "Indigenous Australian cultural capital such as Dreamtime myths and spirituality are popular tropes explored in numerous Horror films, including *The Last Wave*, and to a lesser extent *Picnic at Hanging Rock* (1979), *The Dreaming* (1988), *Kadaicha* (1988), *Zombie Brigade* (1988) and *The Min-Min* (1990)" (2007, 91). Additionally, *Min Min* (2012) is a short Horror film by Matt Bird about mythological beings called min min lights that terrorize trespassers of sacred sites in the Blue Mountains. *Kadaichi* (1988) is a lackluster commercial Horror film with vengeful Aboriginal spirits that are consumptive and destructive. The paucity of scholarship about Aboriginal vampires is a facet of the cultural conditions of Australia, as much as a mistranslation of what this vampire would look like in film.

Consider a few modern examples to illustrate the state of Australian Horror and Aboriginal vampirism. They exist on a spectrum from ultra low-budget (*Zombie Brigade*) to internationally funded blockbuster (*Daybreakers*). *Zombie Brigade*, also known as *Night Crawl*, and *Zombie Commando*, was one of the few Australian zombie movies in the 1980s. In "Aboriginal Horror Films," McKee calls *Zombie Brigade* "a complex (and confused?) film" (1997a, 121). The plot revolves around a troop of zombie-vampires made up of fallen soldiers that terrorize a community—in Lizard Valley. Local Aborigines use shamanistic magic to help fight the invasion, but they are ultimately contaminated and consumed with the town. As McKee notes, Aboriginality is "invariably linked to the supernatural," as "part of the horror genre" (1997a, 123). The Dreaming becomes a vehicle for vampires to consume the land, and white and Indigenous figures alike.

The 2009 film *Daybreakers* is a sci-fi dystopia in which vampirism has spread across the world and contaminated most of humanity. Those people that remain must be conserved, along with their blood, as the last resources. In this big-budget film, co-produced with Hollywood for a transnational viewership, Aboriginal Australian vampires are assimilated into a global gestalt. The apocalyptic setting, catalyzed by a mass-extinction event, recalls themes of eco-Horror—a common extension of the way Aboriginal vampires are read through wilderness.

General absorption of Aboriginal culture and vampires in Western and Australian films is also visible in *The Last Wave* (1977), released as *Black Rain* in the USA. In an article on forms of Horror in Australian cinema, Jonathan Rayner explores Aboriginality through the main character, who is plagued by apocalyptic visions of water that stem from "the magic of the Aborigines" and the Dreaming—as elemental aspects of the environment "and the Aborigines characterized as Other" (2005, 106). *The Last Wave* capitalizes on supernatural misinterpretations of concepts of the Dreaming and primal fear that often infiltrates Australian Horror films. Other films more directly reference the vampiric forms of Aboriginal myth. *Hunting for Shadows* (2016) incorporates Mythological Horror, adapting Dreaming figures into "ghoulish nightmares in the wilderness" (Hardy 2018). Consumptive or tenebrous creatures are Dreaming monsters like the Bunyips and Kadaitcha, or Quinkans. From oral tradition depicted in cave paintings around Quinkan (or spirit) country, the Imjin and Timara represent the split personae of the Quinkan. The darker, slender Imjin is suggestive of the Yara-ma-tha-who. Shadowy hands silhouetted on a tent at night, in the film, are reminiscent of vampiric winds of the Namorroddos combined with depictions of Yawk Yawk maidens as macabre sirens of the Dreaming, imbued with bloody, homicidal aspects of the Kadaitcha (executioner).

In film, the Aboriginal vampire is usually consumed by a classic vampire figure that is produced for a non–Indigenous audience, often for a non–Australian audience as well. The colonial representation of disembodied and preternatural horrors of the outback landscape is still connected to Aboriginal vampires, superimposed over the urban defilement of contemporary life. Vestiges of the authentic Aboriginal vampire are trapped in manifestations of ominous shadows, ancestral or spiritual figures, the dark sun, and Australian fear rhetoric.

Conclusion: Digitizing Aboriginal Vampires

The dilution and adaptation of the Aboriginal Australian vampire from oral myth to film increases through transmedia practice. Aboriginal vampires are represented in various capacities across these media. In print, vampires created by Indigenous authors often hybridize mythic Dreaming narratives and mechanisms with Stoker-esque qualities. Tinctured by Dreaming metaphysics, these vampires are used to play with authorial subjectivity. Non-Indigenous texts often represent vampires in line with Western traditions of autochthonism. Dreaming, which helps constitute the Aboriginal vampire in Aboriginal fictions, is reconceptualized for magical and supernatural purposes in much of the white tradition. In film, there is a lack of authentic Aboriginal vampire figures. Vampiric qualities are ascribed to Indigenous mythology and culture, and often adapted to a transnational audience. The paradoxical effect of transmedia practice and the adaptation process is to claim and reclaim, and redistribute narratives. In the context of the Aboriginal vampire, it amounts to an extension of the politics of transmediality as much as the politics surrounding Aboriginality.

There is potential in the literary vampire for film adaptation. However, Aboriginal vampires (as Horror figures) are largely unacceptable in both Indigenous and white production due to racial and economic tensions, influenced by power structures that dictate what is available. Aboriginal vampires characterized by Dreaming mythology are more often found in lower-budget films, small presses, or digital publications and releases. Digitization allows for non-mainstream representations to be circulated and produced. Through new media, Aboriginal Horror and vampiric figures are increasingly represented, which may offer a new repository of reproducible images and themes.

There is a clear movement, from types of vampirism that exist in Aboriginal orality to a hybrid form that incorporates Western vampires. In new media, Aboriginal vampires retain a reflection in land—trees, shadows, wind—and in ontological systems that become part of the mise-en-scène. Aboriginals describe the Dreaming and their subjective relationship to it through the photographic stills. In vampire fiction, the image encompasses the monstrous individual, their often-demonic totem, and the consumptive landscape. Aboriginal vampires are created by, and are a part of, the land, and this is obvious in various adaptations in print and film, but in different proportions across the spectrum. The constantly adaptive yet immutable quality of the figure, constituted in blood, resonates powerfully with the structure of the Dreaming.

"In need of vitamin sea"
The Emergence of Australian Identity Through the Eyes and Thirst of Kirsty Eager's Vampires

PHIL FITZSIMMONS

Introduction: Foundation and Form

This essay seeks to unpack the nature and associated symbolic meanings of the vampires in Kirsty Eager's *Saltwater Vampires* (2010). Eager's text still remains a bestselling text for young adults in Australia, roughly corresponding to a time period in which it became increasingly clear that this country's meta-narrative was itself in a state of flux. As a vampire narrative its emphasis is naturally linked to "the symbolics of blood" is already located in a "liminal position" (Stephanou 2014, 5). However, this Young Adult fiction is even more so in that it also lies between several intersecting urtexts related to the Australian context and its underpinning history. In particular Eager has used the destruction of the Dutch East India trading vessel the *Batavia*, which ran aground off the coast of Western Australia on the fourth of June 1629 as an entrée and mimetic foundation for her vampire narrative. As is often the case with historical narratives, and in particular vampire accounts, an initial destructive event then "fans forward, ... to become different moments of the one process of sensing" (Taussig 1992, 21). To further elaborate on this process and the context of this essay, "the connection between humans and vampires—whether constructed within fantasy, fiction, fandom or real-life emulation—is a symbiotic one, and one which is sustained by the umbilical cord of memory" (Bacon and Bronk 2013, 2). Wherever blood and memory are comingled in text, understanding the context is an imperative (Gilders, 2004). Therefore, as summarized in ensuing sections, in the Australian socio-historical and literary contexts the linking thread of actuality and memory is "the imperative of blood" (Brisbane 2009, 400), of which the *Batavia* disaster is the first recorded instance.

From Carnage to Culture: Foundational Aspects of Vampiric Mimesis

Up until recently the actual floundering of the *Batavia* in 1629 and the ensuing carnage was a little-known historical incident in the Australian metanarrative, with the exception of a select few maritime historians. It is only recently that the accounts surrounding this disaster have surfaced in which it has been realized that this entire event "made the sinking of the Titanic look like a Sunday school picnic" (FitzSimons 2011, 9).

The wreck of the *Batavia* was set in a nexus of an interlocking advances in Dutch ship design, explorative zeal and religious change, which gave birth to a peculiar mixture of colonialism and the corporatization of Southeast Asia. The discovery of the Spice Islands by the Dutch, with the subsequent exportation of exotic spices such as pepper, cloves and nutmeg back to Holland gave rise to the world's first multinational firm, the Dutch East India Company. Now emboldened with a "thirst for conquest and riches" (Rivers Editors 2016, 1) this company provided the means for the development of the "golden age of the Dutch Republic" (Dash 2002, 1). While on the one hand it was one of the most powerful empires of all time, it was also "destroying itself through religious zealotry, ... and the fervent embrace of a new creed: corporate power" (FitzSimons 2011, 1).

The *Batavia* was the first of an intended larger fleet that would bring Dutch colonizers to the Far East and return with their holds full of unimaginable wealth. It is in these first forays into the Great Southern Ocean, that the myth of the great unknown Southland, "Terra Australis Incognita," came into being. With only vague rumors of the continent's existence arising from the handful of captains who had found their way into this unchartered southern ocean, straying to far and to long in the southern latitudes before turning north to Spice Islands would appear to have been disastrous for many.

With "fragments of charts that were useless in the extreme, and all but useless navigational aids" (Dash 2002, 1) the *Batavia* ran aground on the Abrolhos Archipelago off the coast of Western Australia in June 4, 1629. Of all the wrecks in these waters in the 16th and 17th centuries, this particular maritime incident has become truly infamous, labeled as the story of an "Indian Ocean Anti-Christ" (Mead 2009, 557).

Following the initial grounding the Francisco Palseart, *Batavia*'s captain,

The Emergence of Australian Identity (Fitzsimmons) 179

left a group on board, including Jeronimus Cornelius, and with a group of soldiers, sailors and passengers managed to secure a precarious foothold on a nearby sandy atoll. Using a small sailboat, Captain Palsaert then sailed on to Java, Indonesia in order to secure a rescue. In the meantime Cornelius, named as an apothecary, took control of the survivors, and with a small cohort further separated the survivors and then killed 115 men, women and children. Palsaert returned on a larger frigate, and then proceeded to hang Cornelius after cutting off his hands. The testimony of those finally rescued, and from some who were later executed, was that all that ensued once the ship became snarled on the coral was gruesome in the extreme.

Goodwin (1986, 145) describes it as a "descent into rebellion and bestiality, full of brutality, rape, murder and torture, the lust for power, due to the weakness of those in command, and the unjust commercial and judicial power of the company that instituted the ill-fated voyage." It remains one of the bloodiest recorded first contacts with previously undiscovered lands in international seafaring history (Dash 2002). The absolute horror of this incident remains seared into the mind frames of specialist maritime historians up until this day.

However, as one reads further into the subsequent colonial history of Australia, it does not take long to realize that the same colonial ideology of violence which spawned the Batavian massacre took a firm foothold in Australia as a cultural pandemic with the arrival of the British in the 1700s. Indeed, in discussing the links between Dutch and British colonialism and lingering colonial remnants of British violence, Dwyer and Nettlebeck contend this relationship is insidious, and has now "become invisible, sanctioned in law and normalized as an aspect of everyday life" (2018, 14). This colonial violence was not by any stretch of the imagination invisible once the British arrived in 1770, followed by the First Fleet of convict outcasts in 1776. While nearly destroying this imperial force and its rag tag group of convicted criminals, albeit for many charged with petty crimes, the harshness of this driest continent on earth ensured an enduring struggle launching the myth of the outback desert survivor. Never divesting itself of the British pastoral view of the world, in which the land and indigenous communities were there for the taking, this mythic perspective was rampant for over two hundred years. Huggan (2007, 19) paints a bleak picture of this entire period, stating that "indigenous abuse occurred even into the late twentieth century in that there were grave human rights abuses, deaths in custody, serial rape, the forced removal of Aboriginal children, ... and the road to indigenous self determination firmly blocked."

Throughout this entire period, the "white settler voice" morphed into the Australian identity narrative of the "outback bushman soldier" during the Boer War in South Africa. This became further concretized in the bloodshed of young Australians in World War I, and in the narrative of the battlefield of Gallipoli. Unable to push back the Turks on the narrow beach, this military failure designed by British generals has become socio-culturally reframed and "recast into a 'baptism of fire' proving Australia's worth for nationhood, seeing in bloodshed the expunging of the convict stain and the birth of nation consciousness" (Porter 2005, 103).

This glorification of the Britishness of the Australian "bush man soldier" encouraged a celebration of the colonial contribution to Britain's global contribution, the embodiment of this progress in the bushman figure lent Australia its distinctiveness. In this "atavistic rough-hewn image lay the myth of the white Australian nativity. The mythology was problematic" (Hutchinson 2018, 105).

As the Antipodean "social imaginary" (Taylor 2004, 91) struggles "to come to terms with his colonial past, Aboriginal heritage and its new Asian orientation and multicultural identity" (Pursiegle and Macleod 2004, 4) a deep-seated sociocultural tension has arisen. To paraphrase Trigg, it is in these individual and national socio-psycho places and times of unknowing that "identity and time become bathed in a strange uncanny light" (Trigg 2012, xiv). It is precisely at such a time of unknowing or absence of knowing that monsters and vampires appear in a culture's narrative as a "construct and projection, the monster exists only to be read: the monstrum is etymologically that which reveals, that which warns, a glyph that seeks a hierophant" (Cohen 1996, 4).

From Paratext to Intertext: Threads of Blood and Bane

Every aspect of the historical account of the wreck of the *Batavia* has provided Eager with a "ring of truth" narrative platform that provides a logical account for the arrival of European vampires on what previous Dutch sailors and explorers had previously termed "Terra Australis Incognita" or "Unknown South Land." The grounding of the narrative in a "ring of truth" includes the use of the actual names of those involved in the mayhem, madness and excess of slaughter on the Abrolhos coral Islands: Cornelius, Zeevanck, Haas, Pelgrom. Although Cornelius is the leader, it is only much later in the text we learn that he is an old vampire and part of an ancient clan. Eager uses the Batavian slaughter event as a further "rhizome-like space where everything interconnects" (Eco 2014, 12), and as stated, overlaying and inserting vampires as the destabilizing force of "absence." As discussed in the following sections these vampires attempt to enter the new world by fusing death with life, creating an undead space where the living and the dead coexist. Eager fleshes out these spaces enlarging on vampire imaginaries through the use of two key themes: negating spaces of belonging and negating spaces of being.

Salt Water Vampires touches on critical details that make up the current shift of Australian narrative from the desert frames of people and places to "limitless horizons of the ocean" (Marin 1997, 7). Willem, a Goth with a Dutch background in this narrative, makes allusions to this when he makes the connection that vampires are behind the issues in the small coastal town: "The vampiric bite is not about the horror movie bullshit undead" (Eager 2010, 94). From the outset the previous connection of male-female fusion and reversal is continued as the reader is introduced to the head vampire on board the *Batavia*, Jeronimus Cornelius, who is first shown clinging to the bowsprit of the ship as the vessel is battered to pieces on the coral atoll by the gathering swell and dropping tide. Just as the initial paratextual illustration was a signpost of what was to come in this novel, so to this is an initial "can opener of meaning" (Fetterman 2009, 41) as it is a direct intertextual link to Géricault's preparation and subsequent painting of *The Raft of Medusa* (Huet 2007, 29). In this painting Géricault blended history and an artistic representation of the Medusa mythological figure.

The historical-textual linkage reveals a stunningly similar pattern to the wreck of the *Batavia* as Géricault's painting was a mythic representation of another shipwreck, subsequent mutiny and cannibalism. In the first few days of July 1816, the French frigate *Meduse* was on her way to formally re-establish French colonial rule in Saint Louis, Senegal, when it ran aground on the Arguin Banks off the coast of Mauritania. Due mainly to the incompetence of the ship's captain, this farcical attempt at navigation was then compounded when approximately 400 passengers boarded the ships launches, which then towed a ramshackle raft with 151 soldiers, sailors and some male passengers on board. The heavy seas and size of the raft made headway impossible and it was cut loose after several days. After thirteen days adrift, only ten survivors were left: cannibalism had taken a heavy toll. After interviewing several of the survivors, Géricault painted the *Raft of the Medusa*, which depicts three African slaves waving at a distant French ship, with a figure of the Medusa on the bowsprit overseeing the desperate scene. Obsessed with the ideas of pain, death and suffering in preparation for this painting and others, Géricault stole body parts from the local hospital. As Huet (2007, 29) contends, this painting has become an archetypal representation of male-death by the monstrous feminine as "art historians have long noted the figure of Medusa on the bowsprit." As the last vestige of the earth goddess, she resisted Greek order and religion. With the power of her gaze to turn men into stone, she is also representative of men's fear of castration and death. Although killed and beheaded by Perseus, her gaze was still able to turn men to stone. In this undead state, Medusa is the representation of the double-other, the monstrous feminine and an image of death. Frozen as a death mask, she was crying a silent scream in order to be heard above the removal of all boundaries, and in Géricault's painting she was a cry against the re-establishment of the brutality of colonial rule.

Also arising out of Géricault's painting, the bowsprit has become a metonymic extension of the female as evil. With the Medusa's head on the bowsprit in this artwork leading slaves back to their colonial captors, it has also become representative of the foundational support and mythological marker of colonial contamination. In Eager's text, this European and vampiric colonization becomes full blown contamination. The narrative sequences that immediately follow on from Cornelius' viewpoint from the bowsprit, are very closely aligned with the historical records of the final destruction of the *Batavia*. With the ship pulverized into wooden splinters the survivors become trapped on the coral atolls that at first appear as their salvation. Using the religious language and metaphor that echoes the blood-filled death of the Christ figure, Cornelius uses the associated baptism-resurrection of conversion when he cries out "the ocean has delivered me" (Eager 2010, 5). In this "born again" scene he "looks to the sky, a downpour, some sign from the heavens that should refuse the abomination contained in a flask, but all he saw was the bloated white face of the moon smiling down on him, mocking him in the sky with scolding clear its rabid mouth" (Eager 2010, 11). The abyss, ocean and moon triptych now connected, the space below is cast as a void or Hades (Rowlandson and Voss 2013). With the arrival of these new vampires the alignment of sea and moon are also portents of chaos or carnage (French 1972). Terra Australis is now a place of the limitless bounds of the undead, and as a new space for vampires, is a "birth of a new space, which mends as it ruins ... associated with castration and enigma of the female" (Botting 1995, 149).

With the captain of the vessel sailing away to find water and a safer haven, Cornelius "turns" three of the crew. This new cohort then separates the survivors, and begins to feast: "They made this circle of blood. The moon witnessed the slaughter that followed" (Eager 2010, 12). In mythological frames of thinking, "attention must be paid to the warnings of the moon" (Rowlandson and Voss 2013, 249). In only a few sentences after the initial killing has been completed, we find that this cohort of four "new arrivals" actually made it to the mainland of Western Australia by walking on the sea bottom, and after emerging from the ocean fed on only a few Aboriginal inhabitants. Given the harshness of the environment their new space was in that extremity or "in between" zone between the sea and a desert that stretches almost across the entire continent to the east. While the narrative makes it clear that the aridity and lack of sufficient food was not to their liking, Eager omits any details regarding ho how they travelled, when they arrived on the east coast and where they were for over four hundred years before arriving on the east coast. Just as this continent had remained silent for eons before their arrival so it remained silent after their arrival. This particular locational silence is deafening in regard to the implications it carries. In the first instance, in casting the commencement of this narrative of this new desolate and driest of all continents, Eager "returns to the original Gothic landscape, which is typically desolate and menacing" (Botting 1995, 2). The old world's ways of knowing now finds an even older world, one of an immense scale and limitless space in which the silence and displacement of the Medusa trope finds an opportunity for a new, wider voice.

In respect to this notion of space, Eager also uses the compressed narrative process of juxtaposing the historical background with the current context of her narrative. Running through transformational shifts between Cornelius's personal history, his treasonous act of drinking the blood of an ancient Dutch vampire, the floundering of the *Batavia* and the blood-lust assault on young people in Australia is the literal and implied notion of violence. In regard to the latter, shifts in historical focus, time and landscapes narratively carry the mythological and Gothic time-space ideals of invasion and war (Marin 1997). As another form of "doubling" the movement between these two narrative forms in *Salt Water Vampires* also melds the underpinning original Gothic trope of space and landscape with the historical shift in the meaning of the word "horizon." The original Gothic etymological semantic implication was related to notions of "limit, limit of the gaze and limit of sea and sky" (Marin 1997, 7). For the peoples who had begun to explore beyond the immediacy of their own shores, this linguistic mindset was formed in order to grasp the possibility of a place that transcended the known in which contained the "others." The attempt to make sense of the infinite involves the partition of the horizon so that space can be distinguished from anti-space, "here" can be separated from "there."

As has occurred in other narratives, through their short burst of rapacious appetite, the vampires in Eager's text also represent a focus on rampant capitalism and displacement of indigenous peoples. However, their initial foray in this new land, and subsequent long delay in arriving on the east coast of Australia was a "harbinger of category crisis" (Cohen 1996) that was to come. In their narrative movement from east to west, which in Australian literature has come to signify the shift in the national white misogynist and racist masculine centered narrative of desert survivor to a more open multicultural world view, these vampires were also pointing to a time when another European colonial power would arrive in the east with similar colonial ideals.

Eager's initial historical recount through to current day moves through several juxtapositions that reflect an ongoing narrative and social mimesis.

184 Asia and Australia

As also summarized briefly, a key missing ingredient is that once the cohort of vampires onto terra firma proper, only the briefest of mention is given to the indigenous inhabitants. The flourishing indigenous culture of 40–60,000 years prior to European colonization is completely negated. This Dreamtime culture in which history and geography are combined "is slow motion 'island time,' the singing into being of evolving landscapes through myths of transformation" (Cranston 2007, 253). In the backward and forward motion of Eager's narrative, the absence of Aboriginal voice is fully realized when it becomes clear that the first land of this cohort of Dutch vampires has become a closed cult centered in Sydney almost four hundred years later. The mutineer's base in Australia is in King's Cross, a red-light district where prey is easy to garner.

The interplay between historical fiction and vampire narrative reaches a critical focus point when the reader learns that the Cornelius is called "the apothecary" and that his vampiric evolution commenced in Amsterdam in 1628. At that time, he was an apprentice vampire who drained the blood from a 500-year-old founding member who was in some form of frozen state, and took it with him on the *Batavia*. With the Batavian-based vampires, called Mutineers, now a global entity in open revolt with the older founding group, the enmity between them reaches a new level when Cornelius remerges in the older European city. In order to achieve ongoing immortality and a more powerful form, he once again returns to Amsterdam to steal more blood of this founding vampire father. In Eager's text, the "ancients" can die if their blood, termed amp, is completely drained. The narrative thread of this book centers around the search for the vial of amp that was in the hands of the Batavian vampires, and after it has been stolen by newly and accidentally turned young Australian surfers living in a narrow-minded small town as outcasts. Their hedonistic drug taking lifestyle does not fit with most townspeople. Interestingly, it is made clear that an eyedropper of amp has the effect similar to cocaine. In parallel to the surfers who crave to be on the water, the core group of Mutineers are now forced to live under water in order to escape both the light of sun during the day, and avoid detection from the ancients. The Mutineers have become just as marginalized as the surfers who are have secreted the last vial of amp and are now seeking to destroy them as well.

As outlined in the introduction to this section, it would appear that narratively Eager has reintroduced another mirroring effect in that the vampires who instigated a global network are now the marginalized. Those which destroyed are now on the verge of being destroyed, which eventually occurs within the crashing waves of the east coast of Australia: a counterpoint to their beginning. Just as the Mutineers began with extreme violence, which in many ways pointed to their demise, so too the remnants of the British colonizers are on the same path. While it may seem counterintuitive, the multifaceted violence wrought on the Australian landscape and on the indigenous people has a deep-seated and long running socio-psychological effect and affect. Termed the "colonial mirror effect" by Banivanua-Mar (2007, 33), this process is enduring enaction of memory and deeply held tacit beliefs in which the underlying institutional elements of "civilization sniffs out the enemy, uses smell against itself in an orgy of imitation" (Taussig 1992, 67).

Just as the vampire is an emblematic code that "allows the past its eternal return" (Cohen 1996, ix) because the human condition seems incapable of learning from its history, so too the vampires in Eager's book are both representations of the British colonial "war of extermination" (Ishiguro 2017, 130) as well as "grotesque mirrors for disturbed inner states" (Botting 1995, 109). While it has only recently been acknowledged that violence was a key force in colonial spheres, an even more recent realization is that it is still an ongoing issue. With the notion that violence was the core operational force in all colonial settings given little attention, even less research has been paid to its actuality and long-term effects whereby initial realty became an all-encompassing world view. It is only relatively recent realization that such was the nature of colonial power in Australia that brutality morphed into "symbolic violence" (Bourdieu, 1991), becoming embedded in the entire fabric of social, legal and religious institutions, long after British power appeared to wane and disappear.

However, the concept of violence was not just a leftover institutional framework; more importantly, several researchers have come to the conclusion that the ideal of violence has become a melded component and social force despite centuries after Australia was discovered, or as indigenous Australians believe, invaded. As Rojas (2001, 111) notes, the "process that made 'civilization' an element of the national self-consciousness of the West was the same process that authorized violence in the name of civilization. The self-consciousness of civilization authorized bringing civilization to others by violent means." Césaire believes that this original colonial underpinning of subjugation through extremely violent means had the same psychological effect on those seeking to take control of the land and its indigenous peoples. "The de-civilization and brutalization of the colonizer colonization works to *decivilize* the colonizer, to *brutalize* him in the true sense of the word, to degrade him, to awaken him to buried instincts, to covetousness, violence, race hatred, and moral relativism" (2000, 2).

In linking the concept of the monster in general to its symbolism in narrative, Botting makes the connection that "the disturbing parts of human identity became the stock devices. Signifying the alienation of the human subject from the culture and language in which s/he was located, these devices increasingly destabilized the boundaries between psyche and reality, opening up an indeterminate zone in which the differences between fantasy and actuality were no longer secure" (1995, 8). The vampires in Eager's text highlight the historical threads of fabrication that exist in the Australian metanarrative, which unless acknowledged and reframed will only server to engender insecurity.

Conclusion

The vampire in literature has always been a metaphoric constructionist and a constructivist marker relating to how humans are unable to make sense of their world and have created or wandered into a liminal zone of their own making. Thus like "a letter on the page, the monster signifies something other than itself: it is always a displacement, always inhabits the gap between the time of upheaval that created it and the moment into which it is received, to be born again" (Cohen 1996, 4). The vampire is the penultimate social semiotic. The very nature of its actions, deeds and being beckons us to realize that everything we know is a social product, that all our words, worlds, concepts, and ideas were created and passed along by people at various times and places (Berger & Luckmann, 1966), all with the same ongoing faults and failings.

Like all human failings, the problem with the lingering vestiges of colonialism is that unless the remnants of the "symbolic violence" underpinning every language form and institutional component it created are confronted erased, the anxiety and fear grown out of ignorance will compound exponentially. The shift in the Australian social imaginary from one littoral zone to another, with an absence of recognition of the violence that had occurred in the interior, has and will lead to an ignorance of the interior of self. The salve of the sea, which looms large in the "national imaginary, ... and where the most significant events in their lives occur" (Zeller and Cranston 2007, 21, 22) could once again be a boundary encircling the "vulgarization of the island" (Devanney 1994, 29).

Globalism: Real and Virtual Worlds?

The Ecohorror of *The Strain*
Plant Vampires and Climate Change as a Holocaust

TATIANA PROROKOVA-KONRAD

Introduction: The Vampire After 9/11

In their book *Monstrous Nature: Environment and Horror on the Big Screen* (2016), Robin L. Murray and Joseph K. Heumann (2016) underline the important role that the vampire plays in horror films, claiming that "[t]he vampire has served as one of the most prevalent monsters of focus since the inception of the horror film genre" (44). The vampire is, indeed, one of the most popular horror characters. The creatures that live in the dark and suck human blood are easily recognized by viewers worldwide, and, therefore, are frequently used by filmmakers. Yet, since Tod Browning's classical portrayal of a vampire in *Dracula* (1931), this monster has undergone a considerable transformation. This essay explores one of the most recent portrayals of the vampire in the TV show *The Strain* (2014–2017), and argues that in response to multiple ecological concerns that have become particularly urgent in the post-9/11 era of climate change, the vampire transforms into an eco-monster that humanity has to fight. To specify, the new type of a vampire is a monstrous plant that illustrates the mutation of the natural world. Through the new image of the vampire, *The Strain* explores the relationship between humanity and nature, primarily characterizing it as colonization and war.

Multiple scholars have already commented on the irrevocable consequences of 9/11 on the United States and the global world in general from military and political perspectives, yet cultural production has largely transformed since the terrorist attacks, too. For example, numerous cinematic texts have been decoding messages about good and evil employing the painfully familiar scenario of 9/11; Terence McSweeney labels such texts as "challenging 'remakes' of September 11th 2001" (2014, 136). Yet, the post-9/11 era is affected not only by the terrorist attacks but also by other crises. Anna Froula writes, "The aftermaths of 9/11 have compounded chaos in warzones and increased national and international surveillance. They intersect with crises in climate change and infrastructure readiness (or lack of readiness), global hunger, increasingly hypertoxic environments, and 'superbugs,' such as the Zika virus. Such intersections suggest a wider scope of 'post-9/11 texts[apost]'" (2016, 113). The horror of the 21st century is so diverse and multifaceted that the traditional monsters that audiences worldwide are used to undergo fascinating metamorphoses to speak politically and reveal the horrors of our current world. The vampire is one of such "tools" through which the genre of horror can communicate crises, including climate change. Kevin Wetmore notes that the "post–9/11 world—fraught with terrorism, war, disease, financial meltdowns, and global climate change—proves an extremely fertile ground for vampire films" (2017, 86).

Imagining the vampire today is a process that differs considerably from how it was a century ago. *The Strain*, for example, on the one hand, invites the viewers to meditate upon the problem of climate change through this traditional monster; yet, on the other hand, it illustrates the transformation that the vampire is literally forced to undergo at a time of ecological decline. Moreover, through the eco-representations of the vampire, the series inevitably comments on the risks of the transformation of the human body, too. Selmin Kara argues: "while recent examples of eco-cinema often project the anxieties related to this new epoch on terminal landscapes ravaged by human activity, a small cluster of films evoke an Anthropocene imaginary at the metabolic level, showing the impact of ecological change on human bodies" (qtd. in Froula 2016, 114). In *The Strain*, this deadly effect is depicted in two ways. First, the vampire who, as this essay argues, represents a monstrous plant, is physically transformed—as can be noticed, for example, in its skin color and a special appendage for biting. Second, the human being him/herself is transformed, once having been bitten. Yet this transformation is enabled not exactly because of the bite but rather because of the parasitic worms that the vampire transmits. Vampirism is thus displayed as a form of an (almost) inevitable disease that the human faces at the time of the environmental transformation and ecological decline.

Interpreting the vampire as a mutated plant or an eco-monster helps us understand the cultural treatment of climate change. Focusing on the transformation of perhaps one of the most traditional monsters on screen, *The Strain* attempts to reveal the intricacy of the current environmental problems. Mutation as the key process that characterizes the existence of vampires and humans stands for larger cultural and ecological anxieties of humanity today, when literally everyone/everything has to adjust to the changing environment.

The Strain *as Plant Horror*

The Strain accurately follows the traditions of ecohorror, i.e., horror that "deals with our fears and anxieties about the environment" (Tidwell 2018, 115), although it might be not so easy to grasp that at first sight. The series starts with a mystic yet horrifying event in New York: a landed plane is suspected to be infected with an unknown virus, for everyone on board is dead. Dr. Ephraim Goodweather (Corey Stoll) is asked to investigate the case. As he and his team soon realize, the virus does not kill people but rather turn them into vampires. The virus starts to spread throughout the city, while the main characters attempt to prevent the apocalypse.

The vampire evidently portrays evil in *The Strain*, for it poses a threat to the very existence of humanity, whereas humanity is represented as a (potential) victim. Whether this relationship is so transparent, however, can be questioned once having deconstructed the image of the vampire. I interpret the concept of the vampire in *The Strain* as a metaphor for the ecological decline. This reading, however, complicates the straightforward classification of vampires as evil, positioning them, as victims, too.

Humanity's exploitation of nature, climate change, and the irrevocable transformation of the environment are among humanity's most urgent problems today. Various cultural artifacts analyze these issues, providing unique views on the role of humanity in the emergence of current ecological problems. Crucially, in *The Strain* it is Nature that gives birth to the vampires. The audience finds out about the existence of the so-called Master—the father of all vampires (or, as they are usually referred to in the series, *strigoi*). The Master is an ancient evil existing in soil and primarily constructed of worms. The worms can be interpreted as a mechanism of reproduction, a weapon or a means to infect, and as life-sustaining substance, for with the help of the worms the Master can create new vampires, he can fight humans, turning them into vampires, and, he can prolong human life, transforming the worms/his blood into an elixir of eternal youth. Using the worms as the vampire's key weapon, *The Strain* not only plays with the issue of parasitism—the pattern frequently used by 21st-century ecohorror that "draw[s] upon our fear of parasites" (Larsen 2017, 60) in order "to effectively entertain and simultaneously horrify the audiences" (61)—but it also directly connects the vampire to nature, presenting the monster as part of the natural world. Moreover, the Master can be interpreted as Nature itself, for he is the creator of the vampires. Yet, crucially, while Nature is usually characterized as female through its life-giving function, *The Strain* reveals what happens once Nature mutates due to the wrongdoings of humanity—it becomes aggressive, terrifying, and masculine/male.

Infecting humans with parasitic worms that originally live in soil, Nature/the Master creates monsters that suck human blood with the help of their throat appendages. Yet I contend that the green color of these vampires, the form of their throat appendages that closely resembles flowers, as well as the "blood" of the vampires that looks like white-green juice, turn the vampire into a mutated plant. Such an interpretation does not necessarily refute a conventional understanding of the physical appearance of the vampire: "The physical representation of the vampire is traditionally human in nature, making it familiar and relatable, the mythic lore malleable enough to adapt to a wide range of rapidly changing cultural, social, and entertainment needs, evidenced by the survival of the undead in the western consciousness since Bram Stoker put ink to paper" (Peacock 2015, xviii). Rather, it adds another dimension to our understanding of the vampire in the age of climate change.

The vampire in *The Strain* has been strikingly misinterpreted as "just" monsters, whose portrayal is not even complex enough to call them vampires:

> In *The Strain*, the central concept defining the character of the vampire is its monstrousness. These creatures are clearly designed as physically repugnant mutants, bearing more of a resemblance to zombies, or evocative of aliens, as the most characteristic feature of vampirism, that of sucking human blood, is carried out by means of an absolutely repulsive artificial second tongue. Apart from this aspect, the definition of the vampire character in *The Strain* is extraordinary weak, as the main plotlines depict them as living dead creatures with no ability to feel or express anything and with no sign of self-awareness [Pérez and Canet 2018, n.p.].

While I completely refute this argument, I speculate that this difficulty to define the new type of a vampire lies in rather controversial views regarding the ecological decline today, and climate change in particular that is still considered a myth by many and is thus frequently not recognized as a powerful and important pattern in cultural narratives.

Why is the new vampire depicted as a plant? Natania Meeker and Antónia Szabari interpret plants as follows: "plants have been defined as defective and incomplete beings. In their position as 'lower' life-forms, plants are subject to being manipulated and consumed by humans who accordingly impose their own goals on them (by cultivating them as food, decoration, shelter, and commodities, among other things)" (2012, 33–34). The powerlessness of plants has drawn attention of numerous filmmakers who experimented with this issue, inviting the audience to imagine what might happen once plants are given the power that they seem to lack. The monstrous plants that one can view in plant horror have been frequently linked to the problem of ecological decline.

Angela Tenga, for example, claims that "[t]he association between the vegetal world and horror" (2016, 56) can be interpreted as a manifestation of "fears of ecological and environmental crises" (2016, 57). Agnes Scherer summarizes the cultural portrayals of monstrous plants into one definition: "The typical 'monster plant' is almost the opposite of a plant: it grows rapidly, often menacingly so; it walks around and chases its human victims with snatching arms like a predator; it often sucks their blood or eats them, occasionally with a mouth full of fangs; and sometimes it even wants to merge with the human body" (2016, 31). Therefore, the invasion of plants is viewed as "an absolute rupture not only of normality (as always happens in horror), but of the entirety of the known world and its fundamental structuring rules" (Keetley 2016, 22).

Interpreting the vampire from *The Strain* as part of nature, a (monstrous) plant, on the one hand, expands the cultural understanding of a vampire. From a "traditional" vampire that is described as "a reanimated corpse that rises from the grave to suck the blood of living people and thus retain a semblance of life," we now move to explore the potential of a vegetal vampire, which only underscores that "[t]hat [the previous] description certainly fits Dracula, the most famous vampire, but is only a starting point and quickly proves inadequate in approaching the realm of vampire folklore. By no means do all vampires conform to that definition" (Melton 2015, 3). Yet on the other hand, a metaphorical portrayal of a vampire as a plant opens a pivotal discussion on climate change and the role of humanity in the destruction of nature. Considering the fact that "the vampire is most commonly viewed as a symbol of sin, temptation, Satan, and even God" (Peacock 2015, xix) is crucial when attempting to understand the relationship between nature and humanity as portrayed in ecohorror. The vampire as a sin is a figurative projection of what humanity has been doing to nature and the environment, exploiting, using, and destroying the natural world that we all live in. Hence, what we see in *The Strain* is "how our exploitation of the natural world may come back to bite us in unexpected but direct ways" (Murray and Heumann 2016, 41). Murray and Heumann argue: "The direct relationship between environmental exploitation and a destructive nature comes to the fore in the vampire film, when the living dead literally arise from the grave" (2016, 42). Humanity's exploitation of nature can itself be compared to a form of vampirism, for "vampirism most readily compares with consumption, a greed for resources, land, and blood that separates humans from the natural world that provides their home" (Murray and Heumann 2016, 42). In this respect, my interpretation of the vampire bite "as a means of feeding, i.e., sucking blood, or as a way of turning the victim into the vampire" (Prorokova 2017, 161) can be applied to both human vampirism toward nature and the vampirism of mutated nature toward its main offender, humanity.

While "[t]he direct relationship between blood, soil, and vampires is overlooked in most representations of vampires in popular culture" (Murray and Heumann 2016, 43), it is, indeed, crucial in *The Strain*. Through this relationship, *The Strain* directly addresses the problem of ecological decline. The series introduces Nature as both life-giving and life-taking. Humans are depicted as victims in the series, yet it is difficult to confidently claim that the audience fully sympathizes with them. The viewer traditionally identifies with the characters that are like him/her; in *The Strain* these are obviously the humans (and not the vampires). And while we realize that the vampires are the humans' enemy, it is still hard to classify them as traditional evil. *The Strain* suggests that humans are directly connected to that evil—humans *gave birth* to it. Consider, for example, the complex relationship between Dr. Goodweather's son Zach (Max Charles) and his mother, Kelly Goodweather (Natalie Brown) who was turned into a vampire. Despite her being a "monster," she remains Zach's mother, for the Master preserves maternal feelings and intellect in her. She searches for her son, hoping to keep him away from his human father. In turn, Zach continues to treat his mother as a parent and not as a monstrous being. He does everything to reunite with her and finally chooses her over his father. While the relationship between Kelly and her son can be interpreted in multiple ways, I suggest considering it a metaphor for the connection between humans and the ecological decline. We are directly connected to nature, and the mutated natural world is the new environment that we will ultimately have to adjust to. It is, therefore, crucial that while everyone else is trying to fight *against* the new "nature," Zach is the only one willing to *accept* this new reality, instead of considering it abnormal and dangerous for humans. Thus, "the eco-trauma associated with a lost connection with nature and a shattered human ecology" (2016, 42) discussed by Murray and Heumann is viewed in *The Strain* from an interesting perspective: the trauma as the main characteristic of the unfolding reality is stark, yet there are ways to overcome it by means of accepting the unwanted transformation.

The Strain is a vivid example of ecohorror that illustrates what happens when "a damaged Earth fights back, turning humans into vampires and ghouls, literal monsters that concretize monstrous treatment of the natural world and magnify the actual consequences of environmental exploitation" (Murray and Heumann 2016, 42). Yet it is also a *vampire* horror film; thus, the exploration of the body in it is inevitable. While "in horror to be human is to be above all a body, and hence materially vulnerable—to fears and pleasures alike" (Austin 2012, 99), in plant horror these traditional concepts are distorted. It happens due to the very connection between humans and vampires/nature. Scholars claim that "while plants have nothing of the human within them, humans all contain a little something of the vegetal order: the nutritive faculty is present in the human life principle (*psuchē*), while intellect and desire are not present in the plant" (Meeker Szabari 2012, 36), thus underlining the direct connection of humans to plants. Therefore, bearing in mind my contention that the vampire in *The Strain* is a monstrous plant, I claim that the humans in the series are directly connected to the evil embodied by the vampires. Through these connections, *The Strain* skillfully and persuasively outlines the similarities between the humans and the vampires, making them part of one world, insisting on the co-existence of the two and the necessity of adaptation—something that is rarely done in traditional vampire films but is, indeed, key in vampire ecohorror. The series constantly reminds us that "human desecration of the Earth may create the very monsters that drink their blood" (Murray and Heumann 2016, 42). And just like in Roger Corman's *The Little Shop of Horrors* (1960) "[n]ature can make some outrageous demands, as when the plant with a taste for blood ... insists that the hero, Seymour (Jonathan Haze), feed people to it" (Kawin 2012, 80), in *The Strain*, where nature is transformed due to the actions of humanity, the border between the life-giving and life-taking functions of nature is diluted.

The Strain directly deals with "the real trauma humans experience when their earthly home is destroyed, illustrating the sometimes horrific effects environmental degradation may have on humanity" (Murray and Heumann 2016, 42). Yet it also straightforwardly explores the problem of physical degradation of the human being *and* the plant as a representative of the natural world. Hyun-Jung Lee makes an interesting observation:

> The dead body, as the final excrement of life and the ultimate reminder of the ego's eventual extinction, is where the abject becomes infinitely potent: eliciting the most visceral reactions, the human corpse perpetually draws and repels our gaze. Reading the un-dead vampire in terms of abjection therefore uncovers intense struggles over the limits and conceptions of self, as well as over the troubling split between dreading death and desiring it. The vampire as animated corpse, material death circulating among the living, and liminality incarnate is a figure *characterized by* its equivocal, composite nature [2016, 31; italics in original].

The vampire in *The Strain* can, indeed, be read as an "animated corpse," for technically these are infected humans. However, interpreting the series from an eco-critical slant, the vampire is not a dead human but rather a mutated plant. Examining the eco-vampire from the perspective of "abjection"—the term that Lee borrows from Julia Kristeva, who, in turn, characterizes "abjection" as "that which does not 'respect borders, positions, rules' ... that which 'disturbs identity, system, order'" (qtd. in Creed 1986, 45)—is helpful here. While Kristeva tries "to explore the different ways in which abjection, as a source of horror, works within patriarchal societies, as a means of separating the human from the non-human and the fully constituted subject from the partially formed subject" (Creed 1986, 45), *The Strain* moves the concept of abjection even further. The series certainly explores the relationship between the human and the vampire from the position of life/death. But, even more importantly, it attempts to uncover the difficulties for the co-existence of the two once the vampire is not a living dead but rather a *mutated* being. The vampire as abjection thus turns into a signifier of our (un)readiness to interact with the evolving world.

The series explicitly poses the question of whether humanity is ready to accept the mutated environment, and if yes then to what extent. It gives the answer through different human characters: some do not see these creatures as monsters while others start a war against them. In doing so, *The Strain* opens a much broader and much more serious discussion on ecology and the environment, on our (in)ability to adapt, and on the issue of home. Whether it is "the connection between soil and home and … their link to ecology" (Murray and Heumann 2016, 43) that stands for Nature's home (the vampires are born from worms that live in soil), or the new world of humans that is invaded by the mutated Nature, home is crucial to our understanding of the environment that unites humans and plants but not separates them. *Co-existence* thus seems to be one of the most important issues that *The Strain* explores, attempting to deal with the current ecological crisis.

Climate Change as a Holocaust

Described as "the vampire apocalypse" (Peacock 2015, 102), *The Strain* plots a possible scenario of what humanity might deal with when mutated nature dominates. Exploring the reasons for the vampire invasion, the series questions the actions of human beings toward both nature and themselves. It does so referring to the most recent wars as well as resurrecting the memories of the atrocities committed during World War II, specifically through the images of the atomic bomb and concentration camps.

Allen Thompson (2009) claims:

> Through the last decades of the twentieth century we became accustomed to the idea that human beings are responsible for the extinction of this or that particular species of plant and animal, the destruction of one or another irreplaceable local or regional ecosystem, and more generally a significant loss of global biodiversity. But part of the threat posed by global warming appears to be something else—a threat to the entire world of nature. The sense that many people have is of an impending apocalypse. Not unlike the threat of a nuclear holocaust during the Cold War, global warming has aroused profound concerns about the future of humanity and the planet as a whole [80].

The apocalypse that climate change is frequently equated to is an equivocal term to deal with. On the one hand, it underscores the scale of the climate change issue. Yet on the other hand, the portrayals of an inevitable end of the world not only reduce the potential of humans to minimize the effects of climate change, but they also risk introducing a pattern of non-action, as action is seen as ultimately leading nowhere.

Yet the apocalypse that *The Strain* displays to its audience differs from the images that other dystopian narratives have already offered. *The Strain* attempts to illustrate the environmental apocalypse as a catastrophe similar to the ones that humanity has already witnessed in history. In doing so, the series by no means reduces the significance of climate change; rather, it attempts to communicate the problem that Amitav Ghosh (2016) wittingly characterizes as "unthinkable," discussing the difficulty to imagine the ramifications of climate change, through the familiar atrocities committed by certain people in order to dominate or exterminate other groups of people. While *The Strain* makes references to the most recent military interventions of the United States in the Middle East, it is through the images of World War II that the series most skillfully constructs the horror of climate change.

The connection to World War II is continuously shown in the series through the character of Abraham Setrakian (David Bradley) who, as the audience learns from various flashbacks, encountered the Master and other vampires while he was a prisoner in one of the Nazi camps. Yet the World War II subplot fully develops only in the fourth and final season of the series. The third season ends with Zach detonating a nuclear bomb, thus "avenging" his father who has murdered Zach's mother in self-defense. Because the explosion ultimately obscures the sun, the vampires can walk freely during the day. In the fourth season, the audience witnesses how the group of humans attempts to confront the vampires. The vampires are now depicted as a powerful dictatorial group. Calling themselves "The Partnership," they propagandize the necessity of the human/vampire collaboration for the preservation of a peaceful co-existence. The humans are forced to donate their blood to feed the vampires. They queue in longer lines to perform their new duty, and those with the B+ blood type are considered particularly precious; women with this blood type are even forced to breed to eventually "produce" more of this delicacy. In addition to that, the vampires build "farms" that will be used to quickly and regularly emulge blood from the humans. These farms overtly stand for the concentration camps used by the Nazis during World War II. Yet they also remind one of slaughter houses for animals. Through these camps, *The Strain* opens a serious discussion of how humanity treats nature. The reference, even if only metaphorical, to the problem of animal abuse is powerful in the series because of the reversal of the roles: the vampires (that I discuss in this essay not necessarily as evil but rather as part of the natural world) exercise full power over humans, slaughtering them for food. In doing so, *The Strain* invites the viewer to look at the problem of animal abuse through the eyes of the victim. Moreover, portraying the slaughter houses as concentration camps, the series openly claims that the abuse of nature is as horrifying as the actions of the Nazis toward selected groups during World War II. *The Strain* compares the two events, thus suggesting that the destruction of the environment is a holocaust that humanity commits toward nature.

The viewer, indeed, considers the vampires in *The Strain* as repulsive and dangerous beings. Primarily because of the means by which they infect the others, i.e., the worms, or rather, as the audience views them, parasites. "While biologists would agree that parasites are a necessary part of our biosphere, the general public tends to view parasites as complicated, dangerous, and deadly" (Murray and Heumann 2016, 125). Yet what this series most successfully illustrates is how "[h]umans may also become like parasites when their hunger for flesh and resources grows voracious" (145). This is certainly achieved through the references to the military invasions by the Nazis during World War II, as well as the use of a nuclear bomb by Americans—another terrifying event that became part of World War II. Humanity's actions toward nature that lead to its mutation and destruction are overtly linked to the consequences of the Holocaust and the use of the Atomic Bomb during World War II—some of the most horrifying events in the human history—in order to convey the seriousness of the problem, illustrate its scale, and draw everyone's attention to the inevitable ramifications that we all will have to deal with. In doing so, *The Strain* becomes one of the few examples to successfully communicate the issue of climate change—the issue that we either refuse to discuss at all or simply do not know how to do that.

Conclusion

The vampire as one of the most popular monsters in the horror genre has been largely exploited to discuss various issues pertaining to sexuality, masculinity, power, body, and many more. Yet in the age of climate change, the vampire as a cultural phenomenon acquires a new dimension, being able to tackle the questions related to the ecological decline. *The Strain* is an excellent example of how the vampire with its traditional characteristics related to decay, fear, and death can be used in order to discuss the problem of the changing environment, mutating plant and animal species, and fading ecology. Making the vampire part of the world that we all live in, the series effectively discusses the multifaceted nature of evil, arguing that it is not necessarily supernatural but rather it is very real and around us; moreover, it is evil that we crafted ourselves with our own wrongdoings.

Portraying the vampire as a monstrous plant, *The Strain* makes a valuable contribution to the discussion of the vampire in general and of the horrors of climate change in particular.

Drawing on the horrors from World War II, including the dictatorship of the Nazis, prosecution of certain groups, existence of concentration camps, and the use of a nuclear bomb, the series makes a laudable attempt to deal with the problem of ecology and the environment that culturally and cinematically has proved to be hard to imagine. While using vampires to discuss climate change might seem far-fetched and almost disrespectable with regard to such a serious issue, *The Strain* demonstrates how through the use of familiar villains and historical calamities one can effectively talk about such an "invisible" phenomenon as climate change, helping general audiences imagine the scale of the problem, educating them about the issue, and spreading eco-awareness. This, along with direct actions aimed at minimizing the ramifications of climate change, is humanity's primary task today.

"Set to drain"
Vampirism as Mechanic and Metaphor in The Elder Scrolls IV: Oblivion

TREVOR DODGE

Popular culture seems to have always had it out for the vampire. The vampire is almost always an expression of a kind of Otherness that doesn't dramatically deviate from the way vampires have largely been presented in other media, an Otherness that is, yes, physically and even emotionally menacing, but also an Otherness that is out of joint with most official notions of community. The vampire, most of the time, is an expression of an extreme individualism that doesn't ultimately derive its identity from within a tribe; the vampire is often a radically isolated individual whose existence is a direct threat to the official culture's idea of community, and might especially be threatening to any existing or emerging expression of a global community.

In plenty of vampire novels, films, comics, and television programming, there is usually some portrayal of a grand clash of civilizations, wherein a radical individual must not just be contained, but erased entirely from existence. This is something we see happening in the pages of Bram Stoker's *Dracula*, where the title character of Stoker's epistolary novel is the only major character in the book not allowed to speak (or write) directly for themselves; everything we come to know about the Count is relayed to the reader via the wide variety of epistles created by *other* characters in the book, all of which begin because there is a foreign national (the Count) who wants to buy himself a healthy chunk of proper English real estate. Any physical/emotional menace the Count might pose, then, is in addition to the most menacing notion of all: yes, the Count would be more than happy getting to have Jonathan Harker as his permanent guest/prisoner at Castle Dracula in dreary, decrepit Transylvania, but the Count would be made even more happy getting to have Harker as his permanent neighbor at Cottage Dracula in merry old England.

In his book *From Demons to Dracula: The Creation of the Modern Vampire Myth* (2008), writer and archaeologist Matthew Beresford provides an entertaining history of how various visions and versions of the vampire have appeared in popular culture. "Although *Dracula* was the catalyst for the modern vampire myth it was almost uniquely the theatre, cinema and television exploitation of the being that ultimately caused the shift towards the modern conception of the vampire," Beresford writes. "Whereas in the superstitions and myths of the Middle Ages or within folklore it was the lack of knowledge that fueled the existence of the vampire, the technological advancement and mass-market productions of modernity eradicated the unknown and transformed the vampire into a household product" (Beresford 2008, 140).

If a "lack of knowledge" in fact and throughout history gave rise to the existence of a "vampire myth" that mostly lived in "superstitions" and/or "within folklore," Beresford argues that a substantially less fearful version of the evolving "myth" has largely been the one reflected and promoted by 20th century stage and screenplays. "Today the vampire is no longer the feared being that he once was," Beresford insists.

> In the hundred years or so post–*Dracula* the vampire's transformation has been like a star turning into a supernova.... The fear created by the vampire has dissipated, and the vampire himself has become a parody of what he once was. The reason for this is quite simple: we no longer fear the vampire [Beresford 2008, 140].

It is this "fear" that might have initially fueled the creation of vampire myths in the first place, but if Beresford's claims are correct, it may very well be the case that the mass production of vampire stories and distribution of them across different forms of popular media have in large measure de-fanged the vampire as that aforementioned radical, isolated individual. Take for example the commercial blockbuster that Anne Rice's *Interview with the Vampire* (1976) became in both the publishing and film industries well over a quarter century ago, wherein vampires are portrayed in far more nuance than fear. "It was society's fear of the vampire that allowed him to exist through the ages," Beresford continues. "But how did the fear subside after so long? And what does this mean for the vampire in the twenty-first century?" (Beresford 2008, 140).

It is later in the same chapter of his book where Beresford appears willing to engage answering these questions in particular. "The increased popularity of the vampire," he writes, "coupled with new mass-communication technology such as the Internet, boosted the growing appeal of the Gothic lifestyle" (Beresford 2008, 150). Beresford's book is primarily interested in examining the connections between what he terms "vampire myths" and various performances of "vampiric" identity through much of European history (up to the point of the contemporary, to what he calls the "modern vampire myth"; and as briefly explained here earlier, this myth is one largely informed and underwritten by post-*Dracula* works in prose, film, and television). This primary interest takes a casual glance forward toward what the relaxing of fear might "mean for the vampire in the twenty-first century," and at least asks the question. This is ultimately a question, however, that Beresford either is unwilling or unable to answer. To be fair, looking toward what is next in the evolution of vampire myths is not Beresford's concern. And the most obvious evidence of this could very well be that he is not looking at all at the medium which best captures and performs what it means and feels like to live in the contemporary: games.

Enter Masquerade

If Beresford's book is any indication, yes, it most definitely seems that popular culture has indeed always had it out for the vampire. Within popular culture, however, games can be incredibly effective epicenters for the instruction and practice of empathy. Beresford contends that "this understanding of, or empathy with, vampires created by works such as *Interview With the Vampire* or the psychic analyses of vampirism allowed for people to become more involved in vampire role-playing or lifestyles." He goes on to mention the classic 1991 pen-and-paper role-playing game *Vampire: The Masquerade* (*V:TM*), and argues that the one-two punch of intellectual properties like *Interview* and *V:TM* "were perhaps a precursor for the vampire being adopted by numerous societies, interest groups and subcultures" (Beresford 2008, 158).

In writing about pen-and-paper RPGs himself, A. Scott Glancy describes *V:TM* as "one of the most successful role-playing games of the 1990s" which "created its own vast narrative—a secret world of supernatural forces that exist just below the surface of known history" (Glancy 2009, 81). Categorically, RPGs not only tend to offer a "vast" narrative experience, but a multiplicity of possibility as well. In the academic discipline of games studies, much of the core conversations regardless of subject or example has been (and probably always will be) how any given subject/example is reflective of (or performed as) the player's intentionality and/or agency. To oversimplify these conversations, this emphasis on intent and agency for the player is what most separates games from other media; this emphasis also might be what gives games a potentially more global appeal than other media.

However, Glancy points out something of a paradox, if not a high irony, in the possibility that games may not promote certain forms of empathy, especially when it comes to completing objectives or solving puzzles inside the game. "While this vast narrative did provide a wide, varied, and endlessly unfolding world for the players to explore," Glancy writes, "all too often that world was already populated by interesting non-player characters with a myriad of agendas and motives, who were already having adventures" (Glancy 2009, 81).

Because games almost always have win-states (i.e., capturing an opponent's king in a game of chess), a player's success in (and, assumedly, enjoyment of) the game is dependent on completing the game's main quest(s) and, effectively, being the protagonist at the center of whatever narrative the game presents. In describing *V:TM*'s mechanics and principal quests, Glancy laments that "the scenarios (and in my opinion, the game mechanics) too often cast the players in the roles of supporting characters.... This situation always felt like the equivalent of being reduced to the role of sidekick to the real protagonists" (Glancy 2009, 81). The paradox and irony is that a medium with such tremendous potential to perform and practice empathy might, in some cases, perform and practice little to no empathy at all. "No one wants to have to play one of Doc Savage's sidekicks or one of the 'red shirts' from *Star Trek*," Glancy declares. "People play role-playing games to be the heroes, to take center stage, to feel as if they are changing the course of events, rather than being swept along by them" (Glancy 2009, 81).

Some of this failure to provide a clear path to empathy is likely due to the competitive nature of games that is inherent to the entire medium. But another part of this failure might have a fair amount to do with potential Others the game designers are either deliberately or inadvertently asking us to empathize with, and especially when game designers choose to invite a vampire to the proverbial table for a pen-and-paper RPG session in a game like *V:TM* or *Dungeons & Dragons*. This failure could also be particularly true of videogames, where any nuanced take on the vampire can be pretty hard to come by. Even in 2018, character design and sprite animations are still much closer in appearance to the principal antagonists and mini-bosses of video games like Konami's 1986 classic *Castlevania*, which takes most of its cultural cues from the same "modern vampire myth" explicated by Beresford.

Enter Oblivion

Oblivion is the fourth installment in Bethesda Studio's *Elder Scrolls* series of role-playing games (RPGs). It is an action-adventure RPG published in 2006, in which the PC (player character) is a prisoner, who in the game's opening scene witnesses the assassination of the Emperor of the fictional kingdom of Cyrodiil. Before the Emperor is murdered, he gives the prisoner a royal amulet for safekeeping, and the adventure proverbially begins from there. But before any of these events occur, and as with any traditional RPG, the player is allowed to customize their PC/avatar in the game.

In *Oblivion*, vampirism isn't a race or identity that can be chosen the same way other RPG elements can be chosen, i.e., at the very beginning of the game, when the player can spend an infinite amount of time customizing their PC before even a title screen or quick tutorial for the game loads. Vampirism in *Oblivion* isn't a skill or an ability, either; rather, it is presented as an affliction, as a disease, a condition that manifests and progresses and can become permanent if the player does nothing to alter its advancement (or even is aware of an infection). In most cases where we see videogame vampires, for all intents and purposes they are designed and programmed to be little more than an exotic albeit one-dimensional antagonist.

This is a somewhat slanted way to say that the Vampire and various representations of vampirism already existed in videogame culture well before *Oblivion* was published. In *Oblivion*, there are two ways for the PC to become infected: (1) taking on "The Dark Brotherhood" sidequest or (2) randomly encountering/fighting other characters in the world who are already infected. The PC can only contract the disease through a melee exchange in which the PC takes damage from a vampire. Once this damage is incurred, a simple text phrase appears at the top of the screen: "You have contracted Porphyric Hemophilia."

It's important to the analysis underway here that the PC does not have to kill a vampire in order to contract Porphyric Hemophilia, nor has to be killed by one in order to register the condition. Again, the disease is contracted when the PC takes any amount of melee damage from an infected combatant; even the slightest damage incurred from the melee results in the PC becoming infected. It's also important that contracting Porphyric Hemophilia does not automatically transform the PC into a vampire proper. The game affords a window of three in-game days for the PC to cleanse themselves of the disease. This is accomplished by visiting any chapel in the game world. If the PC does not pray in a chapel within the three-day window, the next time the PC rests in any bed in the world for any amount of time, upon waking, the following message will pop up on the screen:

> You dream of someone sleeping peacefully in his bed, when a shadowy, gaunt figure silently enters the room. Approaching the bed, the figure leans down and sinks its fangs into the sleeping person. After a few moments, the pale figure rises, blood dripping down his/her chin. As color flows back into the vampire's face, and his/her features fill out, you recognize the face as your own. You awake screaming.

In *Oblivion*, Porphyric Hemophilia is not an identity, ability, or special power; rather, it is categorized as a "Disease" inside the game engine, and it is one of over thirty other conditions which can adversely affect the PC in the game. Vampirism in the game, then, is not only separate from Porphyric

Hemophilia, but is a special attribute/augmentation with direct impact on how the PC looks (eyes redden, facial features and hair become older, paler), which in turn affects how the PC interacts with both friends and foes in the game world. The PC also experiences increased weakness to fire and sunlight, which makes both combat and travel in the world substantially more difficult once these conditions take full effect.

When a PC is afflicted by vampirism in *Oblivion*, the game world changes in some fairly drastic ways. NPCs in the game try to avoid contact or communication, and most NPCs can also tell how long it has been since the vampire has last fed. The vampire can only feed upon sleeping NPCs (who, ironically, are not harmed or turned themselves into vampires in the process); if a feeding is witnessed by another (awake!) character, the game categorizes the incident as a crime, and issues a monetary bounty. Beresford would likely categorize the kind of vampire the PC becomes in *Oblivion* as a "psychic vampire," which "go as far back as the ancient spirit (demon) forms, the Incubus or Succubus, who would drain people of life, energy or blood" and "also visited sleeping people ... who are generally happy in life with good relationships, jobs, friends and so forth" (Beresford 2008, 156). Beresford further describes psychic vampires as "those in society that are deemed 'loners' or 'misfits,' or those who cannot maintain stable relationships and jobs and who flit from social group to social group in a 'vampiric' fashion. The coined term is perhaps too conveniently used to describe those in society who are different from what is acknowledged as 'normal,' and who seek ways to gain some of this social structure for themselves" (157).

The World Is a Vampire

Playing as a vampire in *Oblivion* means almost always encountering increased difficulty in virtually every aspect of the game that matters (travel, barter, combat), if not experiencing an outright fight at every turn. Other characters inside the game world who would otherwise be helpful to the non-vampire PC will automatically try to shun the vampire and resist any kind of engagement at all, rendering the PC as substantially more of an Other than they had been before becoming infected with Porphyric Hemophilia. What I might suggest is that in *Oblivion*, Porphyric Hemophilia is the not-quite-dead-yet corpse of old-world nationalism in the wake of a global community. The PC will encounter plenty of Otherness in the game world, but becoming a vampire proper requires either the willful intent to become one (electing to complete "The Dark Brotherhood" sidequest) or derelict attention on the player's part as to what is happening to the PC once infected, avoids going to chapel (or simply doesn't know this is possible) for three in-game days, and wakes up with nightmares relayed as pop-up text messages. Becoming a vampire in *Oblivion*, then, is the PC's fall into a specific kind of Otherness that only temporarily/situationally rewards situational and percentage-based forms of invisibility, yet *permanently* punishes the PC by making some of the game's most crucial elements (travel, barter, conversation) much more difficult as a reflection of (if not directly in service to) that Otherness.

In the preface to their book *Retaking the Universe: William S. Burroughs in the Age of Globalization,* Davis Schneiderman and Philip Walsh write, "there is also dispute about the salient features of globalization ... the term may be understood in its current context, broadly speaking, to refer to the flow of capital, goods, technologies, ideas, forms of culture and people across previously minimally related spaces, to create an intensified form of interconnectedness" (2004, 3). *Oblivion* is not only an RPG, where the player's typical first order of business is to consider and decide upon skillsets and character attributes of/for the avatar they will pilot through the game world as a unique PC within that world, but *Oblivion* is also an open-world game, wherein the PC is not bound to experiencing the game's quests in a linear sequence that is consistent regardless of who the player is or how they customize their avatars.

Why this matters is fairly straightforward: among contemporary forms of popular media, open-world RPGs (and especially those which comprise *The Elder Scrolls* series) are easily among the most commercially successful and culturally recognizable texts which require the player/viewer/reader to consider their ludic experiences as deeply connected to a more globalist mindset. In *Oblivion*, acquiring material resources is just as critical as leveling the PC's core attributes, and the game's bartering economy is heavily impacted by the PC's reputation in the game world (reputation in *Oblivion* is based largely upon interactions with NPCs). In essence, how others regard the PC *matters*. And it especially matters when it comes to buying/selling/upgrading/repairing the game's myriad drop and reward items.

Ken Rolston, the lead game designer for both *Oblivion* and *Morrowind* (the 2002 CPRG and third installment in *The Elder Scrolls* series), writes about both games in an essay titled "My Story Never Ends":

> In both *Morrowind* and *Oblivion*, the leading character is the landscape, and the supporting characters are the culture and history of the land. In *Oblivion*, however, we made a conscious decision to present more elaborate narrative rigging than we did in *Morrowind*, and concerned ourselves less with exotic cultures and obscure histories. Compared with *Morrowind*, *Oblivion* greatly improved the quality and presentation of plots and characters in individual quests. Given the critical and market success of *Oblivion*, perhaps that was a wise decision. Unfortunately, *Morrowind* was far superior in its sense of place, richness of theme and culture, and coherence and integration of characters and plots with history, cultures, and landscapes. *Morrowind* is to

Oblivion as the novel *Moby Dick* is to the movie *Titanic*. *Oblivion* is slick, entertaining, and satisfying. *Morrowind* is rough going, often slow paced, wordy, and exhausting, but deep and textured in its visual and literary narrative [2009, 119–120].

Why Rolston's comments matter in the context and concerns of globalization is because *Oblivion* was intentionally designed to be less concerned with "exotic cultures and obscure histories" than its predecessor *Morrowind*, a game that Rolston clearly feels is "far superior" in its portrayal of "history, cultures, and landscapes." That he phrases these items as plural—particularly "cultures" and "landscapes" is also particularly noteworthy. Furthermore (and to the application of the vampire as not just Other, but as an effective metaphor for some of the more abject side effects of globalism), where *Morrowind* may have opted for slow pacing and an exhaustive sense of encyclopedianism in service to the game's depth and textures, *Oblivion* not only is the more "slick" and "entertaining" game, but one that apparently punishes any performance of Otherness that shows its face as that of a vampire in the PC.

"A first axis of globalization—and for some, the only axis—is that of economics," Schneiderman and Walsh write (2004, 3). As in the real world, the globalist nature of virtual worlds in videogames is also more nuanced and complex than serving up a laser focus on economics (2007's *BioShock* and its brazen critique of Ayn Rand and her various "virtues" of selfishness notwithstanding). Especially in open-world RPGs, where what a PC has in their inventory and how they acquired it is monitored by the game itself. "Opposed to such reductionism, but with a similar emphasis on economics," Schneiderman and Walsh continue, "contemporary Marxist theorists such as Immanuel Wallerstein agree that capitalist social relations tend towards universality and totality, but see this process as marked by increasing social conflict and the polarization of economic resources, with political and military conflict as 'lag effects' of this general process" (2004, 3).

Upon the PC's waking up for the first time as a vampire proper in the virtual world of *Oblivion*, the entire game pauses to deliver its own special epistle: "You dream of someone sleeping peacefully in his bed, when a shadowy, gaunt figure silently enters the room." Both the "You" and the "someone," of course, are the PC, who has spent at least three full in-game days suffering Drain Fatigue, a suffering so slight that the player could very easily have no idea even as to its existence. The "shadowy, gaunt figure" who "silently enters the room" is, of course, a metaphor for vampirism in a number of ways, not the least of which is how this "figure" is a future projection of how the PC, too, will appear to others in the game world. And when this projection is denied recognition and transaction as anything other than an economic unit, the game world's globalist agenda imposes itself upon the radical individual.

In *Oblivion*, the PC's autonomy and influence is drastically impacted by their transition to Otherness, and any temporary, percentage-based advantages are vastly counterweighed by a physical and economic existence that is permanently set to Drain. Like the vast majority of open world, sandbox-style games, daytime travel in the game world of *Oblivion* offers far less menace and difficulty than traveling the exact same parts of the world during nighttime. A wide variety of videogames have similar depictions of night travel (to borrow a line from *Game of Thrones*: "The night is dark and full of terrors"), but especially other games also published by Bethesda, games like the mainstream blockbuster *Fallout 3* (2008) (which, like its cousin *Oblivion*, was also awarded Game of The Year), and even the slightly older and more obscure *Call of Cthulhu: Dark Corners of the Earth* (2005).

In their introduction to *Controversies in Globalization* (2010), political scientists Peter M. Haas, John A. Hird and Beth McBratney write,

> Globalization includes a host of problems or issues that do not respect national boundaries—they are, as some have written, "problems without passports." ... The consequences of globalization are also significant. Just as Charles Lindblom defined politics as a matter of who gets what, when, how, and why, globalization forces influence the systematic distribution of who gets what, when, how, and why [2010, xxv].

If we are willing to consider the vampire as a metaphor for those disempowered, marginalized, and/or in some way made (to quote Rolston here again) "exotic" or "obscure" by the "consequences" of globalization, we need look no further than how *Oblivion* reinforces a sort of first-worldism that has no place nor purpose for Otherness.

The next sentence of the PC's waking dream reads like this: "Approaching the bed, the figure leans down and sinks its fangs into the sleeping person." As mentioned before, if the PC continues their existence as a vampire proper in the game world, the player will face the inevitable consequence of having to feed the PC outside the normal mechanics of finding/consuming food and/or drink drop items. The only way for the PC to regain health is, as mentioned previously, to attack a sleeping NPC.

Then the next two sentences: "After a few moments, the pale figure rises, blood dripping down his/her chin. As color flows back into the vampire's face, and his/her features fill out, you recognize the face as your own." The first two of these three sentences cement a kind of tutorial quality to this chunk of text, whose appearance has halted the entire game in order to directly communicate with the player that their PC is indeed now a vampire proper in the game world; the game will/does not resume until the player clicks the OK button, requiring from the player an actual physical response. In writing about gamic action, new media theorist Alexander Galloway calls moments of interruption like these "diegetic machine acts," for they are acts initiated by the program/machine/computer/console/etc so as to continue, extend, and enhance the fiction(s) presented by the game.

This is a very different experience than the onset of Drain Fatigue, which takes hold during combat. When the machine flashes the phrase "You have contracted Porphyric Hemophilia" in the top/left corner of the screen, it is neither punctuated with a period, nor does the machine pause the game and wait for the player to respond in any way. Contracting the disease is not an occasion the program/machine deems important enough to stop the game world for, and/or to wait for the player's acknowledgment. In other words, contracting the disease does not stop the game world; in fact, the game world does not seem to be slowed at all when the player is notified that their PC has contracted Porphyric Hemophilia.

Last, the final sentence: "You awake screaming." While *Oblivion* provides players the opportunity to explore its game world with PCs who are vampires proper, it does not mandate that every player must do so (and, in many ways, punishes players who do). Playing as a vampire in *Oblivion* is entirely optional, and, furthermore, becoming a vampire in *Oblivion* is both preventable *and* reversible. Once the PC becomes a vampire proper, the game affords an option for the PC to "cure" themselves of the condition. In fact, there are multiple options that would cure a PC of the condition. The most involved of these cure options is the "Vampire Cure" sidequest, activated when the PC visits Raminus Polus (an NPC) at the Arcane University inside the game world. To cure the PC of their vampirism, Polus requires (as many sidequests do) a lengthy amount of arbitrary ingredient/resource-gathering. Polus follows this directive up with an even more arbitrary one, which is to kill, scavenge and render to dust the corpse of Hindaril, another vampire in the game world, whose existence in *Oblivion* is to enable afflicted PCs to rid themselves of their disease. The least visible of cure options is a hack in the game wherein the player suspends playing entirely, drops to the command line, and inputs a short string of code which, upon resuming the game, gives the PC a vial of "Vampirism Cure Potion" that 100 percent reverses the condition (Galloway would likely consider this a nondiegetic player act).

And while *Oblivion* provides players these cure opportunities through its gameplay and throughout its game world, it is beyond clear that being a vampire in the game is something players should definitely avoid. Again, there is that final sentence of the PC's waking dream: "You awake screaming." Where all the other sentences in the "first nightmare" serve dual functions as (1) a confirmation the PC is indeed a vampire proper and (2) a light tutorial for the player to understand how to feed now that the PC is indeed a vampire proper, the final sentence is indisputable in its affectation that either being or becoming a vampire is a horrific and categorically undesirable thought to even consider.

This essay, then, may seem to seek empathy for the vampire, or at the very least, to ask us to consider the vampire's plight as something worth our consideration. The vampire is almost always that strange and frequently perceived-as-perverse radical individual whose relentless pursuit of their own needs and desires make them impossible to empathize with, not unlike the way popular fictions starring zombies might very well do much the same thing. If this essay does that, I hope it is mostly as a side effect of analyzing how the metaphors and even mechanics of vampirism connect to a larger appraisal/exploration of 21st century globalism.

As Schneiderman and Walsh write, in dealing with the "flow of capital, goods, technologies, ideas, forms of culture and people across previously minimally related spaces," globalization (as metaphorized by the game world of *Oblivion* in general and problematized by the vampire in particular) aspires "to create an intensified form of interconnectedness," yet nevertheless demonizes, ostracizes, and destroys The Other in that aspiration (2004, 3). For vampires to even survive in the game world of *Oblivion*, they must operate in the shadows and rely on various forms of chance, manipulation and violence in order to do so. Radical individualism is possible, but it is clearly not preferable. Even Gregor Samsa, upon waking to learn that he has metamorphosed into a giant insect, isn't encouraged to scream at and disregard himself in such a manner as the player is in *Oblivion*. In Kafka's famous novella, the infusion of the monstrous is, at least in part, a call for empathy. In *Oblivion*, there are far more menacing forms of monstrosity, the ultimate of which hinges on what many inhabitants of its game world deem to be an inevitable certainty: that the world is hopelessly hurtling toward destruction, and old-world notions of radical individualism will do nothing to prevent it.

Afterword

Amanda Jo Hobson
and U. Melissa Anyiwo

The vampire is a traveler, a real undead globetrotter, moving across continents and cultures and through time, a shapeshifter taking on the aesthetics and ideologies of the culture, time, and genre of its context. In Neil Jordan's film adaptation of *Interview with the Vampire* (1994), we see Louis and Claudia board an ocean liner in New Orleans setting off on a global search for other vampires. We watch as they enter port after port around the world only to be disappointed that the rumors of vampires produce none in reality, until they settle briefly in Paris. Their journey is an attempt to discover the roots of their existence, while separating the folklore and fiction from their experiences of vampirism. This fictional voyage of vampires replicates the way the vampire as an idea travels across borders and beliefs as tales to titillate and terrify.

We have previously examined the appeal of the vampire. It is a figure that rises from the cultural graveyard of icons over and over again to haunt our collective imaginations. Anyiwo writes, "The joy of the vampire tale is that it perfectly mirrors that search for identity, offering a figure on which to mirror everything we desire and fear" (2015, 1). The vampire is the monster that is most like humans; they used to be us, and they maintain parts of their human acculturation, even as they become atavistic cultural markers. They engender our concerns about those who lie outside of societal norms, and these categories shift and change over time and across physical and ideological boundaries. Across cultures and times, human being's attraction to the vampire has been consistent, and even the ideas for which the vampire stands have remained, from an explanation and exploration of the mysteries of the human body and disease, to our never-ending fears about ageing, death, and the afterlife, to our concerns about those identities that fall outside of the perceived norm.

212 Afterword

As editor Cait Coker explores in the introduction to this book, every culture contains lore of a creature that sustains by feeding on the blood or energy of other beings. The stories of these supernatural beings often rely on narrative tropes that become familiar to the reader but then juggle and jumble the elements, remixing the expected features of the vampire tale, and taking on cultural aspects of the context in which they are created. The global phenomenon of the vampire is neither a recent trend nor is it some type of solely American cultural export. The teen-driven juggernaut of *Twilight Saga* (book series 2006–2009 and film series 2008–2012) expanded beyond the borders of the United States and influenced contemporary visions of a young (at least on the surface) "romantic" vampire around the globe. Yet it was the import of *Dracula* (1897) into the U.S. that laid the groundwork for the "American" vampire, and even the Count himself was a (mis)reading of the history of Transylvania and vampire myths from Eastern Europe, the Greeks, and the Ottoman Empire by the Irish émigré to London Bram Stoker. By the time Dracula makes it to the shores of the United States onto the New York stage and Hollywood film through Tod Browning's authorized adaptation, the Count—as Count Orlok—had already made his unauthorized film debut, becoming an icon of vampire fiction and of anti–Semitism and xenophobia in 1922 with a German spin on the British trope (Hobson). This import/export cycle of the vampire has been true throughout the history and folklore of the preternatural creature, meaning that idea of the "global vampire" is one that is dependent upon socio-cultural historical contexts.

In the oft-cited *Our Vampires, Ourselves*, Nina Auerbach analyzes British and American cultural representations of and reactions to the vampire, focusing on the manner in which fear and power shape the idea its image. She writes, "Vampires go where power is: when, in the nineteenth century, England dominated the West, British vampires ruled the imagination, but with the birth of film, they migrated to America in time for the American century" (1997, 6). Though Auerbach's characterization appears on the surface to be indicative of the vampire itself following the power, it is more that, in the cultural exportation cycle, colonial power has greater access to the means of ideological dissemination. In the case of Britain, the colonies established physical, governmental, military, and cultural control over the colonized states, and in the 20th century the United States' cultural and intellectual colonization of the globe created the physical embodiments of capitalist institutions as well as the cultural replications and the eventual adaptations of those cultural products. As such, the United States exported both McDonald's and sparkling vampires during its position as global cultural leader.

Yet when we return to Anne Rice's source novel, *Interview with the Vam-*

pire (1976), we are reminded that the colonial traveler actually seeks only images of himself and destroys or simply ignores the unfamiliar. Thus, missing from the movie, Louis and Claudia do in fact find the vampire as they journey through Europe, but he is not the type of vampire they seek. Instead of a romanticized mirror image, they are horrified and disappointed with the shambling revenant they discover and tear him to pieces never to be spoken of again. Like the predominant image in cinema, the vampire must at least have the surface appearance of the romantic European Dracula archetype to be considered "acceptable." Sweden's *Let the Right One In* (2008), the German *We Are the Night* (2010), the Iranian *A Girl Walks Home Alone at Night* (2014), even the New Zealand parody *What We Do in the Shadows* (2014) rely on British and American iterations of the vampire despite the very different vampires that exist within their national imaginations. As a result, as Coker's text elegantly illustrates, to find authentic decolonialized International representations of the vampire one must look beyond the mainstreaming halls of Hollywood and the American film distribution industry.

In many ways, the vampire remains the visualization of a nation's darkest impulses whether romanticized or demonized. Just as the vampire was used in the Medieval world as an excuse to marginalize, discriminated against, and torture those who were visually different, today this undying murderer remains an easy scapegoat that reveals racial and class barriers. For example, in 2017, the village of Mulanje Malawi had a "vampire outbreak" with citizens claiming they had been attacked at night by creatures who sucked their blood. This triggered a wave of vampire hunters to seek out the suspected menace and destroy it. Somehow it is no surprise that the accused as bloodsuckers were the wealthy members of this struggling nation while the hunters were the poor. At its height, a thousand villagers armed with torches, machetes, and stones, attacked the home of entrepreneur Orlendo Chaponda searching for the monsters who were sucking their lives dry (Agence France-Presse 2017).

Today, we engage in a technologically aided global society with porous cultural borders in which you can watch vampire teen dramas from Korea (*Orange Marmalade*, 2015) or vampiric political satires from Cameroon (*Les Saignantes*, 2005), or if you would rather, read narco-trafficking gangster vampires in Mexico City (*Certain Dark Things*, 2016) or perhaps yaoi vampire manga (*Vampyre's Portrait*, 2008). All you need is an internet connection. The global vampire, though, is more than simply being able to access the popular culture and vampire stories of other countries than the one in which the audience sits. The contemporary global vampire demonstrates that the means of cultural production have expanded in this technological global culture, opening the narrative for voices that have often been left out of the mainstream vampire narrative, especially on film. This has allowed the distribution of artistic projects by individuals who may not have been able to afford to make a film or who were unable to find a traditional publisher for their novel or comic. In this way, the vampire of these independently created series are able to explore issues that they would not have been able to do via mainstream distributors, specifically these indie texts demonstrate a deeper and more explicit engagement with issues of race, gender, and sexuality. For instance, Audre's Revenge, a collective working to raise the visibility of queer, trans, Black, people of color in horror and science-fiction, is raising money for the production of *Bitten, A Tragedy* (forthcoming). The directors, Monika Estrella Negra and Miriam Bastani, write on the crowdfunding page that the film deals with "microaggressions and transgenerational trauma" using the vampire as a "means of exploring the intersections within movements that are often overlooked" because vampires bring "the past right along with them" (Negra and Bastani, 2018). This film, like Audre's Revenge's other film projects, explores explicitly the idea of the vampire as cultural outsider and the connection to socio-cultural racism from the perspective of individuals that have experienced racism in its many incarnations. Additionally, *Bitten*, like many indie queer vampire novels—such as Rebekah Weatherspoon's *Vampire Sorority Sisters* series (2011–2013) or Jordan Castillo Price's *Hemovore* (2017), explores queer identities and sexualities unequivocally, whereas much of mainstream vampire fictions uses queer eroticism either implicitly or by cataloguing the perceived looming threat of queerness. As self-publishing and crowdfunding films grow, these modes of creation will continue to offer greater diversity of vampire stories.

This, therefore, demonstrates the future of vampire studies: it is global and diffuse, and at the same time, it is also local and specific. The vampire tells immense narratives about what it means to be human, and micronarratives about the experiences of specific groups and individuals, most of whom have been historically and cultural marginalized. Our vampire is, as Auerbach wrote, ourselves. It is the idea about just who the "ourself" is that we continue to explore in vampire studies.

About the Contributors

U. Melissa **Anyiwo** is a professor and the Coordinator of African American Studies at Curry College, Massachusetts, and co-chair of the Vampire Studies Area of the national Popular Culture Association. She has published multiple texts on the vampire as ethnic and gendered archetype, including *Buffy Conquers the Academy* (Cambridge Scholars Press, 2013) and *Gender Warriors: Reading Contemporary Urban Fantasy* (Sense, 2018).

Simon **Bacon** has coedited books on various subjects including *Undead Memory* (2014), *Little Horrorsosity* (2016), *The Gothic: A Reader* (2018), and *Growing Up with Vampires: Essays on the Undead in Children's Media and Horror* (2018). He is working on his second monograph.

Candace R. **Benefiel** was an associate professor and humanities librarian at Texas A&M University for many years. She had an MLIS from the University of Texas at Austin and an MA from West Texas State University. She was also a doctoral candidate at Texas A&M at the time of her death in 2017. Her scholarship included numerous articles in the *Journal of Popular Culture, College and Research Libraries*, among others, and the book *Reading Laurell K. Hamilton* (2011).

Naomi Simone **Borwein** holds a Ph.D. in English from the University of Newcastle. She works at Western University. Her research appears in volumes like *From Analysis to Visualization, The Palgrave Handbook to Horror Literature*, and *Horror Literature Through History*. Chapters are forthcoming in *Horror Literature from Gothic to Post-modern*, the Palgrave Gothic Handbook series, and elsewhere. She is head poetry editor for Swamp Writing and has a secondary specialization in Mathematics Education and Curriculum and Pedagogy.

Cait **Coker** is an associate professor and the Curator of Rare Books and Manuscripts at the University of Illinois, Urbana-Champaign. She is also an associate editor at *Foundation: The International Review of Science Fiction*, and is on the editorial board of *The Journal of Fandom Studies*. Her research focuses on genre history, women's writing, and the history of women in publishing. She has published numerous essays and articles on popular vampire fiction in *Slayage* and *TXT Magazine*, as well as various chapters in edited collections.

216 About the Contributors

Trevor **Dodge** teaches courses in authoring and literature at Clackamas Community College, as well as courses in games studies and new media in the Creative Media and Digital Culture program at Washington State University–Vancouver. His fourth and latest book is *He Always Still Tastes Like Dynamite* (Subito 2017).

Julien **Drainville** is a graduate student of comparative literature at Université de Montréal in Québec, Canada, and a teacher of English as a Second Language to French-speaking students. His research focuses on popular culture and transmedial studies, and, more specifically, interactive storytelling in video games.

Phil **Fitzsimmons** is an independent researcher. Prior to this he was an Assistant Dean—Research at Avondale College (Australia), Director of Research (San Roque Research Institute, Santa Barbara, USA) and senior lecturer at Wollongong University (Australia). His research interests are in the fields of popular culture and adolescent spirituality.

Marta María **Gutiérrez-Rodríguez** has been a lecturer in English at the University of Valladolid (Spain) since 2007. She has a Ph.D. in English. The theme of her doctoral thesis was the representation of the Salem witchcraft trials in 19th century Anglo-American fiction. She is working on the representation of this historical event in novels and plays written in the 20th and 21st centuries.

Amanda Jo **Hobson** is the Assistant Dean of Students and Director of the Women's Resource Center at Indiana State University. Her doctoral work at Ohio University's School of Interdisciplinary Arts centers on feminist genre film. Her published work includes chapters in *Race, Gender, and Sexuality in Post-Apocalyptic TV and Film* (2015) and *Race in the Vampire Narrative* (2015). She is the coeditor, with U. Melissa Anyiwo, of *Gender in the Vampire Narrative* (2016).

Natalie **Krikowa** is a media scholar and practice-led researcher at the University of Technology Sydney. She researches and teaches in media, participatory and fan culture, genre studies (science fiction and fantasy), and Australian cultural histories of lesbian and queer media. She also works as the Creative Director of Zenowa Productions, writing and producing queer female focused works including *The Newtown Girls* (2012) and *All Our Lesbians Are Dead!* (2017).

Miranda Ruth **Larsen** is a Ph.D. candidate at the University of Tokyo and a lecturer at Bunkyo Gakuin University. She studies K-pop, affect, and fandom, specifically male K-pop idol groups and how they operate in Japan. Her work includes essays in *A Companion to Media Fandom in Fan Studies* (2018), *[REC] Terror* (forthcoming), and *Media Keywords* (forthcoming).

Maureen-C. **LaPerrière** is a professor of literature and culture at the Université du Québec à Trois-Rivières. Although her teaching and research interests range from gender issues to the uses and representations of violence in the media to the metaphoricity of popular culture, the vampire *always* seems to influence whatever serious topic she is covering.

Marie **Levesque** is a Ph.D. student in comparative literature at the University of Montreal. Her research interests center around the figure of the vampire, gender studies and popular culture in general. She is also a lecturer of English literature and an English as a Second Language teacher.

Fernando Gabriel **Pagnoni Berns** is a Ph.D. student and works as a professor at the Universidad de Buenos Aires (UBA), Argentina. He teaches courses on international horror film and has published essays in *Divine Horror*; *Critical Insights: Alfred Hitchcock*; *Dreamscapes in Italian Cinema*; *Reading Richard Matheson*; and *Time-Travel Television*, among others. He is working on a book about Spanish horror TV series.

Kendra R. **Parker** is an assistant professor of English in the Department of Literature at Georgia Southern University. She is the author of *She Bites Back: Black Female Vampires in African American Women's Novels, 1977–2011*.

Thomas **Prasch** is a professor and chair of history at Washburn University. His publications include chapters on F.W. Murnau's *Faust* (in *Terrifying Texts*), Alfred Russel Wallace's Spiritualism and his evolutionary thought (in *Perplext in Faith*), and ethnicities in Henry Mayhew's *London Labour and the London Poor* (in *Fear, Loathing, and Victorian Xenophobia*), among others.

Tatiana **Prorokova-Konrad** is a postdoctoral researcher at the Department of English and American studies, University of Vienna, Austria. She holds a Ph.D. in American studies from the University of Marburg, Germany. She was a visiting researcher at the Forest History Society (2019), an Ebeling Fellow at the American Antiquarian Society (2018) and a visiting scholar at the University of South Alabama, USA (2016). She is the author of *Docu-Fictions of War: U.S. Interventionism in Film and Literature* (University of Nebraska Press, 2019) and a coeditor of *Cultures of War in Graphic Novels: Violence, Trauma, and Memory* (Rutgers University Press, 2018).

Karen E. **Viars** is the Humanities and Science Fiction Librarian at the Georgia Institute of Technology Library, and the liaison to the School of Literature, Media and Communication. She has previously published and presented on *Star Wars* and *Lord of the Rings* fandoms, instructional design, and learner motivation. Her research interests include educational psychology, managing science fiction collections, and fan studies.

Works Cited

Abbott, Stacey. *Celluloid Vampires: Life After Death in the Modern World.* Austin: University of Texas Press, 2007.

_____. "Urban Vampires in American Films of the Eighties and Nineties." Vampires: Myths and Metaphors of Enduring Evil Conference Proceedings. Budapest: May 22–24, 2003.

Adams, William M. "Nature and the Colonial Mind." In: *Decolonizing Nature: Strategies for Conservation in a Post-Colonial Era,* edited by William M. Adams and Martin Mulligan. London: Earthscan, 2003, pp. 16–50.

Adib-Moghaddam, Arshin. *A Metahistory of the Clash of Civilizations: Us and Them Beyond Orientalism.* London: Hurst and Co., 2011.

Agence, France-Presse. "Panic and Vengeful Mobs as Vampire Scare Rattles Malawi." 05 December 2017. Retrieved from https://www.malaymail.com/s/1525383/panic-and-vengeful-mobs-as-vampire-scare-rattles-malawi.

Aker, Laurena, editor. *Fan Phenomena: The Twilight Saga.* Chicago: Intellect Books, 2016.

Alfredson, Tomas, director. *Let the Right One In.* Sweden: EFTI, 2008.

Allard, Meredith. *Her Dear and Loving Husband.* Copperfield Press, 2011.

Allen, David W., and Kel Dolen, directors. *Reign in Darkness.* Australia: Cajun Pictures, 2002.

Almereyda, Michael, director. *Nadja.* Feature Film. U.S., Kino Link Company, 1994.

"Also, Adv. and N.," Oxford English Dictionary (OED), 28 Nov. 2016, http://www.oed.com/view/Entry/5740?redirectedFrom=also#eid.

Amirpour, Ana Lily, director. *A Girl Walks Home Alone at Night.* United States: Logan Pictures, 2014.

Andreacchio, Mario, director. *The Dreaming.* Australia: South Australian Film Corporation, 1998.

Andreescu, Raluca. "A Portrait of the Artist as a Vampire in Jim Jarmusch's Only Lovers Left Alive." In: *Gothic Peregrinations: The Unexplored and Re-Explored Territories,* edited by Agnieszka Lowczanin and Katarzyna Malecka. New York: Routledge, 2018, 92–105.

Andrews, Nigel. "Dracula in Delft." *American Film* vol. 4, no. 1, 1978, pp. 32–38.

Anyiwo, U. Melissa. "Introduction." *Race in the Vampire Narrative.* Rotterdam: Sense Publishers, 2015, pp. 1–6.

Aranda, Vicente, director. *The Blood Spattered Bride.* Feature Film, Spain, Morgana Films, 1972.

Arthur, Jay Mary. *The Default Country: A Lexical Cartography of 20th Century Australia.* Sydney: University of New South Wales Press, 2003.

"As, adv. and Conj.," Oxford English Dictionary (OED), 28 Nov. 2016, http://www.oed.com/view/Entry/11307?rskey=PYniAq&result=6&isAdvanced=false#eid.

Ashcroft, Bill, et al. *The Empire Writes Back: Theory and Practice in Post-Colonial Literature.* New York: Routledge, 1989.

Ashton, Paul. *From the Brink: Experiences of the Void from a Depth Psychology Perspective.* Karnac Books, 2007.

Works Cited

Auerbach, Nina. *Our Vampires, Ourselves*. Chicago: University of Chicago Press, 1995.
_____. *Woman and the Demon: Life of a Victorian Myth*. Cambridge: Harvard University Press, 1982.
Austin, Guy. "Biological Dystopias: The Body in Contemporary French Horror Cinema." *L'Esprit Créateur* vol. 52, no.2, 2012, pp. 99–113. Accessed June 19, 2018. https://doi.org/10.1353/esp.2012.0023.
Bacon, Simon, and Katarzyna Bronk. *Undead Memory: Vampires and Human Memory in Popular Culture*. Oxford: Peter Lang, 2013.
Baker, Emmerson W. *A Storm of Witchcraft: The Salem Trials and the American Experience*. New York: Oxford University Press, 2015.
Baker, Roy Ward, director. *The Vampire Lovers*. Los Angeles: American International Pictures, 1970.
Ball, Alan, director. "Strange Love." *True Blood*, season 1, episode 1. HBO, 7 Sep. 2008.
Banivanua-Mar, Tracey. *Violence and Colonial Dialogue*. Honolulu: University of Hawaii Press, 2007, pp. 33–34.
Barthes, Roland. *Le Neutre: Cours au Collège de France (1977–1978)*. Paris: Éditions du Seuil, 2002.
Bekolo, Jean-Pierre, director. *Les Saignantes*. Cameroon: Quartier Mozart Films, 2005.
Benjamin, Walter. "Critique of Violence." In: *Reflections: Essays, Aphorisms and Autobiograpical Writings*, edited and translated by Edmund Jephcott. New York: Schocken Books, 1978.
_____. *Illuminations*. Translated by Harry Zohn, New York: Schocken Books, 1968.
Beresford, Matthew. *From Demons to Dracula. the Creation of the Modern Vampire Myth*. London: Reaktion Books, 2008.
Berger, Peter, and Thomas Luckmann. *The Social Construction of Reality*. London: Penguin Random House, 1966.
Bhabha, Homi. "Of Mimicry and Man: The Ambivalence of Colonial Discourse," *October* 28 (Spring 1984), pp. 125–133. Reprinted in: *Discipleship: A Special Issues on Psychoanalaysis*. 28 (1994), pp. 125–133.
Billig, Michael. *Banal Nationalism*. London: SAGE, 1995.
_____. *Laughter and Ridicule: Towards a Social Critique of Humour*. Los Angeles: Sage, 2005.
Bini, Andrea. *Male Anxiety and Psychopathology in Film*. New York: Palgrave, 2015.
Bird, Matt. *Min Min*. Blue Mountains, Australia: Chesterfilm, 2012. Blanchot, Maurice. *L'Entretien infini*. Paris: Éditions Gallimard, 1969.
Blood. Written by Park Jae-bum. KBS2. 2015.
Blume, Mary. "Shadowboxing with Werner Herzog." *Los Angeles Times*, 24 February, 1979: 9.
Bogle, James, director. *Kadaicha*. Australia: Premier Film Marketing, 1988.
Bondanella, Peter. *A History of Italian Cinema*. New York: Continuum, 2009.
_____. *Italian Cinema: from Neorealism to the Present*. New York: Continuum, 2007.
Boscarino, Mary. "Desiring Japan: Transnational Encounters and Critical Multiculturalism." MA Thesis. Oxford: Miami University, 2011.
Botting, Fred. *Gothic*. London: Routledge, 1995.
Bourdieu, Pierre. *Language and Symbolic Power*. Cambridge: Polity Press, 1991.
Brass, Tom. "Nymphs, Shepherds, and Vampires: The Agrarian Myth on Film." *Dialectical Anthropology*, vol. 25, nos. 3–4, 2000, pp. 205–237.
Brisbane, Katharine. "Theatre from 1950." In: *The Cambridge History of Australian Literature*, edited by Peter Pierce. Cambridge: Cambridge University Press, 2009, pp. 391–418.
Brown, Carolyn. "Figuring the Vampire: Death, Desire, and the Image." *The Eight Technologies of Otherness*, edited by Sue Golding. New York: Routledge, 1997.
Browning, John, and Caroline Picart, editors. *Dracula, Vampires and Other Undead Forms*. Lanham, MD: Scarecrow Press, 2009.
Brudnage, Anthony. *Going to the Sources: A Guide to Historical Research and Writing*. Chichester: Wiley-Blackwell, 2013.
Bullock, Marcus P. "Germany's Lost Son, Germany's Dark Dream: Werner Herzog, Ecstasy, and *Einfühling*." *Discourse* vol. 36, no. 2, 2014, pp. 232–60.

Butler, Judith. *Gender Trouble: Feminism and the Subversion of Identity*. 1990. New York: Routledge, 2006.
———. *Undoing Gender*. New York: Routledge, 2004.
Calef, Robert. "More Wonders of the Invisible World." In: *Narratives of the New England Witchcraft Cases*, edited by George Lincoln Burr, Mineola, NY: Dover Publications, 2002, pp. 289–391. (Orig. pub. 1914.)
Calhoon, Kenneth S. "Werner Herzog's View of Delt: Or, *Nosferatu* and the Still Life." In: *A Companion to Werner Herzog*, edited by Brad Prager. Chichester, UK: Wiley-Blackwell, 2012, pp. 101–126.
Call of Cthulhu: Dark Corners of the Earth. Bethesda Softworks/ZeniMax, 2005.
Camden, Jennifer, and Kate Faber Oestreich. *Transmedia Storytelling: Pemberley Digital's Adaptations of Jane Austen and Mary Shelley*. Newcastle: Cambridge Scholars Publishing, 2018.
Campbell, Beatrix. *Goliath: Britain's Dangerous Places*. London: Methuen, 1993.
Campbell, Joseph. *The Hero with a Thousand Faces—Commemorative Edition*. Princeton: Princeton University Press, 2004.
———. *The Inner Reaches of Outer Space: Metaphor and Myth as Religion*. Novato, CA: New World Library, 1986.
———. *The Masks of God: Primitive Mythology*. London: Secker and Warburg, 1960.
Canby, Vincent. "Screen: *Nosferatu*, Herzog's Dracula: Nip on the Nape," *New York Times*, 1 October 1979.
Casper, Kent, and Susan Linville. "Romantic Inversions in Herzog's *Nosferatu*." In: *German Quarterly* vol. 64, no. 1, 1991, pp. 17–24.
Castlevania. Konami, 1986.
Césaire, Aimé. *Discourse on Colonialism*, translated by Joan Pinkham, Monthly Review Press: New York, 2000.
Chaffin-Quray, Garrett. "HORROR an Adaptation with Fangs: Werner Herzog's *Nosferatu: Phantom Der Nacht (Nosferatu the Vampyre, 1979)*." *Kinoeye* 2 (20): December 2002.).
Chaplin, Susan. *The Postmillennial Vampire. Power Sacrifice and Simulation in* True Blood, Twilight *and Other Contemporary Narratives*. Cham, Switzerland: Springer, 2017.
Charles River Editors. *The Dutch East India Company: The History of the World's First Multinational Corporation*. Sydney: Charles River Editors, 2016.
Chawla, Devika, and Amardo Rodriguez. *Liminal Traces: Storying, Performing, and Embodying Postcoloniality*. Rotterdam: Sense Publishers, 2011.
Clark, Maureen. "Postcolonial Vampires in the Indigenous Imagination: Philip McLaren and Drew Hayden Taylor." In: *Transnational and Postcolonial Vampires*, edited by Tabish Khair and Johan Höglund, London: Palgrave Macmillan, 2013, pp. 121–37.
Claydon, Phil, director. *Vampire Killers*. Feature Film. U.K., Alliance Films, 2009.
Clement, Jemaine, and Taika Waititi, directors. *What We Do in the Shadows*. New Zealand: Resnick Interactive, 2014.
Cohen, Jerome. "Monster Culture (Seven Theses)." In: *Monster Theory: Reading Culture*, edited by Jerome Cohen. Minneapolis: University of Minnesota Press, 1996, pp. 3–25.
Condon, Bill, director. *The Twilight Saga: Breaking Dawn, Part 1*. United States: Summit Entertainment, 2011.
———. *The Twilight Saga: Breaking Dawn, Part 2*. United States: Summit Entertainment, 2012.
Cornell, Michaela. "KCP Loft Announces Kim Turrisi to Write YA Adaptation of Award-Winning LGBTQ Digital Series *Carmilla*" *Chorus Entertainment*. 18 Jan 2018, Accessed November 1, 2018. https://www.corusent.com/news/kcp-loft-announces-kim-turrisi-write-ya-adaptation-award-winning-lgbtq-digital-series-carmilla/
Corrigan, Timothy, editor. *The Films of Werner Herzog: Between Mirage and History*. New York: Methuen, 1986.
———. 2012. "The Pedestrian Ecstasies of Werner Herzog: On Experience, Intelligence, and the Essayistic." In: *A Companion to Werner Herzog*, edited by Brad Prager. Chichester, UK: Wiley-Blackwell, 2012: pp. 80–98.
Craddock, Michael Dolf. *The Yara-ma-yha-who: An Australian Beasts Story*. Eskdale, Victoria: Kindle Direct Publishing, 2016.

Craft, Christopher. "'Kiss Me with Those Red Lips': Gender and Inversion in Bram Stoker's *Dracula.*" *Representations* Vol. 8, autumn 1984: pp. 107–133.
Cranston, C.A. "Islands." In: *The Littoral Zone: Australian Contexts and Their Writers*, edited by C.A. Cranston and Robert Zeller. New York: Rodopi, 2007, pp. 219–260.
Craven, Wes, director. *Vampire in Brooklyn.* Paramount, 1995. Amazon Video.
Creed, Barbara. "Horror and the Monstrous-Feminine: An Imaginary Abjection." *Screen* vol. 27 no. 1, 1986, pp. 44–70.
_____. *The Monstrous-Feminine: Film, Feminism, Psychoanalysis.* London: Routledge, 1993.
Critchley, Simon. *On Humour.* New York: Routledge, 2002.
Cronin, Paul, editor. *Herzog on Herzog.* London: Faber & Faber, 2002.
Curran, Bob. *American Vampires: Their True Bloody History from New York to California.* Pompton Plains, NJ: New Page Books, 2013.
Dahl, John, director. "Mine." *True Blood*, season 1, episode 3, HBO, 21 Sep. 2008.
Dash, Mike. *Batavia's Graveyard.* New York: Crown Publishers, 2002.
Davidson, John E. "Hegemony and Cinematic Strategy." In: *Perspectives on German Cinema*, edited by Terri Ginsber and Kirsten Moana Thompson. New York: G.K. Hall & Co., 1996, pp. 48–71.
Davies, Christie. *Ethnic Humor Around the World: A Comparative Analysis.* Bloomingtom: Indiana University Press, 1996.
Dawkins, Marcia Alesan. *Clearly Invisible: Racial Passing and the Color of Cultural Identity* Waco: Baylor University Press, 2012.
Deardorff, Daniel. *The Other Within: The Genius of Deformity in Myth, Culture, and Psyche.* White Cloud Press, 2004.
Demos, John. *The Enemy Within: Years of Witch-Hunting in the Western World.* New York: Viking, 2008.
Devanney, Jean. *By Tropic Sea and Jungle: Adventures in North Queensland.* Sydney: Angus and Robertson, 1944.
Dickstein, Morris. "The Aesthetics of Fright." In: *Planks of Reason: Essays on the Horror Film*, edited by Barry Keith Grant and Christopher Sharrett. Lanham, MD: Scarecrow Press, 2004, pp. 50–71.
Doig, James. "The Horror Novel Since 1950." In: *Sold by the Millions: Australia's Bestsellers*, edited by Toni Johnson-Woods and Amit Sarwal. Newcastle upon Tyne: Cambridge Scholars Press, 2012, pp. 112–27.
Doty, William. *Mythography: The Study of Myths and Rituals.* Alabama: University of Alabama Press, 2000.
Douglas, Ian. *Cities: An Environmental History.* London: I.B. Tauris & Company, Limited, 2013. ProQuest Ebook Central.
Douglas, Mary. *Implicit Meanings: Selected Essays in Anthropology.* New York: Routledge, 1999.
Dowd, Tom, et al. *Storytelling Across Worlds: Transmedia for Creatives and Producers.* Burlington, MA: Focal Press, 2013.
Down, Barry, et al. *Rethinking School-to-Work Transitions in Australia: Young People Have Something to Say.* Cham, Switzerland: Springer, 2018.
Dwyer, Philip, and Amanda Nettlebeck. "'Savage Wars of Peace': Violence, Colonialism and Empire in the Modern World." In: *Violence, Colonialism and Empire in the Modern World*, edited by Philip Dwyer and Amanda Nettlebeck. Cham: Palgrave Macmillan, 2018, pp. 1–24.
Eager, Kirsty. *Salt Water Vampires.* Sydney: Penguin Books, 2010.
Ebert, Roger. "*Nosferatu the Vampyre* (1979)." 5 October 1979. "*Nosferatu the Vampyre* (1979)." 24 October 2011. https://www.rogerebert.com/reviews/nosferatu-the-vampyre-1979.
_____, and Werner Herzog. *Images at the Horizon: A Workshop with Werner Herzog Conducted by Roger Ebert.* Chicago: Facets Multimedia, 1979.
Eco, Umberto. *From Tree to the Labyrinth: Historical Studies on the Sign and Interpretation*, translated by Anthony Oldcorn. Cambridge MA: Harvard University Press, 2014.
Edelstein, Dan, and Bettina R. Lerner. *Myth and Modernity.* New Haven, CT: Yale University Press, 2007.

Eder, Jens. "The Politics of Transmediality." In: *The Politics of Adaptation*, edited by Dan Hassler-Forest and Pascal Nickals. London: Palgrave Macmillan, 2015: pp. 66–81.
Eder, Jens, et al. "Introduction." In: *Characters in Fictional Worlds*, edited by Eder, Jannidis, and Schneider. Berlin: de Gruyter, 2010: pp. 3–67.
Eggleston, Colin, director. *Outback Vampires*. Yarralumla, Australia: Somerset Film Productions, 1987.
Eisenbach, Ronit. "Fast Forward, Play Back." *Journal of Architectural Education* vol. 62, no. 1, 2008, pp. 56–63. doi:10.1111/j.1531-314x.2008.00216.x.
Eisner, Lotte, *The Haunted Screen: Expressionism in the German Cinema and the Influence of Max Reinhardt*, translated by Roger Greaves. Rev. ed. Berkeley: University of California Press, 1969.
_____. *Murnau*. Translated by Martin Secker. Revised ed./English translation. Berkeley: University of California Press, 1973.
The Elder Scrolls III: Morrowind. Bethesda Softworks/ZeniMax, 2K Games, 2002.
The Elder Scrolls IV: Oblivion. Bethesda Softworks/ZeniMax; 2K Games, 2006.
Elfman, Richard. director. *Modern Vampires* (a.k.a. *Revenant*). Storm Entertainment, 1998.
Eliasburg, Jan, director. 2010. *Supernatural*. Season 6, episode 5, "Live Free or Twi-Hard." Aired October 22, 2010 on CW.
Erwin, Ethan, producer, and Kira Snyder, writer. "Sonata" *Moonlight*, season 1, episode 16, CBS, 16 May 2008.
Evans, Elizabeth. *Transmedia Television: Audiences, New Media, and Daily Life*. New York: Routledge, 2011.
Fallout 3. Bethesda Softworks, 2008.
Ferrara, Abel, director. *The Addiction*. Feature Film. U.S., Fast Films, 1995.
Fetterman, David. *Ethnography Step by Step*. Thousand Oaks: SAGE, 2009.
FitzSimons, Peter. *Batavia*. Sydney: Ransom House, 2011.
Fleissner, Jennifer. "Dictation Anxiety: The Stenographer's Stake in Dracula." *Nineteenth-Century Contexts* vol. 22, no. 3, Fall 2000, pp. 417–455.
Foot, John. *Modern Italy*. New York: Palgrave Macmillan, 2003.
Franco, Jesús, director. *Vampyros Lesbos*. Feature Film, West Germany, Fénix Films, 1971.
French, Peter J. *John Dee: The World of an Elizabethan Magus*. London: Routledge, 1972.
Freeze. Written by Ha Seon-jae and Lee Jin-woo. Channel CGV. 2006.
Freud, Sigmund. *The Joke and Its Relation to the Unconscious* [1940]. London: Penguin Classics, 2002.
Froula, Anna. "What Keeps Me Up at Night: Media Studies Fifteen Years After 9/11." *Cinema Journal* vol. 56, no. 1, 2016, pp. 111–118. Accessed February 19, 2018. https://doi.org/10.1353/cj.2016.0056.
Galloway, Alexander R., *Gaming: Essays on Algorithmic Culture*. Minneapolis: Minnesota University Press, 2006.
Gandy, Matthew. "The Melancholy Observer: Landscape, Neo-Romanticism, and the Politics of Documentary Filmmaking." In: *A Companion to Werner Herzog*, Brad Prager. Chichester, UK: Wiley-Blackwell, 2012, pp. 528–546.
Gansel, Dennis, director. *We Are the Night*. Germany: Rat Pack Filmproduktion, 2010.
Gates, Raymond. "The Little Red Man." In: *Dead Red Heart*, edited by Russel B. Farr. Greenwood, Australia: Ticonderoga Publications, 2011, pp. 379–395.
Gateward, Frances. "Daywalkin' Night Stalkin' Bloodsuckas: Black Vampires in Contemporary Film." *Genders* no. 40 (2004): no pag.
Gelder, Ken. *Reading the Vampire*. London and New York: Routledge, 1994.
"Genderqueer." Pride.com, 15 Aug. 2018, https://www.pride.com/genderqueer.
Genette, Gerard. *Paratexts: Thresholds of Interpretation*, translated by Jane Lewin. Cambridge: Cambridge University Press, 1997.
Ghosh, Amitav. *The Great Derangement: Climate Change and the Unthinkable*. Chicago: University of Chicago Press, 2016.
Gibson, Marion. *Witchcraft: The Basics*. London and New York: Routledge, 2018.
Gilders, William. *Blood Sacrifice in the Hebrew Bible: Meaning and Power*. Baltimore: John Hopkins University Press, 2004.

224   Works Cited

Ginsberg, Elaine K. "Introduction: The Politics of Passing." In: *Passing and the Fictions of Identity*, edited by Ginsberg, Durham: Duke University Press, 1996, pp. 1–18.
GLAAD. "Where We Are on TV Report—2017." *GLAAD*. Accessed September 12, 2018. https://www.glaad.org/whereweareontv17.
Glancy, A. Scott. "World Without End: The *Delta Green* Open Campaign Setting." *Third Person: Authoring and Exploring Vast Narratives*. Edited by Pat Harrigan and Noah Wardrip-Fruin. Cambridge, MA: MIT Press, 2009.
Godbey, Frank. *Salem Lost*. Kindle eBooks, 2010.
Godbey, Frank R., Jr. *Jonathan Hale: The First American Vampire*. Baltimore: PublishAmerica, 2009.
Goethe, Johann Wolfgang von, *Italian Journey 1786–1788*, translated by W.H. Auden and Elizabeth Mayer. New York: Schocken Books, 1968.
Goodnow, Katherine. *Kristeva in Focus: From Theory to Film Analysis*. New York: Berghahn Books, 2010.
Goodwin, Ken. *A History of Australian Literature*. London: Macmillan, 1986.
Gordon, Joan, and Veronica Hollinger. "Introduction: The Shape of Vampires." In: *Blood Read: The Vampire as Metaphor in Contemporary Culture*, edited by Joan Gordon and Veronica Hollinger. Philadelphia: University of Pennsylvania Press, 1997, pp. 1–7.
Green, Mary Jane. "Locating Québec on the Postcolonial Map." In: *Postcolonial Thought in the French Speaking World*, edited by Charles Fosdick and David Murphy. Liverpool: Liverpool University Press, 2009, pp. 248–258. doi: 10.5949/UPO9781846319808.021.
Gutelle, Sam. "Vampire Web Series 'Carmilla' Adds to Its Franchise with Book Deal." *Tubefilter*, 19 June 2017. Accessed November 13, 2018. https://www.tubefilter.com/2017/06/19/carmilla-book-deal-kids-can-press/.
Gutenberg, Andrea. "Shape-Shifters from the Wilderness: Werewolves Roaming Twentieth Century." In: *The Aestheticization of the Unaesthetic in Contemporary Literature and Culture*, edited by Konastanz Kutzbach and Monika Mueller. Amsterdam: Brill, 2007.
Haas, Peter M., et al., editors. *Controversies in Globalization: Contending Approaches to International Relations*. Washington, D.C.: CQ Press, 2010.
Haefele-Thomas, Ardel. *Queer Others in Victorian Gothic: Transgressing Monstrosity*. Cardiff University of Wales Press, 2012.
Halberstam, Judith. *Skin Shows: Gothic Horror and the Technology of Monsters*. Durham: Duke University Press, 1995.
Hall, Stuart. "Cultural Identity and Diaspora." In: *Identity: Community, Culture, Difference*, edited by Jonathan Rutherford, London: Laurence and Wishart, 1990, pp. 222–237.
Halliwell, Leslie. *The Dead That Walk: Dracula, Frankenstein, the Mummy, and Other Favorite Movie Monsters*. New York: Continuum, 1988.
Hamilton, Laurell K. *Guilty Pleasures*. New York: Berkley Books, 2002.
_____. *Kiss the Dead*. New York: Berkley Books, 2012.
Han, Hye Chung, and Chan Hee Hwang. "Adaptation and Reception: The Case of the "Twilight" Saga in Korea." In: *Genre, Reception, and Adaptation in the 'Twilight' Series*, edited by Anne Morey. Farnham: Ashgate, 2012, pp. 215–227.
Hanofi, Zakiya. *Monster in the Machine: Magic, Medicine and the Marvelous in the Time of the Scientific Revolution*. Durham: Duke University Press, 2000.
Hardwicke, Catherine, director. *Twilight*. United States: Summit Entertainment, 2008.
Hardy, Davo, director. "Digging in Your Heels: The Story of My Low-Budget Mythological Horror Film." Filmmakers Stories, *Filmmaker Freedom*. 2018. https://filmmakerfreedom.com/blog/filmmaker-story-davo-hardy-mythological-horror-film.
_____, director. *Hunting for Shadows*. Australia: Davo Hardy Productions, 2016.
Hardy, Rob, director. *Thirst*. Australia: New South Wales Film Corp, 1979.
Harper, Frances Ellen Watkins. *Iola Leroy, or Shadows Uplifted*, New York: Oxford University Press, 1988.
Harris, Charlaine. *Dead Until Dark*. New York: Ace Books, 2001.
Harron, Mary, director. *The Moth Diaries*. Houston: Media Max Productions, 2011.
Harvey, Colin. B. *Fantastic Transmedia: Narrative, Play and Memory Across Science Fiction and Fantasy Storyworlds*, London: Palgrave Macmillan, 2015.

Hastie, Amelie. "Blood and Photons: The Fundamental Particles of *Only Lovers Left Alive.*" *Film Quarterly*, vol. 68, no. 1, 2014, pp. 63–68.
Haynes, Roslynn D. *Seeking the Centre: The Australian Desert in Literature, Art and Film.* Cambridge: Cambridge University Press, 1998.
Hefner, Brooks E. "Rethinking *Blacula*: Ideological Critique at the Intersection of Genres." *Journal of Popular Film and Television*, vol. 40, no. 2, May 2012, pp. 62–74.
Heller, Tamar. "The Vampire in the House: Hysteria, Female Sexuality, and Female Knowledge in Le Fanu's *Carmilla.*" In: *The New Nineteenth Century: Feminist Readings of Underread Victorian Fiction*, edited by Barbara Harman and Susan Meyer, New York: Garland Publishing, 1996, pp. 77–95.
Hendrix, Duke, director. *Bloodspit.* Sydney Australia: Troma Entertainment, 2008.
Hendrix, John. *History and Culture in Italy.* Maryland: University Press of America, 2003.
Hermes, Joke. *Re-Reading Popular Culture.* Oxford: Blackwell Publishing, 2005.
Herzog, Werner. Translated by Martje Herzog and Alan Greenberg. *On Walking in Ice: Munch-Paris, 23 November–14 December 1974.* St. Paul: University of Minnesota Press, 2015.
Hess Wright, Judith. "Genre Film and the Status Quo." In: *Film Genre Reader IV*, edited by Barry Keith Grant. Austin: University of Texas Press, 2012, pp. 60–68.
Hewitt, Jon, and Richard Wolstencroft, director. *Bloodlust.* Victoria, Australia: Windhover Productions, 1992.
Hill, Frances. *Such Men Are Dangerous: The Fanatics of 1692 and 2004.* Hinesburg, VT: Upper Access, 2004.
Hillyer, Lambert, director. *Dracula's Daughter.* Feature Film. Los Angeles, Universal Pictures, 1936.
Hobson, Amanda. "Plague, Shadows, and Antisemitism: Re-thinking the Place of Nosferatu in the Classroom." Review of director F.W. Murnau, *Nosferatu, Eine Symphonie des Grauens.* H-German, H-Net Reviews. October 2009. Retrieved from http://www.h-net.org/reviews/showrev.php?id=26111.
Holden, Robert, and Nicholas Holden. "Black Words on a White Page." In: *Bunyips: Australia's Folklore of Fear.* Canberra: National Library of Australia, 2001, pp. 11–38.
Hollinger, Karen. "Theorizing Mainstream Female Spectatorship: The Case of the Popular Lesbian Film." *Cinema Journal* I, vol. 37, no. 2, 1998, pp. 3–17.
Holte, James Craig. *Dracula in the Dark.* Westport, Connecticut: Greenwood, 1997.
Horak, Jan-Christopher. "W.H. or the Mysteries of Walking in Ice." In: *The Films of Werner Herzog: Between Mirage and History*, edited by Timothy Corrigan. New York: Methuen, 1986, pp. 23–42.
Horrocks, Roger. *Male Myths and Icons: Masculinity in Popular Culture.* London: Palgrave Macmillan, 1995.
Hough, John, director. *Twins of Evil.* Feature Film, London, Hammer Films, 1971.
Howe, Andrew. "*Harry Potter* and the Popular Culture of Tomorrow." In: *Transforming Harry Potter: The Adaptation of Harry Potter in the Transmedia Age*, edited by John Alberti and P. Andrew Miller. Detroit, Michigan: Wayne State University Press, 2018, pp. 19–37.
Huang, Chien-Jen, Ping-Heng Tsai, Chia-Ling Hsu, and Reuay-Ching Pan. "Exploring Cognitive Difference in Instructional Outcomes Using Text Mining Technology." IEEE International Conference on Systems, Man, and Cybernetics. Taipei, Taiwan, 2006.
Huddleston, Tom. "*Nosferatu the Vampyre.*" *Time Out*, 29 October 2013. https://www.timeout.com/london/film/nosferatu-the-vampyre.
Huet, Marie-Helene. "The Face of the Disaster." *Myth and Modernity—Yale French Studies*, vol. 111, 2007, pp. 7–31.
Hughes, Langston. "Jokes on Our White Folks." *Langston Hughes and the Chicago Defender: Essays on Race, Politics, and Culture, 1942-62*, edited by Christopher C. De Santis, Urbana: University of Illinois Press, 1995, pp. 97–99.
Hughes, William. *Beyond: Bram Stoker's Fiction and Its Cultural Context.* London: Macmillan, 2000.
_____. *Bram Stoker's Dracula: A Reader's Guide.* New York: Continuum, 2009.
Hutcheon, Linda. *A Poetics of Postmodernism: History, Theory, Fiction.* New York: Routledge, 1988.

_____. *A Theory of Adaptation*. Second edition. New York: Routledge, 2013.
Hutchinson, Sam. *Settlers, Wars and Empire in the Press: Unsettling News in Australia and South Africa 1863-1902*. Cham, Switzerland: Palgrave Macmillan, 2018.
Ian, Marcia. *Remembering the Phallic Mother: Psychoanalysis, Modernism and the Fetish*. Ithaca: Cornell University Press, 1993.
Irwin, Matthew J. "'Your Wilderness': The White Possession of Detroit in Jim Jarmusch's *Only Lovers Left Alive*." *Capitalism Nature Socialism*, vol. 28, no. 4, 2017, pp. 78-95.
Isenberg, Noah. "Werner Herzog's Maniacal Quests. *Nation*, 7 January 2016.
Ishiguro, Laura. "Northwestern North America (Canadian West) to 1990." In: *Routledge Handbook of the History of Settler Colonialism*, edited by Edward Cavanagh and Lorenzo Veracini. New York: Routledge, 2017, pp. 125-138.
Ivar do Sul, Juliana, and Monica Costa. "The Present and Future of Microplastic Pollution in the Marine Environment." *Environmental Pollution* vol. 185, 2014, pp. 352-364.
Jackson, Morgan. "Mindless Monsters: The Evolution of Vampire Mythology in Modern Fiction." *The Alexandrian*, Vol. 1, Issue 1 (2012). Web.
Jacobs, Harriet. *Incidents in the Life of a Slave Girl*. Originally published 1862. Reprint edition. New York: Dover Publications, 2001.
Jarmusch, Jim, director. *Only Lovers Left Alive*. United States: Sony Pictures Classics, 2013. DVD.
Jenkins, Henry. "'Out of the Closet and Into the Universe': Queers and *Star Trek*." *Science Fiction Audiences: Doctor Who, Star Trek, and Their Fans*. Edited by John Tulloch and Henry Jenkins. Routledge: 1995, pp. 237-265.
Johannessen, Chip, director. "Arrested Development." *Moonlight*, season 1, episode 5, CBS, 26 Oct. 2007.
Johnson, Gary. "Nosferatu the Vampyre." *Images: A Journal of Film and Popular Culture* 8 (1999). http://www.imagesjournal.com/issue08/reviews/nosferatu/.
Johnson, James Weldon. *Autobiography of an Ex-Colored Man*. In: *Norton Anthology of African American Literature*, 2d ed., edited by Henry Louis Gates, Jr., and Valerie A. Smith, New York: Norton, 2014: pp. 792-871.
Johnson, Laurie. "Werner Herzog's Romantic Spaces." In: *A Companion to Werner Herzog*, edited by Brad Prager. Chichester, UK: Wiley-Blackwell, 2012, pp. 510-527.
Johnson, Laurie Ruth. *Forgotten Dreams: Revisiting Romanticism in the Cinema of Werner Herzog*. Rochester, NY: Camden House, 2016.
Jones, Ernest. *On the Nightmare*. New York: Liveright Publishing Corporation, 1951.
Jordan, Neal, director. *Interview with the Vampire: The Vampire Chronicles*. United States: Warner Brothers Pictures, 1994.
Kabir, Shameem. *Daughters of Desire: Lesbian Representations in Film*. London: Bloomsbury, 1998.
Kawin, Bruce. *Horror and the Horror Film*. London: Anthem Press, 2012.
_____. "Nosferatu." *Film Quarterly* vol. 33, no. 3, 1980, pp. 45-47.
Keetley, Dawn. "Introduction: Six Theses on Plant Horror; Or, Why Are Plants Horrifying?" In: *Plant Horror: Approaches to the Monstrous Vegetal in Fiction and Film*, edited by Dawn Keetley and Angela Tenga. London: Palgrave Macmillan, 2016, pp. 1-30.
Keft-Kennedy, Virginia. "Fantasizing Masculinity in Buffyverse Slash Fiction: Sexuality, Violence, and the Vampire." *Nordic Journal of English Studies*, vol. 7, no. 1, 2008, pp. 49-80.
Kennedy, Harlan. "Dracula Is a Bourgeois Nightmare, Says Herzog." *New York Times*, 30 July 1978. https://www.nytimes.com/1978/07/30/archives/dracula-is-a-bourgeois-nightmare-says-herzog-bourgeois-nightmare.html/.
Kenny, Glenn. "The Addictive Charms of South Korean Drama." *The New York Times*. 16 Sept. 2017. p. AR13.
Kent, Leticia. "Werner Herzog: Film Is Not the Art of Scholars, but of Illiterates." *New York Times*, 11 September 1977. https://www.nytimes.com/1977/09/11/archives/werner-herzog-film-is-not-the-art-of-scholars-but-of-illiterates.html.
Kim, Scott. *Benang*. Fremantle: FAC Press, 1999.
_____. *That Deadman Dance!* Australia: Picador, 2010. "The Kinsey Scale.," Kinsey Institute, 15 Dec. 2017, https://kinseyinstitute.org/research/publications/kinsey-scale.php.

KindaTV. "The Carmilla Series" *YouTube*. Accessed December 12, 2018. https://youtu.be/h4 QzRfvkJZ4.
"The Klein Sexual Orientation Grid." American Institute of Bisexuality, 16 Dec. 2017, http:// www.americaninstituteofbisexuality.org/thekleingrid/.
Knowles, Claire. "Sensibility Gone Mad: Or, Drusilla, Buffy and the (D)evolution of the Heroine of Sensibility." In: *Postfeminist Gothic*, edited by Benjamin A. Brabon and Stéphanie Genz Basingstoke: Palgrave Macmillan, 2007, pp. 140–53.
Koslow, Ron, and Trevor Munson. "No Such Thing as Vampires." *Moonlight*, season 1, episode 1, CBS, 28 Sept. 2007.
———. "Sleeping Beauty." *Moonlight*, season 1, episode 10, CBS, 14 Dec. 2007.
Kracauer, Siegfried. *From Caligari to Hitler: A Psychological Study of the German Film*. 1947; rpt. New York: Noonday Press, 1959.
Kratter, Matthew. "Twilight of the Vampires: History and the Myth of the Undead." *Contagion: Journal of Violence, Mimesis and Culture*, vol. 5, 1998, pp. 30–45.
Krausz, Peter. "The Rise of Indigenous Film and Television." *Independent Education*, vol. 43, no.1, 2013, pp. 34.
———. "Screening Indigenous Australia." *Australian Screen Education* vol. 32, 2003, pp. 90–5.
Krikowa, Natalie. "Artemis: Foregrounding Queer Voices Using Transmedia Storytelling." DCA Thesis. University of Technology Sydney, 2017. https://opus.lib.uts.edu.au/handle/10453/90293.
Kroger, Brooke. *Passing: When People Can't Be Who They Are*. New York: Public Affairs, 2003.
Kusumoto, Hiroki. *Vampyre's Portrait, Volume 1*. Gardena, CA: Digital Manga Publishing, 2008.
Lannoo, Vincent, director. *Vampires*. Eurozoom, 2010.
Larsen, Kristine. "Monstrous Parasites, Monstrous Selves." In: *Monsters & Monstrosity in 21st- Century Film and Television*, edited by Cristina Artenie and Ashley Szanter, Montreal: Universitas Press, 2017, pp. 59–90.
Larsen, Nella. *Passing*, edited by Thadious M. Davis. New York: Penguin, 1997.
Lawrence, Novotny. "A Cinema of Contradictions: Gay and Lesbian Representation in 1970s Blaxploitation Films." In: *Queers in American Popular Culture, Volume 2*, edited by Jim Elledge. Westport: Greenwood Press, 2010, pp. 103–122.
Leavenworth, Maria Lindgren, and Malin Isaksson. *Fanged Fan Fiction: Variations on Twilight, True Blood, and the Vampire Diaries*. Jefferson, NC: McFarland, 2013.
Lee, Hyun-Jung. "'One for Ever': Desire, Subjectivity and the Threat of the Abject in Sheridan Le Fanu's *Carmilla*." In: *Vampires: Myths and Metaphors of Enduring Evil*, edited by Peter Day, Amsterdam: Rodopi, 2006, pp. 21–38.
Le Fanu, Joseph Sheridan. "Carmilla." [1872]. In: *In a Glass Darkly*. New York: Arno Press, 1977. Also online: The Project Gutenberg eBook, http://www.gutenberg.org/ebooks/10007.
Leitch, Thomas M. "Adaptation, the Genre." *Adaptation* vol. 1, no. 2, 2008, pp. 106–120 10.1093/adaptations/apn018.
———. *Film Adaptation and Its Discontents*. Baltimore: Johns Hopkins University Press, 2007.
———. "Twelve Fallacies in Contemporary Adaptation Theory." *Criticism*, vol. 45, no. 2, 2003, pp. 147–71.
———. "Vampire Adaptation." *Journal of Adaptation in Film & Performance* vol. 4, no. 1, 2011, pp. 5–16 (2011). doi: 10.1386/jafp.4.1.5_1.
Levack, Brian P. *The Witch-Hunt in Early Modern Europe*. London: Longman, 1995.
Lewis, Paul. "You're Being Watched: There's One CCTV Camera for Every 32 People in UK." *The Guardian*. Guardian News and Media. March 2, 2011. https://www.theguardian.com/uk/2011/mar/02/cctv-cameras-watching-surveillance.
Lindqvist, John Ajvide. *Let the Right One In*. 2004. Translated by Ebba Segerberg. New York: Thomas Dunne Books, 2007.
Lockyer, Sharon, and Michael Pickering. *Beyond a Joke: The Limits of Humour*. New York: Palgrave Macmillan, 2009.
Machulski, Juliusz. director. *Kołysanka*. Monolith Films, 2010.
Macleod, Jenny, and Pierre Pursiegle. "Introduction: Perspectives in First World War Studies."

In: *Uncovered Fields: Perspectives in First World War Studies*, edited by Jenny MacLeod and Pierre Pursiegle. Boston: Brill, 2004, pp. 1–2.

Maher, Erin, and Kathryn Reindl, writers. "B.C." *Moonlight*, season 1, episode 6, CBS, 2 Nov. 2007.

Major, William, and Andrew McMurray. "The Function of Ecocriticism; Or, Ecocriticism, What Is It Good For?" *Journal of Ecocriticism* 42(2): 1–7 (2012).

Marin, Louis. "The Frontiers of Utopia." In: *Utopias and the Millennium*, edited by Kumar Krishman and Stephen Bann. London: Reaktion Books, 1993, pp. 7–17.

Maybee, Spencer, director. *The Carmilla Movie*. Feature Film, Canada, Shaftsbury Films, 2017. http://carmillamovie.vhx.tv/.

Mayne, Judith. "Herzog, Murnau, and the Vampire." In: *The Films of Werner Herzog: Between Mirage and* History, edited by Timothy Corrigan. New York: Methuen, 1986, pp. 118–30.

McCallum, Leslie, director. *The Twins*. Australia: Blue Gum Film Co., 1923.

McClelland, Bruce A. *Slayers and Their Vampires. a Cultural History of Killing the Dead*. Rev. ed. Ann Arbor: University of Michigan Press, 2009.

McFarlane, Brian. *Novel to Film: An Introduction to the Theory of Adaptation*. Oxford: Clarendon Press, 1996.

McGraw, Bill. "Life in the Ruins of Detroit." *History Workshop Journal*, no. 63, 2007, pp. 288–302.

McKee, Alan. "The Generic Limitations of Aboriginality: Horror Movies as Case Study." *Australian Studies* vol. 12, no. 1 (1997a), pp. 115–38.

_____. "White Stories, Black Magic: Australian Horror Films of the Aboriginal." In: *Aratjara: Aboriginal Culture and Literature in Australia*, edited by Dieter Riemenschneider and Geoffrey V. Davis. Amsterdam: Rodopi, 1997b, pp. 193–210.

McLaren, Philip. *Sweet Water, Stolen Land*. St. Lucia, Qld: University of Queensland Press, 1993.

McNally, Shari. "Carmilla: A Queerly Fractured Fairy Tale." *Medium*. Accessed October 16, 2018. https://medium.com/@shari.mcnally/carmilla-a-queerly-fractured-fairy-tale-a8f8bf23b4a7.

McSweeney, Terence. *The "War on Terror" and American Film: Frames Per Second*. Edinburgh University Press, 2014.

Mead, Philip. "Nation, Literature, Location." In: *The Cambridge History of Australian Literature*, edited by Peter Pierce. Cambridge: Cambridge University Press, 2009: pp. 549–567.

Meeker, Natania, and Antónia Szabari. "From the Century of the Pods to the Century of the Plants: Plant Horror, Politics, and Vegetal Ontology." *Discourse* vol. 34, no. 1, 2012, pp. 32–58. Accessed June 19, 2018. https://muse.jhu.edu/article/503905.

Melton, J. Gordon. "Introduction." In: *The Vampire in Folklore, History, Literature, Film and Television: A Comprehensive Bibliography*, by J. Gordon Melton and Alysa Hornick. Jefferson, NC: McFarland, 2015, pp. 1–8.

Meyer, Stephenie. *Breaking Dawn*. New York: Little, Brown and Company, 2008.

_____. *Eclipse*. New York: Little, Brown and Company, 2009.

_____. *New Moon*. New York: Little, Brown and Company, 2008.

_____. *Twilight*. New York: Little, Brown and Company, 2006.

Miller, Elizabeth. "Getting to Know the Un-Dead: Bram Stoker, Vampires and *Dracula*." In: *Vampires: Myths and Metaphors of Enduring Evil*, edited by Peter Day. Amsterdam: Editions Rodopi, 2006, pp. 3–20.

Miller, Laura. *Beauty Up: Exploring Contemporary Japanese Body Aesthetics*. Berkeley: University of California Press, 2006.

_____. "Girl Culture in East Asia." *Transnational Asia*, Vol. 1, No. 1. 2017. Rice University. Web.

Mitchell, Bill. "In Detroit, Water Crisis Symbolizes Decline, and Hope." *National Geographic*. August 22, 2014. https://news.nationalgeographic.com/news/special-features/2014/08/140822-detroit-michigan-water-shutoffs-great-lakes/.

Mittel, Jason. "Strategies of Storytelling on Transmedia Television." In: *Storyworlds Across*

Media: Toward a Media-Conscious Narratology, edited by Marie-Laure Ryan and Jan-Noël Thon. Lincoln: University of Nebraska Press, 2014, pp. 253–277.
Modleski, Tania. *Loving with a Vengeance: Mass Produced Fantasies for Women*. New York: Routledge, 1982.
Moffatt, Tracey, director. *Bedevil*. Qld., Australia: Anthony Buckley Productions, 1993.
Mora, Philippe, director. *The Marsupials: The Howling III*. Sydney, Australia: Bancannia Holdings Pty. Ltd., 1987.
Moreno-Garcia, Silvia. *Certain Dark Things: A Novel*. New York: Thomas Dunne Books, 2016.
Moretti, Franco. *Signs Taken for Wonders: Essays in the Sociology of Forms*. Translated by Susan Fischer, David Forgacs and David Miller. London: Verso, 1988.
Morimoto, Lori. "Transnational Media Fan Studies." In: *The Routledge Companion to Media Fandom*, edited by Melissa A. Click and Suzanne Scott. New York: Routledge, 2018, pp. 280–288.
Mosley, Philip. *The Cinema of the Dardenne Brothers: Responsible Realism*. New York: Columbia University Press, 2013.
Moss, Matt, director. *In Blood*. Australia: Matt Moss Films, 2002.
Mudrooroo. *The Kwinkin*. Pymble, N.S.W.: Angus & Robertson, 1993.
_____. *Promised Land*. Pymble, N.S.W.: Angus & Robertson, 2000.
_____. *Underground*. Pymble, N.S.W.: Angus & Robertson, 1999.
_____. *The Undying*. Pymble, N.S.W.: Angus & Robertson, 1998.
_____. *Writing from the Fringe*. South Yarra, Vic.: Hyland House, 1990. Murnau, F.W., Director. *Nosferatu*. Dist. Fine Arts Guild, 1922.
Murray, Robin L., and Joseph K. Heumann. *Monstrous Nature: Environment and Horror on the Big Screen*. Lincoln: University of Nebraska Press, 2016.
Musca, Carmelo, and Barrie Pattison, directors. *Zombie Brigade*. Toodyay, Australia: CM Productions, 1986.
Mutch, Deborah, editor. *The Modern Vampire and Human Identity*. New York: Palgrave Macmillan, 2013.
Nahrung, Jason. *Vampires in the Sunburnt Country Series*. Australia: Clan Destine Press, 2012–2016.
_____. *Vampires in the Sunburnt Country: Adapting Vampire Gothic to the Australian Landscape*. MA thesis, Queensland U of Technology, 2007.
Negra, Monika Estrella, and Miriam Bastani. *Bitten, a Tragedy*. Philadelphia: Audre's Revenge Film, forthcoming.
_____. *Bitten, a Tragedy* Campaign. *Seed & Spark*. September 2018. Retrieved from https://www.seedandspark.com/fund/bitten-a-tragedy#story.
"Neuter, *adj*. and *n*." Oxford English Dictionary (OED), 21. Dec. 2016. http://www.oed.com/view/Entry/126455?rskey=bLyAg6&result=1&isAdvanced=false#eid.
Newman, Kim. *Nightmare Movies: Horror on Screen Since the 1960s*. London: Bloomsbury, 2011.
Nubaumer, Janina. *The Vampire in Literature: A Comparison of Bram Stoker's Dracula and Anne Rice's Interview with a Vampire*. Hamburg: Anchor Academic Publishing, 2014.
Ong, Walter J. *Orality and Literacy: Anniversary Edition*. London: Routledge, 2013.
Orange Marmalade. Created by Seok Woo. Written by Moon So-san. KBS. 2015.
Parkin-Gounelas, Ruth. *Literature and Psychoanalysis: Intertextual Readings*. Basingstoke: Palgrave, 2001.
Peacock, M. Jess. *Such a Dark Thing: Theology of the Vampire Narrative in Popular Culture*. Eugene: Resource Publications, 2015.
Pérez, Héctor J., and Fernando Canet. "Evolution in the Vampire-Centered TV Ecosystems." In: *Reading Contemporary Serial Television Universes: A Narrative Ecosystem Framework*, edited by Paola Brembilla and Ilaria A. De Pascalism, n.p. New York: Routledge, 2018, pp. 43–56.
Perrin, Claude Stéphane. *Le Neutre et la Pensée*. Paris: L'Harmattan, 2009.
Peucker, Brigitte. 1986. "Literature and Writing in the Films of Werner Herzog." In: Timothy Corrigan, editor *The Films of Werner Herzog: Between Mirage and History*. New York: Methuen, 1986, pp. 105–117.

230   Works Cited

Picart, Carolyn, and Cecil Greek. "The Compulsions of Real/Reel Serial Killers and Vampires: Toward a Gothic Criminology." In: *Draculas, Vampires and Other Undead Forms: Essays on Gender, Race and Culture*, edited by John E. Browning and Carolyn J. Picart. Lanham. MD: Scarecrow Press, 2009, pp. 37–62.
Pinkerton, Nick. "The Interview: Jim Jarmusch." *Sight and Sound*: 50–56 (March 2014). Polidori, John William, Kathleen Scherf, David Lorne Macdonald, and John William Polidori.
Porter, Patrick. "New Jerusalems: Sacrifice and Redemption in the War Experiences of English and German Military Chaplains." In: *Warfare and Belligerence: Perspectives in First World War Studies*, edited by Pierre Pursiegle. Boston: Brill, 2005, pp. 101–123.
Praed, Rosa Campbell. *The Soul of Countess Adrian*. London: Trischler & Company, 1891.
Prager, Brad. *The Cinema of Werner Herzog: Aesthetic Ecstasy and Truth*. London: Wallflower Press, 2007.
_____, editor. *A Companion to Werner Herzog*. Chichester, UK: Wiley-Blackwell, 2012.
Prawer, S.S. *Caligari's Children: The Film as Tale of Terror*. Oxford: Oxford University Press, 1980.
_____. *Nosferatu: Phantom der Nacht*. London: BFI Publishing, 2004.
Prest, Thomas Peckett, and James Malcolm Rymer. *Varney the Vampire; Or, the Feast of Blood*. New York: Arno Press, 1970.
Price, Jordan Castillo. *Hemovore*. Sheboygan, WI: JCP Books, LLC., 2017.
Price, Richard, N. "The Psychology of Colonial Violence." In: *Violence, Colonialism and Empire in the Modern World*, edited by Philip Dwyer and Amada Mettlebeck. Cham, Switzerland: Palgrave Macmillan, 2018, pp. 25–52.
Priest, Hannah. "'Hell! Was I Becoming a Vampyre Slut?': Sex, Sexuality and Morality in Young Adult Vampire Fiction." In: *The Modern Vampire and Human Identity*, edited by Deborah Mutch. New York: Palgrave Macmillan, 2013, pp. 55–75.
Prorokova, Tatiana. "Unmasking the Bite: Pleasure, Sexuality, and Vulnerability in the Vampire Series." In: *Monsters & Monstrosity in 21st-Century Film and Television*, edited by Cristina Artenie and Ashley Szanter. Montreal: Universitas Press, 2017, pp. 159–177.
Pursiegle, Jenny, and Pierre Macleod. "Introduction: Perspectives in First World War Studies." In: *Uncovered Fields: Perspectives in First World War Studies*, edited by Jenny MacLeod and Pierre Pursiegle. Boston: Brill, 2004, pp. 1–2.
Rayner, Jonathan. "'Terror Australis': Areas of Horror in the Australian Cinema." In: *Horror International*, edited by Steven Jay Schneider and Tony Williams. Detroit: Wayne State University Press, 2005, pp. 59–113.
Reich, Jacqueline. *Beyond the Latin Lover*. Bloomington: Indiana University Press, 2004.
Rentschler, Eric. "The Politics of Vision: Herzog's *Heart of Glass*." In: *The Films of Werner Herzog: Between Mirage and History*, edited by Timothy Corrigan. New York: Methuen, 1986, pp. 158–181.
Restivo, Angelo. *The Cinema of Economic Miracles: Visuality and Modernization in the Italian Art Film*. Durham: Duke University Press, 2002.
Rice, Anne. *Interview with the Vampire: A Novel*. New York: Knopf, 1976.
_____. *The Vampire Lestat*. New York: Ballantine Books, 1991.
Ricketson, James, director. *Blackfellas*. Australia: Barron Entertainment, 1993.
Rigoletto, Sergio. *Masculinity and Italian Cinema: Sexual Politics, Social Conflict and Male Crisis in the 1970s*. Edinburgh: Edinburgh University Press, 2014.
Robinson, Amy. "To Pass/In Drag: Strategies of Entrance Into the Visible." Ph.D. diss, University of Pennsylvania, 1993.
Rojas, Christina. *Civilization and Violence: Regimes of Representation in Nineteenth Century Columbia*. Minneapolis: University of Minnesota Press, 2001.
Rolston, Ken. "My Story Never Ends." In: *Third Person: Authoring and Exploring Vast Narratives*, edited by Pat Harrigan and Noah Wardrip-Fruin. Cambridge, MA: MIT Press, 2009.
Rothman, Stephanie, director. *The Velvet Vampire*. Feature Film, Atlanta, New World Pictures, 1971.
Rowlandson, William, and Angela Voss. *Daemonic Imagination: Uncanny Intelligence*. Newcastle: Cambridge Scholars, 2013.

Ryan, Mark David. "Australian Cinema's Dark Sun: The Boom in Australian Horror Film Production." *Studies in Australasian Cinema* vol. 4, no. 1, 2010, pp. 23–41.
_____. *A Dark New World: Anatomy of Australian Horror Films*. PhD diss., Queensland University of Technology, 2007.
Rymer, Michael, director. *Queen of the Damned*. Burbank, CA: Warner Brothers Pictures, 2002. DVD.
Sanders, Julie. *Adaptation and Appropriation* (2nd ed.). New York: Routledge, 2016.
Sandford, John. *The New German Cinema*. London: Oswald Wolff, 1980.
Sangster, Jimmy, director. *Lust for a Vampire*. Feature Film, London, Hammer Films, 1971.
Sarbin, Theodore. "Believed in Imaginings: A Narrative Approach." In: *Believed in Imaginings: The Narrative Construction of Reality*, edited by Joseph de Riviera and Theodore Sarbin. Washington, D.C.: American Psychological Society, 1998, pp. 15–31.
Sasdy, Peter, director. *Countess Dracula*. Feature Film, London, Hammer Films, 1971.
Scherer, Agnes. "The Pre-cosmic Squiggle: Tendril Excesses in Early Modern Art and Science Fiction Cinema." In: *Plant Horror: Approaches to the Monstrous Vegetal in Fiction and Film*, edited by Dawn Keetley and Angela Tenga, London: Palgrave Macmillan, 2016, pp. 31–53.
Schneiderman, Davis, and Philip Walsh, editors. *Retaking the Universe: William S. Burroughs in the Age of Globalization*. Pluto Press, 2004. Reprinted Reality Studio, 2014.
Scholar Who Walks the Night. Created by Jo Joo-hee and Han Seung-hee. Written by Jang Hyun-joo. MBC. 2015.
Schott, Gareth, and Kirstine Moffat, editors. *Fanpires: Audience Consumption of the Modern Vampire*. Washington, D.C.: New Academic Publishing, 2011.
Schroeder, Kirby. "Hypermasculinity." In: *Men & Masculinities: A Social, Cultural, and Historical Encyclopedia, Vol. 1*, edited by Michael Kimmel and Amy Aronson, Santa Barbara, California: ABC Clio, 2004, pp. 417–8.
Scott, Tony, director. *The Hunger*. Feature Film. California, Metro-Goldwyn-Mayer, 1983.
Senf, Carol. *The Vampire in Nineteenth Century English Literature*. Madison: University of Wisconsin Press, 1988.
Shaftesbury. n.d. "Carmilla" *Productions*. Accessed November 21, 2018. https://www.shaftesbury.ca/productions/carmilla.
Shipka, Danny. *Perverse Titillation: The Exploitation Cinema of Italy, Spain and France, 1960–1980*. Jefferson, NC: McFarland & Co., 2011.
Showalter, Elaine. *Sexual Anarchy: Gender and Culture at the Fin De Siecle*. London: Virago, 2001.
Slade, David, director. *The Twilight Saga: Eclipse* [Motion picture]. United States: Summit Entertainment, 2010.
Smaill, Belinda. "Filmic Encounters: The Indigenous Struggles on Film Festival." *Metro Magazine* vol. 134, 2002, pp. 136–41.
Sorlin, Pierre. *Italian National Cinema: 1896–1996*. London: Routledge, 1996.
Spicer, Andrew. *Typical Men: The Representation of Masculinity in Popular British Cinema*. London: I.B. Tauris, 2001.
Spierig, Michael, and Peter Spierig, directors. *Daybreakers*. Australia: Lionsgate, Australian Film Finance Corporation, 2009.
Stanton, Gabrielle, and Harry Werksman. "Fated to Pretend." *Moonlight*, season 1, episode 13, CBS, 22 Apr. 2008.
Starrs, D. Bruno. *That Blackfella Bloodsucka Dance!*. Saarbrücken, Germany: Just Fiction Edition, 2011.
_____. "Writing Indigenous Vampires: Aboriginal Gothic or Aboriginal Fantastic?" *Journal of Media and Culture* vol. 17, no. 4, 2014, pp. 1–3.
Stein, Louisa Ellen. "#Bowdown to Your New God: Misha Collins and Decentered Authorship in the Digital Age." In: *A Companion to Media Authorship*, edited by Jonathan Gray and Derek Johnson. Oxford: John Wiley & Sons, Inc., 2013, pp. 403–425.
Steno, director. *Tempi Duri per i vampiri*. CEI, 1959.
Stephanou, Aspasia. *Reading Vampire Gothic Through Blood*. New York: Palgrave Macmillan, 2014.
Stepien, Justyna. "Transgression of Postindustrial Dissonance and Excess: (Re)valuation of

Gothicism in Jim Marmusch's *Only Lovers Left Alive*." *Text Matters*, vol. 6, no. 6, 2016, pp. 213–226.
Stoker, Bram. *Dracula: A Norton Critical Edition*, edited by Nina Auerbach and David Skall, New York: Norton, 1997.
Strasser, Dirk. "Editorial." *Aurealis* vol. 14, 1994, pp. 4–5.
Tannenbaum, Leslie. "Policing Eddie Murphy: The Unstable Black Body in *Vampire in Brooklyn*." In: *The Fantastic Vampire: Studies in the Children of the Night*, edited by James C. Holte. Connecticut: Greenwood Press, 2002, pp. 69–75.
Tarrat, Margaret. "Monsters from the I. D." In: *Film Genre Reader III*, Vol. 3, edited by Barry Keith Grant, Austin: University of Texas Press, 2003: pp. 346–355.
Taussig, Michael. *Mimesis and Alterity: A Particular History of the Senses*. New York: Routledge, 1992.
Taylor, Charles. *Modern Social Imaginaries*. Durham: Duke University Press, 2004.
Tenga, Angela. "Seeds of Horror: Sacrifice and Supremacy in *Sir Gawain and the Green Knight*, *the Wicker Man*, and *Children of the Corn*." In: *Plant Horror: Approaches to the Monstrous Vegetal in Fiction and Film*, edited by Dawn Keetley and Angela Tenga. London: Palgrave Macmillan, 2016, pp. 55–72.
Thomas, Kevin. "New 'Nosferatu' a Tribute to Murnau." *Los Angeles Times*, 12 October 1979, pp. 35–36.
Thomas, Scott. "Culture, Religion and Violence." *Millenium: Journal of International Studies* vol. 43, no. 1, 2014, pp. 308–327.
Thompson, Allen. "Responsibility for the End of Nature: Or, How I Learned to Stop Worrying and Love Global Warming." *Ethics & the Environment* vol. 14, no. 1 2009, pp. 79–99. Accessed June 19, 2018. https://musejhu.edu/article/265107.
Tidwell, Christy. "Ecohorror." In: *Posthuman Glossary*, edited by Rosi Braidotti and Maria Hlavajova. London: Bloomsbury, 2018, pp. 115–117.
Trigg, Dylan. *The Memory of Place: A Phenomenology of the Uncanny*. Athens: Ohio University Press, 2012.
Ball, Alan, director. *True Blood*. United States: HBO. 2008–2014.
Tumini, Angela. "Vampiresse: Embodiment of Sensuality and Erotic Horror in Carl Th. Dreyer's *Vampyr* and Mario Bava's *The Mask of Satan*." In: *The Universal Vampire: Origins and Evolution of a Legend*, edited by Barbara Brodman and James E. Doan. Cranbury: Fairleigh Dickinson University Press, 2013: pp. 121–135.
Turcotte, Gerry. "Re-Mastering the Ghosts: Mudrooroo and Gothic Refigurations." In: *Mongrel Signatures*, edited by Annalisa Oboe. Amsterdam: Rodopi, 2003, pp. 129–151.
Turner, Victor. *The Ritual Process: Structure and Anti-structure*. Cornell University Press, 1991.
Unaipon, David. "Gherawhar." In: *Legendary Tales of the Aborigines*, edited by Stephen Mueke and Adam Shoemaker. Victoria: Melbourne University Press, 2006, pp. 42–52.
____. "Mungingee." In: *Legendary Tales of the Aborigines*, edited by Stephen Mueke and Adam Shoemaker. Victoria: Melbourne University Press, 2006, pp. 145–149.
____. "Yara Ma Tha Who." In: *Legendary Tales of the Aborigines*, edited by Stephen Mueke and Adam Shoemaker. Victoria: Melbourne University Press, 2006, pp. 217–19.
Vail, John, Jane Wheelock, and Michael Hill. "Preface." In: *Insecure Times: Living with Insecurity in Contemporary Society*, edited by John Vail, Jane Wheelock, and Michael Hill. London: Routledge, 1999, pp. i–xi.
Vampire Detective. Written by Yoo Young-seon. OCN. 2016.
Vampire Flower. Written by Kim Eun Jung, Kim Ji Oh, and Myung Min Ah. Naver TV Cast. 2014.
Vampire Idol. Written by Ha Chul-song, Lee Sung-eun, et al. MBN. 2011.
Vampire Prosecutor. Written by Han Jung-hoon, Yang Jin-ah, et al. OCN. 2011.
Vampire Prosecutor 2. Written Han Jung-Hoon and Kang Eun-Sun. OCN. 2012.
Vampire: The Masquerade. White Wolf Publishing, 1991.
The Vampyre: A Tale; and Ernestus Berchtold, Or, the Modern Oedipus. Peterborough, Ont: Broadview Press, 2007.
Van Toorn, Penny. "The Terrors of Terra Nullius: Gothicising and De-Gothicising Aboriginality." *World Literature Written in English* vol. 32, no. 2, vol. 3, no. 1 199287-97 (1992).

Veeder, William. "*Carmilla*: The Arts of Repression." *Texas Studies in Literature and Language* vol. 22, 1980, pp. 197–223.
Vinen, Richard. "Where Did You Leave Them? Historians and 'Losing the 1950s.'" In: *The Lost Decade? The 1950s in European History, Politics, Society and Culture*, edited by Heiko Feldner, Claire Gorrara and Kevin Passmore. Newcastle: Cambridge Scholars Publishing, 2011, pp. 10–27.
Vrbančić, Mario, and Senka Božić-Vrbančić. "Different Adaptations: The Power of the Vampire." *SIC—A Journal of Literature, Culture and Literary Translation*, vol. 2, no. 1, 2011, pp. 1–15. doi: 10.15291/sic/2.1.lc.4.
Wahl, Chris. 2012. "'I Don't Like the Germans': Even Herzog Started in Bavaria." In: *A Companion to Werner Herzog*, edited by Brad Prager. Chichester, UK: Wiley-Blackwell, 2012, pp. 233–255.
Wald, Gayle. *Crossing the Line: Racial Passing in Twentieth-Century U.S. Literature and Culture*. Durham: Duke University Press, 2000.
Wall, Cheryl. *Women of the Harlem Renaissance*. Bloomington: Indiana University Press, 1995.
Walker, Beverly. "Werner Herzog's *Nosferatu*." *Sight and Sound* vol. 47, no. 4, 1978, pp. 202–205.
"Walter Francis White." In: *Encyclopedia of World Biography*, 2nd ed., vol. 16. Detroit: Gale, 2004, pp. 238–239. *Gale Virtual Reference Library*.
Weatherspoon, Rebekah. *Better Off Red: Vampire Sorority Sisters Book 1*. Johnsonville, NY: Bold Strokes Books, 2011.
_____. *Blacker Than Blue: Vampire Sorority Sisters Book 2*. Johnsonville, NY: Bold Strokes Books, 2013.
Weekley, Ayana K. "Now That's a Good Girl: Discourses of African American Women, HIV/AIDS, and Respectability." Doctoral dissertation, University of Minnesota, 2010.
Weinstock, Jeffrey. *Picnic at Hanging Rock*. Australia: British Empire Films Australia, 1975.
_____. *The Vampire Film: Undead Cinema*. London: Wallflower, 2012.
Weir, Peter, director. *The Last Wave*. Australia: United Artists, 1977.
Weiz, Chris, director. *The Twilight Saga: New Moon*. United States: Summit Entertainment, 2009.
Weller, Peter et al., director. *The Strain*. 4 Seasons; Los Angeles: 20th Century Fox, 2014–2017. DVD.
Whedon, Joss, director. *Buffy the Vampire Slayer*. Mutant Enemy Productions. 1996–2003.
_____. 1997. *Buffy the Vampire Slayer*. Season 2, episode 7, "Lie to Me." Aired November 3, 1997, on WB.
Williamson, Milly. *The Lure of the Vampire: Gender, Fiction, and Fandom from Bram Stoker to Buffy*. London: Wallflower Press, 2005.
Wood, Robin. "An Introduction to the American Horror Film." In: *Planks of Reason: Essays on the Horror Film*, edited by Barry Keith Grant and Christopher Sharrett, Lanham: Scarecrow Press, 2004: pp. 107–139.
Woods Carl T., director. *The Min-Min*. Australia: Starlite Films, 1990.
You're Beautiful. Written by Hong Jung-eun and Hong Mi-ran. SBS. 2009.
Zanger, Jules. "Metaphor into Metonymy. The Vampire Next Door." In: *Blood Read: The Vampire as Metaphor in Contemporary Culture*, edited by Joan Gordon and Veronica Hollinger. Philadelphia: University of Pennsylvania Press, 1997, pp. 17–26.
Zeller, Robert, and C.A. Cranston. "Setting the Scene: Littoral and Critical Contexts." In: *The Littoral Zone: Australian Contexts and Their Writers*, edited by C.A. Cranston and Robert Zeller. New York: Rodopi, 2007, pp. 7–30.
Zimmerman, Bonnie. "Daughters of Darkness: The Lesbian Vampire on Film." In: *The Dread of Difference: Gender and the Horror Film*, edited by Barry Keith Grant, Austin: University of Texas Press, 1996, pp. 430–438.

Index

Abbott, Stacey 82, 162
Aboriginal Australians 165
adaptation 51–53, 176
The Addiction (1995) 51
adze 4
Africa 4
African American literature 36
African diaspora 45, 46
Aguirre: The Wrath of God (1972) 126
AIDS *see* HIV/AIDS
Allard, Meredith 5, 31
Almereyda, Michael 51
Alps 117
L'amante del vampire (1960) 106
America *see* United States
Americanization 105, 110
Americas 60
Amsterdam 184
Andreescu, Raluca 128, 129, 133
Andrews, Nigel 116, 122, 124, 125, 127
Anita Blake, Vampire Hunter 15–16
anti-Semitism 126
Aranda, Vicente 50
L'arc-en-ciel 163
Asanbosam 4
Auerbach, Nina 11, 24, 56, 143, 212, 214
Austen, Jane 52
Austin, Guy 194
Australia 3, 6, 167, 177
Austria 53
Autobiography of an Ex-Colored Man 36, 39

BL (Boys' Love) 153, 213
Bacon, Simon 177
Baker, Roy Ward 50, 124
the Balkans 27
Banivanua-Mar, Tracey 185
Barthes, Roland 93, 220
Bassett, Angela 35
Bastani, Miriam 214
Báthory, Elizabeth 61
Bauman, Elise 49, 55, 58
Bava, Mario 106

The Beatles 114
Bedevil (1993) 174
Belgium 5, 77, 82, 83, 84, 88
Benefiel, Candace 145
Bennett, Jay 49
Beresford, Matthew 24, 25, 26, 28, 201, 205
Berger, Peter 186
Bhabha, Homi 35, 43
Billig, Michael 78, 104
Bini, Andrea 108, 110
Bioshock 207
Blackfellas (1993) 170–171
Blacula (1972) 43, 45
Blanchot, Maurice 93, 94
Blood 145
The Blood Spattered Bride (1972) 50
Bloodlust (1992) 3, 174
Bloodspit (2008) 174
Blume, Mary 116, 120
Boer War 179
Bondanella, Peter 106, 108
Botting, Fred 182, 183, 185
Bourdieu, Pierre 185
Božić-Vrbančić, Senka 53
Bradley, David 197
Brass, Tom 121
Britain *see* United Kingdom
Bronk, Katarzyna 177
Brown, Carolyn 154, 159
Brown, Natalie 194
Browning, John 168
Browning, Tod 189, 212
Büchner, Georg 119, 127
Buffy the Vampire Slayer 5, 15, 143, 167
Bunyips 175
Burdett, Sir Francis 130
Burroughs, William S. 136
Butler, Judith 90, 91, 94, 95, 99, 100, 102, 103
Byron, Lord George Gordon 60, 136, 138

Calef, Robert 23
Calhoon, Kenneth 123

236 Index

California 132
Call of Cthulhu: Dark Corners of the Earth 208
Camden, Jennifer 52
Cameroon 213
Canada 62, 71, 84
Canby, Vincent 119, 123
Canet, Fernando 191
Cannes Film Festival 153
Caribbean 4
Carmilla (novella) 5, 13, 25, 48, 50, 51, 53, 55, 56
Carmilla (web series) 3, 49
Carmilla: The Movie 54–55
Carpathians 109
Casper, Kent 120, 121
Castlevania 203
castration 97, 99, 100, 101, 102, 103
Center for Disease Control (CDC) 42
Certain Dark Things (2016) 213
Césaire, Aimé 185
Chaffin-Quiray, Garrett 120
Chaplin, Susan 25, 33
Charles, Max 194
Chicago 38
Christianity 27, 31
cinema studies 154
Claydon, Phil 51, 183
climate change 189, 196–198
Cohen, Jerome 180, 185, 186
Coleridge, Samuel Taylor 60
colonization 63–65, 71, 183
Columbia 4
comics 146, 213
consumerist society 107, 110
controlling images 42–43
Copernicus, Nicolaus 129
Corman, Roger 195
cosmopolitanism 105, 108, 110, 111, 114
Costa, Monica 139
Countess Dracula (1971) 50
Craddock, Michael Dolf 169
Craft, Christopher 13, 102
Cranston, C.A. 184, 186
Creed, Barbara 44, 195, 196
Critchley, Simon 79
Cronin, Paul 116, 119, 121, 123, 125, 127
Cukor, George 79
Curran, Bob 25, 28
Czechoslovakia 123

Darwin, Charles 129
Dash, Mike 178, 179
Davidson, John E. 120, 127
Davies, Christie 78, 79, 81, 85
Dawkins, Marcia 37–38
Daybreakers (2009) 174, 175
Dead Until Dark 16
Delft 125
Demos, John 28

Deneuve, Catherine 51
Denmark 38
Detroit 128, 131, 132, 134, 135, 136, 137, 138
Detroit River 136
Devanney, Jean 186
The Diaries of Adam and Eve 131
Dickstein, Morris 118
disability 37, 46
Doig, James 167
Douglas, Ian 129–130, 132
Douglas, Mary 77
Dowd, Tom 54
Dracula 4, 11–14, 25, 48, 51, 58, 78, 79, 102, 103, 170, 200, 212
Dracula (1956) 105, 111
Dracula (1931) 189
Dracula's Daughter (1936) 50
draugar 4
the Dreaming 166, 167, 168, 170, 171, 176
The Dreaming (1988) 174
dreams 78
Dungeons & Dragons 203
Dürer, Albrecht 123
Dutch East India Company 177, 178
Dwyer, Philip 179

Eager, Kristy 3, 177, 180, 181–184
Ebert, Roger 118, 123, 127
Eco, Umberto 180
Economic miracle 106, 107, 110
Eder, Jens 165, 166, 167
Eisenbach, Ronit 133
Eisner, Lotte 116, 126
The Elder Scrolls IV: Oblivion 6
Elfman, Richard 77, 79, 86, 87, 88
Ellison, Ralph 36
England 53, 136
Enlightenment 60, 121, 127
Éternelle (2004) 5
Europe 4
Expressionism 119

Fallout 3 208
fan fiction 4, 144, 151, 163, 164
fan studies 154
fanzines 150
Fascism 110
Fearless Vampire Lovers (1967) 124
Ferrara, Abel 51
Fetterman, David 181
Fibonacci 131
Fifty Shades of Grey 151
Fischer, Kai 110
Fisher, Terence 105, 111
Fitzgerald, F. Scott 131
FitzSimons, Peter 178
Foot, John 107
Ford Motor Co. 134
The Four Tops 135
France 14, 136

Franco, Jesus 50
Franklin, Aretha 135
Freda, Riccardo 106
Freeze 145
Freud, Sigmund 78, 88
Friedrich, Caspar David 119, 123
Froula, Anna 190

Gackt 153, 154
Galeen, Henrik 126
Galilei, Galileo 129
Gallipoli 180
Game of Thrones 208
Gansel, Dennis 51
Gates, Raymond 165, 170
Gelder, Ken 24, 26, 126, 167, 168
gender 11, 36; binaries 90, 91, 92; performativity 91, 94, 95, 96, 99, 100, 102, 103
genderqueer 91, 96, 97, 98, 99, 100, 102, 103
General Motors Corporation 134
Géricault, Théodore 181-182
Germany 5, 120
Gherawar 165
giangshi 3
Gibson, Marion 34
Gilders, William 177
Ginsburg, Elaine 37
A Girl Walks Alone at Night (2014) 3, 213
GLAAD 56
Glancy, A. Scott 202, 203
Godbey, Frank R. 5, 28-30
Goebbels, Joseph 121
Goethe, Johann 117
Gone with the Wind 20
Good, Sarah 23
Goodwin, Ken 179
Gordon, Joan 25, 26
Gordy, Berry 135
The Great Gatsby 131
Great Lakes 136
Great Southern Ocean 178
Greece 4
Green, Mary Jane 63, 64, 73
guaxa 4
Guilty Pleasures 15
Gutelle, Sam 56
gypsies *see* Roma

Haas, Peter M. 208
Haefele-Thomas, Ardel 57, 58
Hall, Jordan 49
Hall, Stuwart 104
Halliwell, Leslie 118
Hamilton, Laurell K. 15
Hammer Studios 108, 111, 114
Hardison, Kadeem 44
Harlem 38
Harlem Renaissance 38
Harper, Frances E.W. 36
Harris, Charlaine 16

Harron, Mary 51
Hastie, Amelie 139
Haze, Jonathan 195
Hefner, Brooks E. 45
Heller, Tamar 56
Hendrix, Duke 107
Hermes, Joke 115
Herzog, Werner 6, 116, 117, 118, 126, 127
Heumann, Joseph K. 189, 193, 194, 195, 198
Hillyer, Lambert 50
Hird, John A. 208
Hitler, Adolf 120, 121, 126, 127
HIV/AIDS 5, 28, 42-43, 143
Holden, Nicholas 169
Holden, Robert 169
Holderlin, Friedrich 119
Hollinger, Karen 57, 58
Hollinger, Veronica 25, 26
Holte, James Craig 168
homoeroticism 153, 154, 161
Hong Kong 146
Horak, Jan-Christopher 127
horror cinema 105, 167; comedy 104, 106, 108, 114
Hotel Transylvania 15
Hough, John 50
Howe, Andrew 50
The Howling III (1987) 174
Huang, Chien-Jen 154
Huddleston, Tom 118
Huet, Marie-Helene 181
Hughes, Langston 36
Hughes, William 36
Hungary 61
The Hunger (1983) 51
Hunting for Shadows (2016) 175
Hutcheon, Linda 51, 52, 63, 165, 166
Hutchinson, Sam 180
Hyde 153, 154

I Am Legend 25
Iceland 4
immigrants 4, 36, 83, 155
In Blood (2002) 174
Incidents in the Life of a Slave Girl 43
India 4
Indonesia 179
industrialization 106, 107
Interview with the Vampire 14-15, 25, 154, 201, 202, 212
Interview with the Vampire (1994) 211
Invisible Man 36
Iola Leroy 36
Iran 3
Irwin, Matthew J. 133
Isenberg, Noah 127
Ishiguro, Laura 185
Italian cinema 104, 105, 106, 107, 112
Italy 5, 114
Ivar do Sul, Juliana 139

Jacobs, Harriet 43
Japan 4, 6, 7, 163
Jarmusch, Jim 6
Java 179
Jenkins, Henry 151
Jennings, Christina 56
jiangshi 144
Johnson, Colin *see* Mudrooroo
Johnson, James Weldon 39, 40
Johnson, Laurie 119, 120, 127
Johnson, Magic 40
jokes 78
Jones, Ernest 78
Jordan, Neil 211
Joyce, James 131

Kabir, Shameem 57
Kabuki 123
Kadaicha 175
Kadaicha (1988) 174
Kafka, Franz 210
Kara, Selmin 190
Kawin, Bruce 116, 126, 195
Keetley, Dawn 193
Keft-Kennedy, Virginia 154, 159, 161
Kennedy, Harlan 120
Kenny, Glenn 146
Kent, Leticia 121, 126
Kingslow, Janice 36
Kinski, Klaus 124, 125–126
Kiss the Dead 16
Klein, Rachel 51
Klein Sexual Orientation Grid (KSOG) 102
Kolysanka (2010) 77, 85, 88, 89
Korea, South 6, 213
Koscina, Sylva 110
Kracauer, Siegfried 118
Kratter, Matthew 25, 28
Krausz, Peter 174
Krikowa, Natalie 54, 56
Kristeva, Julia 195
Kroger, Brooke 37
kyonshi 144

Lang, Fritz 120
Lannoo, Vincent 77, 82, 83, 86, 87
Larsen, Kristine 40, 191
Larsen, Nella 38, 40, 41
The Last Wave (1977) 174, 175
Latin America 4
Lawes, William 137
Lawrence, Novotny 50
Lee, Christopher 105, 109, 110, 111, 114
Lee, Hyun-Jung 57, 195
Le Fanu, Sheridan 5, 13, 25, 48, 55, 56, 58, 166
Leitch, Thomas M. 50, 52, 53, 167
lesbians and lesbianism 49–51, 57–58
Lestat 154, 164
Let the Right One In 5, 90, 91, 95, 99, 100, 101

Let the Right One In (2008) 213
Levack, Brian P. 34
Lewis, Paul 138
LGBTQ 49, 101
Liebenberg, William 61, 62, 64, 65, 68, 71, 72
Lindqvist, John Ajvide 5, 90, 91, 95, 96, 99, 100, 101, 102
Linville, Susan 120, 121
Little Shop of Horrors (1960) 195
The Lizzie Bennet Diaries 52
Lockyer, Sharon 78
London 84, 130
Lord Ruthven 11
Los Angeles (L.A.) 5, 45, 79, 81
Louisiana 14, 16
Luckmann, Thomas 186
Lugosi, Bela 126
Lust for a Vampire (1971) 50

Macaulay, Charles 45
Machulski, Juliusz 77, 85, 87, 88
Macleod, Pierre 180
Mafia 79
Major, William 140
Malice Mizer 154
manananggal 4
Mandurugo 4
manga *see* comics
Marin, Louis 181, 183
Marshall, William 45
Marshall Aid program 106
Marx, Karl 61, 65
La maschera del demonio (1960) 106
masculinity 105, 110, 111, 112, 113, 114, 115; hyper-masculinity 112, 114
Massachusetts 28
Masuria 85
Mauritania 181
Mayne, Judith 126
McBratney, Beth 208
McClelland, Bruce A. 25, 27
McClintock, Anne 66, 67
McFarlane, Brian 53
McGee, Vonetta 45
McGraw, Bill 134, 135
McKee, Alan 165, 174
McLaren, Philip 172
McMurray, Andrew 140
McNally, Shari 58
McSweeney, Terence 190
Mead, Philip 178
Mediterranean 113, 114
Meeker, Natania 192
Melton, J. Gordon 193
Memmi, Albert 60, 63, 64, 71
Mexico 4
Mexico City 213
Meyer, Stephenie 103
Michigan Theater 135

Middle East 197
Miller, Laura 51, 153
Min Min (2012) 174
The Min Min (1990) 174
Mitchell, Bill 134
Mittell, Jason 56
Modern Vampires (1998) 77, 79–82, 84, 86, 87, 88
Modernity 109, 113, 115
Montreal 5, 62, 66, 71, 84, 85, 89
Moon Child 6, 153
Moonlight 5, 17–21
Moretti, Franco 79
Morimoto, Lori 145
Morocco 5, 136
Morrowind 206, 207
Mosley, Philip 83
The Moth Diaries (2011) 51
Mudrooroo 168, 169, 171, 172
Munich 127
Murnau, F.W. 6, 14, 116, 117, 118, 120, 122, 124, 126
Murphy, Eddie 35, 44
Murray, Robin L. 189, 193, 194, 195, 198
Muslims 28
Mussolini, Benito 106
Mutch, Deborah 25
My Fair Lady (1964) 79

Nadja (1994) 51
Nahrung, Jason 165, 172
Namorrados 165, 168
national identity 104
nationalism 104, 110, 126, 127
Nazis and Nazism 118, 120, 121, 197, 199
Negovanlis, Natasha 49, 55, 58
Negra, Monika Estrella 214
Nelson, Diane M. 66
Neocleous, Mark 61
Néron, Caroline 61
Nettlebeck, Amanda 179
neutrality 90, 91, 92, 93, 94, 95, 97, 98, 99, 101, 103
New France 63
New German Cinema 120
The New Vampire 25–26, 30, 31, 33, 145
New World 81
New York 28, 38, 40, 190, 191
New Zealand 6
Newton, Isaac 129
9/11 28, 189–190
Noir 51
Nosferatu (1979) 6, 116, 119
Nosferatu (1922) 3, 14

Oberhausen Manifesto 120
Oestreich, Kate Faber 52
O'Flynn, Siobhan 51
Old World 4, 81, 87
Ong, Thomas 166

Only Lovers Left Alive (2014) 3
O ange Marmalade 3, 144, 145, 147–149, 213
Otherness 11, 88, 133, 145, 154, 161, 167, 168, 200, 205, 208, 210
Ouaknine, Steph 49
Outback Vampires (1987) 3, 174

Pabst, Georg Wilhelm 120
Pakistan 4
Paris 127, 130, 137
passing 35–36, 37–39, 40–41
Passing 36, 39, 41
Patasola 4
Patriots' Rebellion 63
Payne, Allen 39, 44, 45
Peacock, M. Jess 192, 193, 196
Pérez, Hector J. 192
Perrin, Claude Stéphane 91, 92, 93, 229
Picart, Caroline 168
Pickering, Michael 78
Picnic at Hanging Rock (1979) 174
Pinkerton, Nick 131, 132, 135
Poland 5, 77, 85, 88
Polanski, Roman 124
Polidori, John 12, 25, 60
Polselli, Renato 106
Popol Vuh 117
Porter, Patrick 180
Portrait of the Artist as a Young Man 131
Portugal 136
postcolonialism 68, 167
Postwar era 107
Praed, Rosa 166
Prager, Brad 118, 119
Prawer, S.S. 117, 119, 122, 124, 126, 127
Price, Jordan Castillo 214
Pride and Prejudice 52
Promised Land 171
Prorokova, Tatiana 193
Puritans 30
Pursiegle, Jenny 180
Pythagoras 129

Québec 62–63, 71
Queen of the Damned (2002) 147, 164
queerness 4, 56–58, 143, 148, 213; closeted 51
Quicksand 36, 38, 41
Quiet Revolution 63, 64
Quinkans 165, 175

race 11, 36, 45, 131, 167
racism 28, 45, 77
Rand, Ayn 207
Rascel, Renato 104, 105, 109, 110, 112, 114
Rasulala, Thalmus 45
refugees 161
Regnoli, Piero 106
Reich, Jacqueline 112
Reign in Darkness (2002) 174

Rembrandt 123
Rentschler, Eric 118, 121
Restivo, Angelo 107
Rice, Anne 14–15, 25, 26, 31, 34, 93, 103, 143, 154, 155, 159, 164, 201, 212
Riefenstahl, Leni 118, 121
Rigoletto, Sergio 105
Robinson, Amy 38
Robinson, Smokey 135
Rojas, Christina 185
Rolston, Ken 206, 207, 208
Roma 117, 125
Romanticism 119–120, 121; Romania 123; Romantic literature 118
Rothman, Stephanie 50
Rowlandson, William 182
Ryan, Mark David 170, 173, 174
Rymer, James Malcolm 25

Les Saignantes (2005) 213
Salem, Mass. 5
Salem Witch Trials 5, 23–24, 30, 33
'Salem's Lot 25
Sanchez, Federico 61, 62, 64, 65, 68, 71, 72
Sanders, Julie 52
Sandford, John 118, 119, 122
Sangster, Jimmy 50
Sarandon, Susan 51
Sasdy, Peter 50
Satan 24, 26, 27
Scherer, Agnes 193
Schneiderman, Davis 206, 207, 210
The Scholar Who Walks the Night 3, 144, 145, 149–151
Schreck, Max 124
Schroeder, Kirby 113
Scott, Kim 171, 172
Scott, Tony 51
Segerberg, Ebba 103
Senegal 181
Senf, Carol 128, 129, 139
Seven Years' War 63
sexism 28
Shakespeare, William 131
Shelley, Percy 136
Sheridan Le Fanu, Joseph 48
Shibuya 155, 162, 163
Shipka, Danny 106
Showalter, Elaine 78
Sicily 117
social order 79
Sookie Stackhouse 16, 20–21
Sorlin, Pierre 107
Soucouyant 4
The Soul of the Countess Adrian 166
South Africa 179
South America 4, 163
South Asia 4, 178
South Korea 145
Southern Vampire series 16–17

Spain 4, 136
Spice Islands 178
Spicer, Andrew 111
Star Trek 203
Starrs, D. Bruno 165, 170, 172
Steno 104, 105
Stephanou, Aspasia 111
Stepien, Justyna 129, 133, 137
Stoker, Bram 4, 11, 25, 48, 102, 103, 122, 126, 162, 166, 170, 176, 192, 200, 212
Stoker, Florence 126
Stoll, Corey 191
The Strain 3, 6, 189
Strait of Gibraltar 136
Strasser, Dirk 173
strigoi 191
Styria 53
Super Bowl 134
Supernatural 144
The Supremes 135
Sweden 5, 212
Sweet Water, Stolen Land 172
Sydney 184
Szabari, Antónia 192, 195

Taejo, King 149
Tangier 128, 131, 135, 137
Tannenbaum, Leslie 45–46
Tarrat, Margaret 108
Taussig, Michael 177, 185
Taylor, Charles 180
Tempi duri per i vampiri (1959) 5–6, 104, 105, 107
The Temptations 135
Tenga, Angela 193
Tesla, Nikola 129
That Blackfella Bloodsucka Dance! (2011) 165, 170
That Deadman Dance! 171
Thirst (1979) 174
Thomas, Kevin 123
Tidwell, Christy 191
Tituba 30
Tokyo 155, 162
tourism 107, 109, 110, 111
transmedia 53–56, 145
transnational 145, 153
Transylvania 27, 78, 123, 200
Trigg, Dylan 180
Trinidad 4
True Blood 17–21, 167
Tumblr 52
Tumini, Angela 56
Tunda 4
Turrisi, Kim 56
Twain, Mark 131
Twilight 4, 5, 103, 144, 148, 151, 167, 212
The Twins (1923) 174
Twins of Evil (1971) 50
Twitter 52

Index   241

L'ultima preda del vampire (1960) 106
Unaipon, David 169, 171
Underground 171
Undying 171
United Kingdom (UK) 114, 167
United Nations (UN) 134
United States (U.S.) 7, 77, 163, 167, 212

Vampire Detective 145
Vampire Flower 145
Vampire Idol 145, 146–147
Vampire Killers (2009) 51
The Vampire Lovers (1970) 50, 124
Vampire Prosecutor 145
Vampire Prosecutor 2 145
Vampire: The Masquerade 202, 203
Vampires (2010) 77, 82–85, 86, 88
VAMPS 163
The Vampyre (1819) 12, 25
Vampyre (1932) 3
Vampyre's Portrait 213
Vampyros Lesbos (1971) 50
Van Diemen's Land 168
Van Helsing 31
van Toorn, Peggy 171
Varney the Vampire, or, The Feast of Blood 13, 25
Vautier, Maurie 63
Veeder, William 56
The Velvet Vampire (1971) 50
vetalas 4
Victorian era 52, 53, 55, 114
video blogs (vlogs) 54
Vinen, Richard 114
visual-kei 154
Von Kleist, Heinrich 119
Voss, Angela 182
Vrbančić, Mario 53
vrykolakas 4

Wagner, Richard 118, 121
Wahl, Chris 118, 127

Wald, Gayle 36, 37
Walker, Beverly 116, 117, 123
Walsh, Philip 206, 207, 210
Wang, Leehom 156
Warsaw 86, 87
We Are the Night (2010) 51, 213
Weatherspoon, Rebekah 214
Weekley, Ayanna K. 42–43
Weimar period 120
Weinstock, Jeffrey 111, 173
Wetmore, Kevin 190
What We Do in the Shadows (2014) 213
White, Jack 135
White, Walter 36
Williams, Tennessee 136
Williamson, Milly 11, 233
Winans, Bebe 135
Winans, Cece 135
Witch(es) 23, 24, 27, 28; and vampires 26–28
Wolff, Robert Paul 61
Wollstonecraft, Mary 137
Wonder, Stevie 135
Wood, Robin 108
World War I 180
World War II 81, 86, 106, 120, 196, 197, 198, 199

YA (young adult) 56, 177
yaoi see BL (Boys' Love)
Yara-ma-tha-who 165, 168, 170
Yara-ma-tha-who 169
The Yara-ma-tha-who: An Australian Beasts Story 169
Yarbro, Chelsea Quinn 15
You're Beautiful 151
Youtube 54

Zanger, Jules 25, 26, 31
Zeller, Robert 186
Zimmerman, Bonnie 44
The Zombie Brigade (1986) 165, 174
zombies 165, 210

www.ingramcontent.com/pod-product-compliance
Lightning Source LLC
Chambersburg PA
CBHW032037300426
44117CB00009B/1095